DISTANCE EDUCATION

A Systems View

DISTANCE EDUCATION

A Systems View

Michael G. Moore
Penn State University

Greg Kearsley
George Washington University

Wadsworth Publishing Company

I⟨T⟩P® An International Thomson Publishing Company

Belmont • Albany • Bonn • Boston • Cincinnati • Detroit
London • Madrid • Melbourne • Mexico City • New York • Paris
San Francisco • Singapore • Tokyo • Toronto • Washington

Education Editor: Sabra Horne
Assistant Editor: Claire Masson
Editorial Assistant: Louise Mendelson
Production Services Coordinator: Debby Kramer
Production: Robin Lockwood & Associates
Print Buyer: Karen Hunt
Permissions Editor: Jeanne Bosschart
Copy Editor: Darlene Bledsoe
Technical Illustrator: Impact Publications
Designer: Wendy LaChance/By Design
Cover Designer: Ross Carron
Photos: Courtesy Univ. Photo/Graphics, Penn State
Compositor: Wendy LaChance/By Design
Printer: Quebecor Printing Book Group/Fairfield
Cover Printer: Phoenix Color Corporation

Printed in the United States of America

1 2 3 4 5 6 7 8 9 10

For more information, contact Wadsworth Publishing Company:

Wadsworth Publishing Company
10 Davis Drive
Belmont, California 94002, USA

International Thomson Publishing Europe
Berkshire House 168-173
High Holborn
London, WC1V 7AA, England

Thomas Nelson Australia
102 Dodds Street
South Melbourne 3205
Victoria, Australia

Nelson Canada
1120 Birchmount Road
Scarborough, Ontario
Canada M1K 5G4

International Thomson Editores
Campos Eliseos 385, Piso 7
Col. Polanco
11560 México D.F. México

International Thomson Publishing GmbH
Königswinterer Strasse 418
53227 Bonn, Germany

International Thomson Publishing Asia
221 Henderson Road
#05-10 Henderson Building
Singapore 0315

International Thomson Publishing Japan
Hirakawacho Kyowa Building, 3F
2-2-1 Hirakawacho
Chiyoda-ku, Tokyo 102, Japan

Library of Congress Cataloging-in-Publication Data

Moore, Michael G.
    Distance education: a systems view / Michael G. Moore, Greg Kearsley.
        p.   cm.
    Includes bibliographical references and indexes.
    ISBN 0-534-26496-4
    1. Distance education—United States.   I. Kearsley, Greg   II. Title
LC5805.M66   1996
371.3′078—dc20   95-36555

CONTENTS

Chapter 3 The Scope of Distance Education   36

Chapter 4 Research on Effectiveness   59

Chapter 5   Technologies and Media   78

Chapter 9   Administration, Management and Policy   172

Chapter 10 The Theoretical Basis for Distance Education 197

Chapter 11 International Perspectives 213

PREFACE

Distance education has become a major form of learning and teaching around the world, yet in the training of educators in the United States, little attention has been given to it. Students and practitioners are expressing dissatisfaction with this situation. As professors of education who have a long-standing interest in distance education, we have experienced a growing demand for instruction in this field, especially from graduate students. Such students typically are teachers or trainers in colleges, universities, the health care field, or corporate training, and they increasingly ask themselves or are asked by others how to adopt a distance education approach in their work. It is primarily for graduate students and professional educators and trainers that we have written this book.

For students of teaching and people who teach, this book reviews the nature of teaching at a distance. For educational administrators, we introduce some of the techniques of organizing and managing the provision of teaching to distant learners. For media coordinators, we examine the roles of technology in delivering distance education courses. For instructional developers, we describe the process of designing distance education materials. And we include chapters on the current scope, the history and theory, the international experience, and some of the policy issues involved in distance education that we think should be of interest to all students of the topic.

As teachers we are aware that students have access to many resources in international journals and electronic communications channels. The fugitive nature of many of these resources, the mixed quality of many (especially the electronic), and the confusion of terminologies being employed make it hard for the beginner to discriminate among the many good and bad resources that are available. What is needed is a preliminary framework that can help students find their way, structure their understanding, and provide the basis for more specialized, individual reading, study, and research. That is what we have attempted to provide in this introductory text.

We are conscious that our academic peers will view the book as somewhat superficial. It is. We have not set out to write a book of scholarship or to provide an exhaustive treatment of the subjects included here. It is very much an introductory text, intended to give an overview of the field and, quite frankly, to make a complex subject as simple as is appropriate for a first reading about the field. The book is to be used as the basis for discussion in our graduate and advanced undergraduate courses, and the structure will allow us to use approximately one chapter a week for a regular semester. We hope our colleagues in other universities and elsewhere will find it helpful in this way.

In the hope that we succeed in both stimulating interest and providing a good foundation for further study, we have included appendixes that list books, journal articles, electronic journals and databases, as well as addresses of organizations and institutions that are involved in distance education.

We would like to thank the many individuals who have contributed to the development of this book. They include faculty, staff, and graduate students at The American Center for Study of Distance Education at Penn State University; staff of the Instructional Communications Systems Group and Tom Smith at the University of Wisconsin; and Michael Lambert and Sally Welch of the Distance Education & Training Council. We also thank the following reviewers for their valuable contributions: Connie Dillon, University of Oklahoma; Robert Ford, Houston Community College; Von V. Pittman, The University of Iowa; Farhad Saba, San Diego State University; Ray Steele, Ball State University; Robert Threlkeld, California State Polytechnic University; and Ronald Zellner, Texas A & M University.

CHAPTER 1

Fundamentals of Distance Education

In this first chapter we introduce some basic ideas about distance education, and in particular the idea of a systems approach to the study and practice of this field. A distance education system should include the components of content, design, communications, interaction, learner environment, and management. We suggest that the systems model helps us understand distance education; it helps us analyze and evaluate what is sometimes called distance education but may not be; it provides a model for good practice at all levels.

The fundamental concept of distance education is simple enough: Students and teachers are separated by distance and sometimes by time. This contrasts with the ancient tutorial, in which a teacher and an individual learner met at the same time and place (as they still do at the Universities of Oxford and Cambridge), and the more familiar contemporary model of instruction in a classroom, where a teacher talks to a group of learners, all together at the same time in the same place.

If teacher and students are not together in the same place or together at the same time, they are separated by distance, and as a result it becomes necessary to introduce an artificial communications medium that will deliver information and also provide a channel for interaction between them.

The use of printed and electronic technologies as the primary form of communication is the first and most obvious characteristic that distinguishes distance education from other forms of education. Using such technologies opens up a range of exciting new ways in which instructors can present information and conduct their interactions with the learner. The successful use of communication technologies, however, requires special design techniques and more careful planning and production than is usual in classroom teaching. Being separated from their instructors, students who are learning at a distance often need advice and counseling about their study problems. Furthermore, ways must be found for administering and evaluating both learning and instruction.

We must deal with the questions of where, when, and how students will study if classroom facilities and the structures found in classrooms are not available. As institutions and even states and nations begin to think how to introduce distance education into their existing educational systems, new policies have to be developed. Sometimes new institutions or departments or consortial arrangements have to be set up. As you can see, an idea that is relatively simple and straightforward becomes quite complicated when you start to think about it a little.

A Definition of Distance Education

We will use the following working definition throughout this book:

> Distance education is planned learning that normally occurs in a different place from teaching and as a result requires special techniques of course design, special instructional techniques, special methods of communication by electronic and other technology, as well as special organizational and administrative arrangements.

Because distance education aims to provide instruction in places and times that are convenient for learners rather than teachers or teaching institutions, many people use the term "distance learning" as a synonym for distance education. We understand that this is not strictly accurate, since in education our interest is in learning that is deliberate and planned, and therefore with teaching as well as learning, nevertheless, when we cite authors who use the term "distance learning," we will use it also.

We cannot emphasize too strongly that distance education is much more than simply using technology in a conventional classroom. We will of course describe many technologies in this book, but the book is not really about technology. It is about the consequences of using technology on such subjects as course design and delivery, interaction and learning, management and organization.

Levels of Distance Education

Distance education exists at a number of different levels. To help us sort out these different levels, we will use a typology developed by Michael Mark (1990). Mark (who chose to use the term "distance learning") distinguished these four levels:

1. **Distance Learning Program** These are activities carried out in a conventional college, university, school system, or training department whose primary

Distance education aims to provide instruction in places and times that are convenient for learners rather than teachers or teaching institutions.

responsibilities include traditional classroom instruction. In recent years many faculty have chosen to teach their courses off-campus by means of audio- or videoconferencing, simply adding the distant learners to their conventional class. This is sometimes referred to as the "craft" approach to distance education, since it usually consists of a single teacher working alone, as contrasted to working with a team in a systems approach. A distance learning program does not usually have its own faculty or administrative services.

2. Distance Learning Unit A special and separate unit within a conventional college, university, or school system that is dedicated to distance learning activities. Such a unit will normally have administrative staff whose sole responsibilities are distance education; it may also have dedicated faculty, though most call on the faculty of the parent body to provide most of the teaching for the unit. The extension divisions of most universities are illustrative of this level of distance education.

3. Distance Learning Institution The sole purpose of the institution is distance education. All activities are exclusively devoted to distance education. Such an institution will have a faculty and administrative staff whose duties are different from those at a traditional college, university, school system, or training department. The British Open University (Chapter 2) is a world-famous example of a distance learning institution.

4. Distance Learning Consortia Consortia normally consist of two or more distance learning institutions or units who share in either the design or delivery of programs, or both. The National University Teleconference Network (NUTN) and "Star Schools" are examples of such consortia.

This distinction among the different levels of distance learning providers will be used throughout the rest of the book. It will be useful to you as you read about distance education to try to identify whether what is being talked about is at program, unit, institutional or consortium level, since the term is used carelessly—though not, we hope, in this book!

Since it would have been tedious to refer continuously to programs, units, institutions, and consortia, we have often used the term "distance education organization" to cover them all.

Courses and Programs

In the literature, and also in this book, you will find reference to "courses", and also you will find the term "programs" used with a different meaning from "distance learning program" as explained above.

"Courses" are produced at all levels of distance education. In a distance education program as defined above, the course is based on the practices and standards of the parent institution. In a conventional American university, a graduate course is likely to be around 150 hours of study with about 45 to 50 hours of direct contact between instructor and students. Therefore the distance education course, usually taught by teleconferencing, will be of the same duration. At the British Open University—a distance education institution—a course is around 450 hours of study with little or no direct instructor-learner face-to-face contact. In all cases a course will at least have learning objectives, one or more teachers, a medium of communication, and content, or subject matter.

The word "program" is often used in a number of senses besides those defined above. Sometimes "program" will refer to audio or television programs that make up part of a course. Sometimes an institution, unit, consortium, or program will refer to its "program" as a generic label to indicate its total offering of courses.

Throughout this book we have tried to be as specific as possible in using these terms; the meaning will usually be clear from the context. We hope that this brief discussion will at least alert you to exercise caution as you encounter these words and to pause to ask yourself what different authors mean when they use them.

A Systems Approach

We believe that a systems approach is very helpful to an understanding of distance education as a field of study and is essential to its successful practice. Throughout this book we often refer to distance education systems, and even

This class meets with their instructor and with groups in Mexico, Finland, and Estonia as well as the United States, using audio, video, and computer conference technology.

when we do not use the term, our thinking is influenced by a systems perspective.

A distance education system consists of all the component processes that make up distance education, including learning, teaching, communication, design, and management, and even such less obvious components as history and institutional philosophy. Within each of these broadly named components are subsystems, which are systems in themselves. For example, there is a subsystem in every distance education system that deals with course design, one that includes many component activities working together so that a course is produced with quality, on time and at acceptable cost. The course design subsystem links to the other subsystems to form the total system. While we may choose to study each of these subsystems separately, we must also try to understand their interrelationships. Anything that happens in one part of the system has an effect on other parts of the system, so as we focus on any one part of the system we need to hold in the back of our minds a picture of the total context.

The systems model provides a tool that not only helps us recognize many of the issues that separate distance education from conventional education, but also helps us distinguish good distance education from bad. Historically, neither teaching itself nor the organization of education has been very systematic.

Distance education courses have been developed and delivered in a very piece-meal and unplanned fashion. With a systems perspective we can see why this had unfortunate and unsatisfactory outcomes in terms of students' learning or cost-effectiveness, or both. In future we think it will be better for students, teachers, and educational institutions if every distance education course was designed and developed in a systematic way and if every distance education organization is developed, as other modern agencies are, as a total system.

Systems in Practice

While a systems view is a good conceptual tool that helps us understand and analyze distance education, it is also a tool that must be applied in the practice of distance education at any level.

Following a systems strategy, each component process in a distance education institution, unit, program, or consortium may be developed and operated independently to some degree, but good quality requires that the development and operation of each component be controlled in such a way that it is fully integrated with the development and operation of all other components, making each supportive of the others.

This systematic approach can and should be applied in the development and delivery of every course. When a distance education course is developed in a system, there is a control mechanism that ensures that all the component processes are well integrated and interact with each other. Then the quality of the final product—that is, the course—is greater than could be achieved by any of the component contributors acting alone.

When a systems approach is applied at the level of an organization, a state, or a nation, the majority of the distance education resources of that organization, state, or nation are integrated. In such a system, every course is planned to take into account how it impacts on every other course, every piece of every course is carefully designed to fit with every other piece, every technology is employed in harmony with every other, what an instructor discusses with students fits with the illustrations included in a study guide, the learner support personnel have access to specialists within the providing organization to deal with the issues arising at each step of a course, and so on.

The Need for a Systems View

A common misperception among educators who are not familiar with a systems approach is that it is possible to benefit from introducing technology into education without doing anything to change the other ways in which education is currently organized. They think that by moving cameras, computers, and microphones into the classrooms, schools, universities, and training departments, they can increase enrollments, provide new curricula, and save money without doing anything else. According to this view, once the technology is in place, there is little else to be done except to let teachers get on with practicing their craft as they have always done. They decide what to teach, prepare the lessons, and interact with students via the camera, computer, telephone, or some combinations of these.

Alas, this is a very immature view of distance education, and it won't work. It is not possible to improve quality, provide for more students, and lower costs without reorganizing education according to a systems model. An analogy of the situation we face can be found in the airline industry. In the early days of commercial aviation, passengers were met by the pilot and an assistant on the runway, paid for their tickets, walked with their bags to the airplane, and were then flown to their destination. The organization of the process of passenger transportation was equally primitive to the airplane.

Today, airline organization depends on a systems model in which there is specialization of labor—there are many hundreds of different specialized jobs—and a sophisticated, computer-supported workflow that ensures everyone's work fits with everyone else's. No single individual, not even the pilot, is able to move the passenger without the contribution of hundreds of other workers, including technicians, communications specialists, and administrators of all kinds. The result of this organizational feat is the provision of high-quality service at a lower passenger cost to millions of travelers than could have been imagined at the beginnings of airline service.

When we compare the airline with a school, university, or training department, we arrive at the heart of the misconception about distance education. As with the airline, a distance education system only becomes cost-effective when it can take advantage of economies of scale. This means that the larger the number of users of the system, the lower the cost for each person. This concept, so familiar in other walks of life, comes about as a result of another common practice that the systems approach makes possible—the "division of labor."

In distance education, especially bearing in mind the different technologies that are available, you cannot just "go it alone" and maintain high quality and low costs. Strangely, education is one of the few areas of modern life where division of labor, or specialization, is still not practiced to any great extent. In traditional classrooms, individual teachers develop and deliver their own courses. They try to be effective communicators, curriculum designers, evaluators, motivators, group discussion facilitators, as well as content experts. This is an extremely wasteful use of human resources, when the content and objectives of so many courses are identical, and it produces wide variation in quality of education.

Simply adding a new technology to this "craft" approach to teaching will not give good distance education, and because the capital costs of the equipment needed are so high and the resources and time required to develop good courses are considerable, it is not financially viable either. Instead, courses need to be developed by teams of specialists and taken by many students across a large number of educational institutions. Just as it is not simply the skill of a pilot even when added to new technology that makes an airline work, so neither the teacher alone nor the technology will make distance education work, though of course these are both critical components of any system.

The biggest challenges facing education today are for legislatures to develop policies that require the development of a total systems approach for distance education, for administrators to redistribute human and capital resources into a total system, and for teachers to be trained to work as specialists within such a system.

Components of a Distance Education System

Figure 1.1 presents a general systems model that describes the main component processes and elements of a distance education institution, program, unit, consortium, or course. These are the common components that will be found at all levels and types of distance education. There must be sources of knowledge or skills that will be taught and learned as well as a process for finding out what students need to learn and for deciding what particular content will be taught. There must be one subsystem that arranges the design of courses and another that provides the communications services to teachers, learners, and administrators. Instructors and others interact with students to help the learning process. There must of course be learners in their different learning environments. Finally, at the most general level, there must be an organization with a policy and a management structure that controls and administers the various parts of each of these subsystems.

We will now examine each part of this system briefly, and we will later focus on each of these components in turn.

Content Experts and Other Sources of Knowledge

The responsibility for deciding what knowledge will be taught by an organization (whether it be a university, college, school, or training department of a corporation, government, or voluntary agency) is that of the organization and its faculty—the people who know their field, its literature, theory, contemporary practice, and problems. Decisions will be made in the light of the organization's educational mission and philosophy, reflected by the philosophy of its teachers, and this in turn will be determined by the organization's history and the history of education in the country in which the organization is located.

For most distance education organizations it is also important to know what knowledge students themselves feel they need, and to develop courses that take into account what they want to learn. Students may also be regarded as potential sources and creators of knowledge, and courses may be designed to employ project and other self-directed learning activities. The degree to which a distance education organization or course might draw on students as a source of knowledge will be influenced by the educational philosophies of the organization and its faculty. There are many different ideas about learning and teaching, and before we can understand an educational organization or its courses, or analyze them or evaluate them, it is necessary to be clear about what particular philosophy is being emphasized or adhered to.

Figure 1.1   A Systems Model for Distance Education

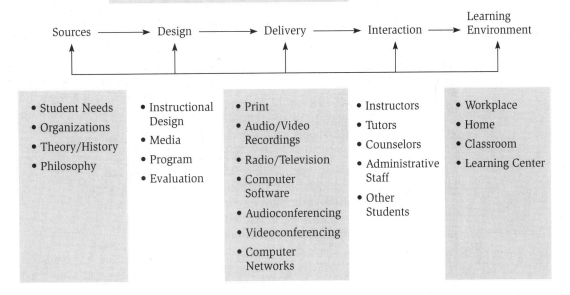

Sources ⟶ Design ⟶ Delivery ⟶ Interaction ⟶ Learning Environment

Sources	Design	Delivery	Interaction	Learning Environment
• Student Needs • Organizations • Theory/History • Philosophy	• Instructional Design • Media • Program • Evaluation	• Print • Audio/Video Recordings • Radio/Television • Computer Software • Audioconferencing • Videoconferencing • Computer Networks	• Instructors • Tutors • Counselors • Administrative Staff • Other Students	• Workplace • Home • Classroom • Learning Center

Design of Courses

Producing distance education courses involves many kinds of design expertise. Since instruction is provided through media and delivered by technology, the media materials need to be designed by individuals with a knowledge of instructional principles and techniques as well as knowledge of the technology. While there are content experts who have both instructional design skills and knowledge of technology, it is better if these responsibilities are carried by different specialists. The instructional designers should work with the content experts and together agree on such matters as the objectives of the course, the exercises and activities the learners will undertake, the layout of textual materials, the content of recorded audio– or videotapes, and the questions for interactive sessions by audio–, video–, or computer conference.

Graphics designers, producers, and other media specialists should be brought in to turn the ideas of the content experts and instructional designers into good–quality course materials and programs. Decisions must be made about which part of the instruction can most effectively be delivered by each particular medium. Finally, evaluation and research experts must plan how to evaluate individual student learning as well as the effectiveness of all aspects of the distance education course in order to ensure that it works—that is, meets the needs of students and the teaching organization and provides cost-effective instruction.

Because so many skills are needed to design a distance education course, one of the key characteristics of most successful distance education courses is that they are designed by course teams in which many specialists work together.

Communication of Information and Interaction via Technologies

In all education there has to be communication between a teacher or a teaching team, and the learner or learners. In distance education this communication takes place via some form of technology. The technology may produce printed media (mainly books and study guides) or programs on audio- or videocassettes, radio or television broadcasts, computer software, audio, audio-graphic or videoconferencing, or computer networks (i.e., computer–mediated communication). The use of technology to carry the messages of teachers and students, rather than relying on face-to-face lecture, discussion, and the blackboard, is what makes distance education so novel to most people. Ironically, the technologies that seem so challenging to so many educators are the same that they are immersed in when seeking information and entertainment.

Distinguishing Technology and Media

When we talk about "technology," we are describing not only the machines that distribute messages but also the organization and the people who make them work. Technologies include the postal system, radio and television broadcasting companies, telephone, satellite, cable, and computer networks. What is distributed through the technologies are mediated messages, or symbol systems, and these we usually refer to as "media." The symbol systems (the media) that carry the messages by means of the distribution systems (the technology) are typically text in books and study guides, sound in audiotapes, pictures in videotapes, or the text, sound, or pictures that make up a teleconference.

For example, the Internet is a technology, an organized network of computers, big and small, and users linked by telephone lines of several types; the messages sent on it are usually in the text medium, though increasingly they are in video and audio media. The technology of mail distributes the media of printed words, data and pictures; sound on audiotapes; moving pictures and sound on videotapes; and all these on computer discs. The technology of radio and television broadcasting distributes messages by sound, and pictures at random through the air. By the technology of satellite, cable, telephone, and computer networks we can distribute text, sound and pictures from point to point or point to multipoints, so the messages may be aimed at particular groups or particular individuals. Correspondence by mail may include sound, text, or pictures by video, but is distributed mainly to individual learners.

Thus, each technology can support the use of a variety of media: print (words and pictures), sound (voice and music), and video (pictures, sound, and motion). Each medium has different characteristics, which also vary according to the technology that distributes it. For example, certain books, audiotapes, or videoconferences are different in the ways they support varying degrees of abstractness and concreteness or how they impact social presence and intimacy. Each of these media support varying degrees of structure in teaching programs, different degrees of dialog between teachers and learners and among learners, as well as differing degrees of self-directedness of the learners. This is an important theme that will be addressed further in Chapter 10.

Interaction: The Role of Instructors

As in all education, it is important for distant learners to have sufficient interaction with their instructors to allow an appropriate degree of exchange of ideas and information. Many educators also feel it is pedagogically important to have interaction between learners. The nature and extent of the interaction that would be deemed appropriate varies according to the organizational and designers' teaching philosophy, the nature of the subject matter, the maturity of the students, their location, and the media used in the course.

One of the key differences between distance and conventional education is that in a distance education system it is common for the interaction in a course to be conducted by an instructor who is not one of the designers or content experts of the course. As explained above, in a total systems approach, courses are usually designed by teams of instructional designers, media experts, and content experts. The cost of such teams and the cost of media is high, and the numbers of students that must take the course for it to be cost–effective is greater than in conventional education. Because of the large numbers, it is not possible for the designers to also be the instructors.

Neither, from a pedagogical point of view, is it desirable they should be, since instruction requires a special set of skills, different from those of designers and subject experts, and is better done when it is the work of persons who devote themselves to the study and development and practice of those skills. Thus the normal procedure in a total systems approach to distance education is that once the courses have been designed and delivered by correspondence, by radio or television, by satellite or computer, students are allocated by the teaching organization to instructors, often referred to as tutors, who interact with them to provide individualized instruction on the basis of the designed materials.

The interactions among instructors and students will be based on issues and questions determined by the course designers and might be conducted in real-time by means of teleconference technologies. While the teleconference provides for very fast interaction, this interaction is usually in a group setting. Outside the United States, even today, interaction is most commonly achieved by means of written communications with a tutor through the mail. In a total systems approach, the course design team sets assignments based on the content of each unit of a course, and the assignments are undertaken by individual students who send them to their personal tutors by mail. The tutors read, comment and return the assignments by mail to the students, and perhaps then discuss by telephone or even in person. Even though the pace of this interaction by mail may be slow, it is inexpensive and allows for a high degree of individualized attention for each student.

In the future we are likely to see more use of desktop work stations that combine both textual interaction by computer and sometimes audio and video communications simultaneously. These provide the same individualization as the correspondence course, together with the teleconference's immediacy of interaction. Such technologies, of course, are still expensive today and not available to most distance learners.

As well as interacting with instructors whose main job is to help them learn the content of the course, students may also interact with counselors who make suggestions about study techniques or help to solve academic or even personal problems that interfere with learning. Students will also interact with administrative staff when registering for courses or checking their progress. Ideally, a distance education course also provides an opportunity for students to interact with each other both synchronously by teleconferences, as they would in a traditional classroom setting, and asynchronously via computer bulletin boards and mailing lists. Correspondence–based distance education courses sometimes include special face-to-face meetings to provide group interaction when designers determine that such interaction is necessary.

Management and Administration

Another aspect of interaction is the administration of distance education courses and programs. Managers are responsible for assessing the needs of learners who are not easily accessible. Since distance education usually uses expensive technologies, the funds required to produce courses are substantial, and management must allocate them among competing proposals. Administrators must ensure that money, personnel, and time are managed so that courses are produced on time and numerous work tasks fit together. Suitable faculty and staff must be recruited and trained. Since instructors are usually at a distance, special procedures must be developed and maintained for monitoring and supervising them. Feedback and evaluation mechanisms are vital because if any part of the system breaks down, the whole system is in jeopardy.

Management must also participate in the political process, helping policy-makers to understand the potential of distance education, obtaining funding, and bringing about the organizational culture change that is needed to accommodate this new form of education.

Learning Environments

In any distance education organization, a great deal of attention must be given to the nature of the learning environment. Students may study course materials and may interact with instructors in their workplaces, at home, in a classroom, at a learning center, or even when they travel. Many stories are told about distant learners on battlefields, in submarines, in lighthouses, and in prisons. Learning in such places and in the workplace or at home presents some real challenges because such settings are subject to many kinds of distractions and interruptions that make learning difficult.

To overcome these potential problems, students must consciously acquire the skills and habits of being effective distant learners. They must, for example, find their own times and places where they can study comfortably. This may mean scheduling a "training period" at work or a "quiet time" at home, with the cooperation of co-workers or family. The proper design of distance education course materials can also affect the success of learning in the workplace or home. Most designers believe that courses should be organized into very short, self-contained segments with frequent summaries and overviews. Some emphasize the need to link academic content to real–life work, community, and home issues that will help students integrate their study with everyday problems, so that instead of being distractions, these become part of their learning. Counselors can be especially helpful in assisting distant learners to make the personal and social adjustments that learning at home requires.

The environment of students whose courses are delivered by teleconferencing is usually that of a small group in a classroom or conference room. To take advantage of such a setting, instructional designers should design activities that involve interaction among the members of each group, and perhaps also interaction with groups at other sites. It is also desirable to have a "site coordinator" who ensures that the teleconferencing equipment is operating properly and the room facilities are satisfactory. Again, there are certain skills that make learning in such environments more likely, and these skills can be consciously modeled by the instructor and monitored by the site coordinator. For example, how much "off microphone" talk to allow in an audioconference site is an issue that should not be avoided.

If possible, learning centers should be located in geographic proximity to the student's home or workplace. These centers can then play many valuable roles, such as providing instructional materials and equipment, carrels for individual study, or rooms for group meetings or private meetings with tutors or counselors. In any event, learning centers need to be run by a knowledgeable administrator who may need a support staff, depending on the center's size.

Interdependence of Elements of a Distance Education System

The elements that we have introduced above—content or knowledge, design communications technologies, interaction, and learning environment and management—are essential to all distance education organizations and courses. Even with this cursory overview, it should be clear that there is a great deal of interdependence among these elements. For example, the exact nature of the design, the communications technology used for delivery, and the interaction depend on the sources of knowledge, the student needs, and the learning environment in a particular course. Selection of a particular delivery technology or combination of technologies should be determined by the content to be taught, who is to be taught, and where the learning will take place. Design of the instructional media depends on the content, the delivery technology, the kind of interaction desired, and the learning environment. All these will be influenced by policy and management. Furthermore, changes in one component of a distance education system have immediate effects on all of the other components.

Unfortunately, in most organizations today the careful design and management that should characterize a total systems approach are nonexistent. In most organizations it is one part of the system that is favored, and usually just one part of one part! Quite commonly, the communications technology receives the money and attention, or more likely, an organization may focus its attention on just one of the many communications technologies that are available. Even the best communications experts will fail if the other elements of the system are neglected. A fundamental message of this book is that distance education should be conceived of and developed as a *total* system, giving equal attention to all the above interacting components if it is to be practiced successfully. Paying attention to one of the components without regard to the others is a recipe for disaster.

System Inputs and Outputs

Another way of looking at the interrelationships among the components in a distance education system is to use a common technique in systems modeling: viewing the system in terms of inputs and outputs. Figure 1.2 identifies some of the inputs and outputs of a distance education system. You can probably think of others.

All the factors listed in the input column affect in some way the output variables we have listed. In some cases the relationship is quite direct, such as the case with instructor/tutor experience and student satisfaction ratings. Other relationships are less direct, such as the link between student access to resources and student achievement scores. Most relationships are multiple in nature; for example, student characteristics affect many of the output variables, whereas student completion rates are a function of many of the input factors. Indeed, with enough understanding of distance education, it is possible to identify a relationship between almost every input and output variable listed in Figure 1.2. The rest of this book is devoted to explaining these relationships in terms of the system components outlined in Figure 1.1.

Different Levels of Distance Education and the Systems Approach

As we pointed out earlier, distance education courses can be offered by institutions with varying degrees of commitment and expertise. The systems approach is more likely to be found in distance learning institutions or consortia than in courses at the program or unit level. While an individual teacher or group in a unit can try to be systematic, following a total systems approach requires more resources and organization than these people have available. As a result, the best distance education courses are more likely to be implemented at the institutional or consortium level than the program or unit level.

Traditional institutions that try to offer distance learning courses typically face significant organizational conflicts, because a systems approach is not very compatible with traditional classroom instruction and the way such instruction

Figure 1.2   Inputs and Outputs of Distance Education

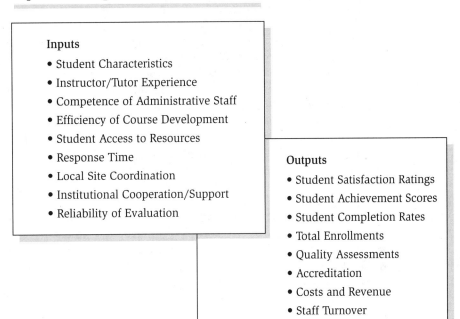

Inputs
- Student Characteristics
- Instructor/Tutor Experience
- Competence of Administrative Staff
- Efficiency of Course Development
- Student Access to Resources
- Response Time
- Local Site Coordination
- Institutional Cooperation/Support
- Reliability of Evaluation

Outputs
- Student Satisfaction Ratings
- Student Achievement Scores
- Student Completion Rates
- Total Enrollments
- Quality Assessments
- Accreditation
- Costs and Revenue
- Staff Turnover

is planned and administered. Traditional schools, colleges, and universities have football fields and classrooms but do not typically have offices full of instructional designers and media specialists, large budgets for materials development and dissemination, and extensive networks of tutors and learning centers. Most faculty who wish to develop distance learning courses are often penalized in the promotion stakes because such work is not highly regarded by academic peers; they are also penalized in their workload, because they have to do for themselves what in a distance learning institution would be the work of a design team.

Distance Education Is About Change

A major theme of this book is that the recognition now being given to distance education portends significant changes in education and how it is organized. To begin with, distance education means that students can have access to more and better learning resources than in the past. Rural and inner-city students can take courses previously available only to students in suburban areas. Handicapped and disabled students can have access to the same courses as everyone else—even if they are homebound or institutionalized. Adults who need specialized training for career enhancement or basic skills can take courses without having to be away from home or their current jobs. Students in one country can learn from teachers and fellow students in others. Courses can be accessed whenever the student wants, at whatever pace is preferred, from almost any location. Overall, distance education opens up many new learning opportunities for many people.

While students will have more freedom and opportunity, they must also assume more responsibility for managing their own learning, in terms of when they will study, how much they want to learn, and seeking out information and resources. Some students may be unwilling or inadequately trained to accept this responsibility and will need help in making the necessary adjustments in their study habits.

The roles of instructors and administrators will be different in distance education systems in the future compared to traditional classroom instruction. In moving to a distance education system, some instructors will have the job of preparing materials without being involved in interaction with students, or if they do, they will have to use the communications technologies and learn to teach quite differently. Some instructors may be very reluctant to give up their physical contact with students or teach via media transmitted through technology. Of course good management will find appropriate positions for those teachers who want to be content specialists, those who prepare to provide interactive support to students, and those who are good at designing and producing mediated communications.

Administrators too will perform different and new duties. Instead of worrying about classroom availability and class scheduling, they will be concerned with ensuring that the various resources are brought together for the design and delivery of courses as well as student support. They have to develop new admissions procedures and find alternatives to "residency" as criteria of excellence. Some administrators may have difficulty understanding the shift in resources and procedures involved.

Distance education also implies major changes within schools and training organizations. With traditional classroom instruction, the student body is primarily defined by geography, with most students in schools and colleges tending to come from the local area. However, with distance education it becomes possible for schools and training to reach students anywhere in the country or the world. So, in theory, every school or training group offering similar instruction will compete with each other. This is by no means a bad thing. A key idea in distance education is the principle of comparative advantage. As applied here this means that each school, university, or training group should decide what subjects it has an advantage in, compared to competing organizations, and should specialize in providing instruction in that subject. The future educational system will have no geographic boundary, but each organization will be more focused and specialized in the range of subjects it offers. This will also mean that all educational providers will need to rethink their marketing strategies.

Without having to worry about designing the content or presenting it, teachers in a distance education system can concentrate their energies on facilitating learning.

As a result of these changes, the quality of distance education will continue to rise. The higher quality will be recognizable. Distance education courses are more open to public scrutiny than traditional classroom instruction because they are delivered by mediated programs that can be accessed easily. This leads to a new emphasis on quality and accountability for educational offerings and to distance education becoming increasingly competitive with conventional education.

Summary

This chapter has introduced some basic ideas about distance education and proposed that a systems model is essential to both the understanding and the practice of distance education. The main points are

- A distance education institution, unit, program, consortium, or an individual course can be analyzed or described as a system. A system includes the subsystems of knowledge sources, design, delivery, interaction, learning, and management. The more integrated these are in practice, the greater will be the effectiveness of the distance education organization.

- As organizations become more understanding about the benefits of adopting a total systems approach to distance education, there will be impact on teachers, learners, administrators, and policymakers and significant changes in the way that education is conceptualized, funded, designed, and delivered. Not least will be opening of access and improvements in quality.

For further discussion about a systems approach to education, see Banathy (1993) or Reigeluth and Garfinkle (1994).

CHAPTER 2

The Historical Context
of Distance Education

Although distance education may seem like a recent development, it is more than a century old. Educators in universities and elsewhere have at different times employed the latest communications technology to deliver instruction to distant learners. In this chapter we review the history of distance education.

Distance education has a history, and this history is not American only, but international. The origins of some of the most important ideas and the techniques we use in distance education today are to be found in events that occurred as long as a century ago, some of which occurred outside our national borders. On the other hand, many developments abroad and the general success of modern distance education around the world can be attributed to ideas and practices invented in the United States. Furthermore, some of the issues that are still emerging overseas, such as the extent of self-direction to be allowed the learner and how to facilitate group learning by teleconferencing, are ones that some Americans have thought about more than their foreign counterparts.

As Figure 2-1 suggests, distance education has evolved through a number of different stages, or generations. The first generation was correspondence study, in which the principal media of communication are printed materials, generally a study guide, with written essays or other assignments being sent by mail. A large percentage of current distance education courses are still conducted by correspondence, and when we look outside the United States, this is by far the most popular form of distance education.

The second generation of distance education began with the appearance of the first Open Universities in the early 1970s. These applied a total systems approach to the design and implementation of distance learning. While open universities relied heavily on correspondence instruction, they also used broadcast and recorded media, especially programs distributed by radio, television,

Figure 2.1   The Evolution of Distance Education

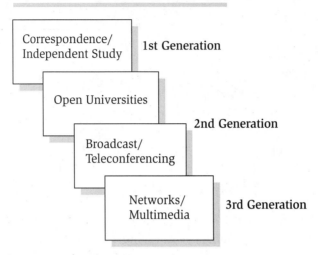

and audiotapes. Thus they represent a transition to the third generation of distance education: delivery of course materials by broadcast television or videotape, with interaction by telephone, or both delivery and interaction by telephone, satellite, cable, or ISDN (Integrated Service Digital Network) lines. In the 1990s a new generation of distance education is emerging based on computer conferencing networks and computer-based multimedia workstations.

Correspondence and Independent Study

The history of distance education in the United States begins with courses delivered by mail. Originally known as correspondence study, the method was called "home study" by private, for-profit schools and "independent study" by the universities (see Glatter and Wedell, 1971; MacKenzie, Christensen and Rigby, 1968; Watkins and Wright, 1992). The earliest documented home study course offered in the United States was in shorthand.

Study at home became interactive with the development of cheap and reliable mail services that permitted students to correspond with their instructors. The academic respectability of correspondence teaching was formally recognized in 1883 when the State of New York authorized the Chautauqua Institute to award degrees through this method. In 1890 the Colliery Engineer School of Mines based in Wilkes-Barre, Pennsylvania, began to advertise a home study course on mine safety which quickly became very popular (see Figure 2-2). The school soon began to offer other courses and in 1891 became the International Correspondence Schools (ICS). As the railroad industry gained importance, ICS offered correspondence courses to workers from as many as 150 railroad com-

Figure 2.2   **Replica of 1890 Newspaper Advertisement for the Colliery Engineer School of Mines.** One of the first home study programs in the U.S. and the beginning of the International Correspondence Schools (Courtesy ICS).

MINING SCHOOL.

Tuition by Correspondence

MR. ALEXANDER DICK, M. E.,
ENGLISH GOVERNMENT CERTIFIED COLLIERY MANAGER,
No. 1 North Fell St., WILKES-BARRE, PA.

is commencing a series of Correspondence Lessons for the purpose of preparing candidates for Mine Foremen's Certificates.

This system of teaching which has worked most successfully in Great Britain has many advantages, a few of which are as follows:

(1). It enables pupils at any distance to participate in the benefits of a large school and to obtain direct connection with the writings of the best authorities on mining.

(2). The pupil may commence his course of tuition at **any time** and may extend his lessons **over any period of time for the same fee.**

(3). No pupil need fear want of sufficient education to begin the course as all subjects are taken from the beginning, and every student's papers are treated independently.

SYLLABUS.

Arithmetic in Relation to Mining.
Ventilation—Theory and Practice.
Modes of Working Coal.
Surveying.
Mechanics of Mining.
The Art of Sketching. Etc., Etc.

PROSPECTUS AND TERMS ON APPLICATION.

panies; in fact, railroad cars were sent around the country to provide hands-on instruction. Today ICS is the largest commercial provider of home study programs in the United States.

In Great Britain, Isaac Pitman began to teach shorthand by correspondence in 1840, soon after the invention of the "Penny Post," which delivered a letter anywhere in the kingdom for a penny. On the Continent, in 1856, a Frenchman, Charles Toussaint, and a German, Gustav Langenscheidt began to teach languages by correspondence. There is, as yet, no evidence of communication between those Europeans and such American pioneers as Thomas Foster, founder of ICS. Certainly there is evidence of a great deal of interaction in the nineteenth century between American and British enthusiasts of the general idea of what we might now call nontraditional higher education.

In the 1880s educators at the University of Cambridge in England tried to establish a degree by correspondence, and when it was rejected by the authorities, Richard Moulton, one of the strongest advocates of the idea, migrated to

Distance education in the form of correspondence teaching was well-established in the United States long before the invention of computers and television.

the United States to help William Rainey Harper set up the new University of Chicago. Harper, a professor of Hebrew, learned the idea of teaching by correspondence as a faculty member at the Chautauqua Institute. Chautauqua was a summer training program for Sunday school teachers, who continued to receive instruction by mail after they returned to their homes. Moving to the University of Chicago as president in 1892, Harper established an extension division to deliver university courses by mail. This was the world's first university distance education program.

In 1906 the Calvert School of Baltimore enrolled four pupils in its home study courses, becoming the first primary school in the United States to offer instruction by correspondence. Today the Calvert School has more than 10,000 students around the world enrolled in its courses.

Correspondence educators have established a tradition of reaching out to learners who are otherwise unprovided for. Among these, in the eighteenth and early nineteenth centuries must be included women. Perhaps for this reason, women have played an important part in the history of distance education. For example, Anna Eliot Ticknor established and ran one of the first home study schools, the Society to Encourage Studies at Home, from 1873 until her death in 1896. The purpose of this "school" was to support women in home studies by providing materials, tutoring, and counseling. Students and their teachers corresponded monthly. A broad range of courses were offered, and a group of eight women helped Ticknor run the Society from her Boston home. During its 24 years of operation, the Society enrolled over 7,000 students from all over the

United States. Most of what is known about Ticknor is found in *Society to Encourage Studies at Home*, published in 1897 by the Riverside Press in Cambridge, Massachusetts. According to Hartley (1992), this publication is available on microfilm from Research Publications, Inc., as number 4801 of the History of Women series.

According to Bittner and Mallory (1933), by 1930 correspondence teaching was offered by 39 American universities. Over time, more and more universities, schools, and for-profit organizations began to offer such courses. Some of the for-profit organizations brought the method into disrepute by dubious sales practices, and to bring order to the business, in 1926 the for-profit schools organized the National Home Study Council. In 1994 the National Home Study Council changed its name to the Distance Education and Training Council. In 1968, in an attempt to distinguish themselves from the home study schools, university correspondence educators decided to call their method "independent study." They became the Independent Study Division of the National University Extension Association, later the National University Continuing Education Association (NUCEA). In 1992 a new organization, the American Association for Collegiate Independent Study (AACIS), was formed to advance the interests of Independent Study professionals, especially in providing continuing education and training.

Problems of Terminology and Concepts

Consideration of the development of correspondence study raises a number of important conceptual and terminological issues.

Independent Study

Not only the historical roots but also the philosophical and methodological roots of distance education lie in correspondence education, and for this reason it is important to understand some of the practices and concepts of correspondence education. Among the most important concepts is that of independent study.

The concept of independent study as used in the United States includes two subconcepts, and both have a part to play in our understanding of distance education. First, correspondence educators, in calling their method independent study, gave us the idea of the student being independent of the instructor in time and place—that is, at a distance. However, the pioneers also developed a second meaning of their students' independence—students making decisions concerning their learning—an independence that was forced on them as a result of their geographic independence. An enthusiastic commentator about learner independence in this second sense was the University of Wisconsin-Madison's Professor Charles Wedemeyer. After a lifetime of teaching and administering university correspondence programs, he wrote:

Independent study consists of various forms of teaching-learning in which teachers and learners carry out their essential tasks and responsibilities apart from one another, communicating in a variety of ways for the purpose of freeing internal learners from inappropriate class pacings or patterns, of providing external learners with opportunities to continue learning in their own environments, and of developing in all learners the capacity to carry on self-directed learning." (1971. p. 550)

By popularizing a term that described distance learning in terms of learner self direction as well as geographic separation, Wedemeyer laid the foundation for the development of an American theory of distance education. Unfortunately, the term independent study also led to American distance education being disregarded by many foreign scholars, because outside the United States the term independent study does not signify that "teachers and learners carry out their essential tasks and responsibilities apart from one another, communicating in a variety of ways." Outside the United States such activity has been defined as distance education. Today the term independent study is only used by members of the National University Continuing Education (NUCEA) Independent Study Division and describes courses using print and correspondence more than other media.

The term distance education is a translation of the German term *fernunterricht*, the French *télé-enseignement*, and the Spanish *educación a distancia*. Interestingly, distance was a term used in the early history of American correspondence education and predates the term independent study; for example, Axford (1963) quotes a University of Wisconsin catalog of 1896 that says the "earnest student may do good work at a distance." The contemporary use of the term can be traced to the German, Otto Peters, who first employed it at the 1969 conference of the International Council for Correspondence Education (ICCE). He attributed it to the British adult educator, Brian Jackson (Peters, 1969).

Learner Autonomy

Whereas in other countries (and, among some educators in the United States) distance education has been regarded as simply a delivery mechanism having little or no philosophical or theoretical foundation, Wedemeyer's idea that learners may be independent not only of "inappropriate class pacings or patterns" but also "to carry on self-directed learning" led to the development of a unique theory. While this theory takes into account the variables that are significant when learners must be in communication with instructors by media, generally found in communications theory, it also takes into account the idea of the self-directed adult learner, which is studied in the field of adult education, and so connects communications theory with the theory of andragogy (discussed in Chapter 8). This gives American distance education a different flavor from that of Europe, where there is little or no emphasis on the concept of learner self-directedness, or autonomy.

In practice also, American distance education is more likely to engage the potential of adult students to control or participate in the conduct of their own distance learning. Outside the United States, as will be seen later, distance education courses are highly structured, and "class pacings" are, in fact, insisted on. In many distance teaching institutions, students are enrolled in annual cohorts and are required to complete all stages of their studies in lockstep fashion (see Henderson and Nathenson, 1984). The focus on self-direction of the individual learner that has been a significant feature of American independent study promises to become even more significant as we move further into the "network" generation of distance learning.

AIM and the Open University

The late 1960s and early 1970s was a time of critical change in distance education. It was a time of experimenting with new media in education and new instructional techniques, which led to the beginning of new educational theorizing. The two most important developments were the University of Wisconsin's AIM Project and Britain's Open University.

The purpose of the Articulated Instructional Media Project (AIM), funded by the Carnegie Corporation from 1964 to 1968 and directed by Charles Wedemeyer, was to find ways of joining (i.e., articulating) various communication media for teaching off-campus students. The media included correspondence study guides and correspondence tutoring, programs by radio, television, and recorded audiotapes; telephone conferences; and local library resources. Personal counseling, discussions in local study groups, and the use of university laboratories during summer periods were integral elements of the project.

AIM Presents a Systems Model

AIM represented a historic milestone in the history of distance education: the beginning of the idea of the total system of distance education and the first test. AIM tested the viability of the idea that the functions of the teacher could be divided, that instruction could be assembled by a team of specialists and then delivered through numerous media. It tested the idea that a learner could benefit from the presentation strengths of the broadcast media, and at the same time, the interaction that was possible by correspondence and telephone. It allowed learners to be self-directed as they worked with the mediated instruction, but human helpers were available to assist when needed (Wedemeyer and Najem, 1969).

In 1965 Wedemeyer gave a lecture about AIM in Wiesbaden, Germany. Afterwards Frank Jessup from the University of Oxford told him about the idea then circulating in Britain for a "University of the Air" that would teach primarily by television. Jessup invited Wedemeyer to Oxford where he met with Professor Harold Wiltshire and Dr. Fred Bayliss of the University of Nottingham. Wedemeyer told them about AIM, and they told him about the work they were doing in teaching economics at the university level in courses that also attempted to integrate correspondence, television, readings, and face-to-face tutorials. This work, they said, was based on American exemplars and clearly had many similarities with AIM.

In London Wedemeyer met Michael Young, founder of the International Extension College, and in Nottingham he met Wiltshire's colleague Walter James, who with Bayliss wrote the Nottingham courses. To all these and others, including the future British Minister of Education, Christopher Chataway, Wedemeyer explained the philosophy and method of what was then the most advanced form of independent study in the United States. AIM, he explained, was based on "the philosophy of correspondence study . . . (which) operates . . . on the individual pursuit of learning . . . to provide integrated sequential learning at a rate and in a place that is most appropriate for adults . . ." (Wedemeyer, 1981, p. 23).

Above all, he drew attention to what he considered the flaws in the AIM structure, and by so doing made what may be regarded as one of America's biggest contributions to distance education. "AIM," wrote Wedemeyer, "was an experimental prototype with three fatal flaws: it had no control over its faculty, and hence its curriculum; it lacked control over its funds; and it had no control over academic rewards (credits, degrees) for its students. The implications were clear: a large-scale, non-experimental institution of the AIM type would have to start with complete autonomy and control" (Wedemeyer, 1981, p. 23).

Birth of the Open University

In 1967 the British government set up a committee to plan a revolutionary new educational institution. It would be a nationwide university system with no resident students. It would be large, well funded, and would employ the fullest range of communications technologies to teach a full university undergraduate curriculum to any adult who wanted such education.

In September 1967 the planning committee began its work, with Harold Wiltshire as a member. In 1968 Walter Perry was nominated as vice-chancellor, or president; Anastasios Christodoulou was named university secretary; and Walter James was appointed one of six directors of studies. In November 1968 Christodoulou visited Wisconsin to study AIM's methods, and two months later Wedemeyer met with Perry and his officials in London.

In September 1969 Wedemeyer moved to the site of the Open University's new campus at Milton Keynes in England to spend several months assisting the British in further developing their plans for the new institution. Even before then, Walter James had written to Wedemeyer:

> You bear some responsibility for the emergence of the Open University in this country. It was your talk on Articulated Instructional Media (AIM) that stimulated us to produce at Nottingham the first university course in this country in which television broadcasts and correspondence instruction were integrated; and it was this experience which produced interest in the University of the Air idea. (Wedemeyer, 1982, p. 24)

According to Wedemeyer, "Almost the entire educational geography of an open educational system was identified in the AIM experiment" (Wedemeyer,

1982, p. 24). In particular, with AIM's three fatal flaws in mind, British policy-makers resisted the pressure from the higher education establishment that they be funded to undertake distance education by setting up units within the conventional universities. Instead, in 1969 the British government made the courageous decision to establish a fully autonomous, degree-granting institution. The British Open University has justified the decision, and having been very successful it has served as a model for similar institutions around the world (see Chapter 3). It also serves as the best example of a total systems approach to distance education.

Broadcasting and Teleconferencing

The third major evolutionary development in the history of distance education was the use of broadcast media (radio and television) which eventually gave way to teleconferencing.

Radio

Broadcasting in education has a long history. Pittman (1986, p. 40) quotes a statement in a 1927 presentation to the Federal Radio Commission from the State University of Iowa that shows the optimism with which radio was then regarded: " . . . it is no imaginary dream to picture the school of tomorrow as an entirely different institution from that of today, because of the use of radio in teaching."

Besides Iowa, a number of other universities, notably Pennsylvania State College, Ohio State University, and University of Wisconsin, began general broadcasting between 1911 and 1922. In February 1925 the State University of Iowa offered its first five radio courses for credit. Of the 80 students who enrolled that first semester, 64 would go on to finish their coursework at the university (Pittman, 1986).

Radio as a delivery technology for education in the United States, however, was to fail. The lukewarm interest shown by university faculty and administrators, and the amateurism of those few who were interested, proved a poor match for the fierce commitment to radio exhibited by commercial broadcasters who wanted it as a medium for advertising. Note that educational radio has been more successful in developing countries (Tilson, 1994).

Television

Educational television was developing as early as 1934. In that year the State University of Iowa presented television broadcasts in such subjects as oral hygiene and identifying star constellations; by 1939 the university's station had broadcast almost 400 educational programs (Unwin and McAleese, 1988). In that same year a high school in Los Angeles experimented with television in the classroom (Levenson, 1945). After World War II, when television frequencies

In the 1960s and '70s many universities acquired licenses for broadcasting Public Broadcasting Services television to their local communities.

were allocated, 242 of the 2053 channels were given to noncommercial use. In addition to programs broadcast on these channels, some of the best educational television was pioneered by commercial stations. The National Broadcasting Company (NBC) aired Johns Hopkins University's "Continental Classroom," which was used by some higher education institutions for credit instruction, and the Columbia Broadcasting System (CBS) broadcast their "Sunrise Semester."

Although commercial broadcasters gave up on these public service offerings, educational television fared better than educational radio because of the contributions of the Ford Foundation. From 1950 onward, Ford gave many hundreds of millions of dollars in grants for educational broadcasting. In 1962 the federal Educational Television Facilities Act funded educational television station construction. In 1965 the Carnegie Commission on Educational Television issued a report that led to Congress passing the Public Broadcasting Act of 1967, setting up the Corporation for Public Broadcasting (CPB).

In 1956 the public schools of Washington County, Maryland, were linked in a closed-circuit television service, and about the same time the Chicago TV College pioneered the involvement of community colleges in teaching by television. In 1961 the Midwest Program on Airborne Television Instruction involved

This university facility in the 1980s transmitted the classroom by video to branch campuses by TI telephone lines.

six states in designing and producing programs that were broadcast from transmitters transported on DC-6 airplanes. According to Unwin and McAleese (1988), this project, which lasted six years, helped break down state barriers and paved the way for future educational broadcasting by satellite.

Instructional Television Fixed Service (ITFS) also came on the scene in 1961 when the Federal Communications Commission (FCC) issued an experimental license to the Plainedge School System on Long Island, New York (Curtis and Biedenback, 1979). ITFS is a low-cost distribution system that limits reception to a distance of about 20 miles. A pioneering effort in use of microwave was the Stanford Instructional Television Network (SITN), which in 1969 began broadcasting 120 engineering courses to 900 engineers at 16 member companies (DiPaolo, 1992).

The first cable television (CATV) began in 1952. In 1972 the FCC required all cable systems to provide an educational channel. One of the first such channels was the Appalachian Community Service Network, based at the University of Kentucky, which developed into today's Learning Channel. One of the first attempts to make a videocourse interactive was in Columbus, Ohio, in 1977, allowing students to respond to tests by means of a special keypad (Baldwin and McVoy, 1983).

Audioconferencing

Audioconferencing means conducting a class by telephone using the public lines. A conference can be conducted by individual students at their homes or offices using regular handsets, but usually when we refer to audioconferencing, we mean teaching that uses special equipment consisting of a speaker (called a convener) and microphones including a number of different distant groups of learners. Almost any number of sites can be joined together, either by an operator or more efficiently by means of a bridge that each site dials so that all sites are joined simultaneously.

One of the oldest, and certainly the largest and most famous, audioconference systems is the Educational Telephone Network (ETN) at the University of Wisconsin. It was set up in 1965 as an outcome of the AIM project, with the immediate purpose of providing continuing education for physicians. Starting with 18 locations and one weekly program, the system expanded to use special equipment, 200 locations, and more than 100 programs every week. Approximately 95 percent of the network time is used for continuing or noncredit education, with considerable emphasis on the professions, mainly doctors, lawyers, pharmacists, nurses, engineers, ministers of religion, librarians, and social workers. (For more on the history of ETN, see Moore, 1981.)

Satellites and the Emergence of Consortia

The age of satellite communications began on April 6, 1965, with the launching of the Early Bird satellite. Early Bird, later designated INTELSAT I, weighed 76 pounds in orbit and offered 240 telephone circuits or one channel of television over the North Atlantic. By the end of 1967, 4 International Telecommunications Satellite Organization (INTELSAT) satellites were in orbit, and today INTELSAT serves virtually every country in the world, operating a global system of 19 operational satellites for public use, each offering 24,000 telephone circuits, which can be boosted to 120,000 circuits by digital multiplication processes.

In the mid-1970s several U.S. universities began to experiment with transmitting educational programs by the Applications Technology Satellite (ATS). One of the first was the University of Alaska, which offered continuing education courses for teachers. NASA (National Aeronautics and Space Administration) used the same satellite to deliver educational programs to more than 2500 villages in India (Rossman, 1992). The Pan-Pacific Education and Communications Experiments by Satellite (PEACESAT) was created in 1971 at the University of Hawaii to provide satellite telecommunications over some 20 Pacific islands. It used the ATS-1 satellite for educational, social, environmental, and health programs.

Fixed satellite services operate at low power, and the equipment required to transmit and receive signals is quite expensive. Programs are usually transmitted to receiving stations that then distribute them by ITFS or terrestrial networks. The newer technology of Direct Broadcast Satellite (DBS) that has been developed in the 1990s allows individuals to receive programs directly in their homes or for individual schools to receive directly at the school. DBS satellite dishes are small and cheap (around $300); however, they are not steerable so must be aimed at only one satellite program provider.

During the 1980s there was an ever increasing availability of broadcast outlets through ITFS, cable television, and satellite channels. Whereas it was the British Open University that led to an explosion of interest in distance teaching in the rest of the world, what caused a similar interest in the United States was the availability of new technology, especially satellite technology. The American organizational device for using this new technology was the consortium, a voluntary association of independent institutions that share the costs, the work, and the results of designing, delivering, and teaching educational courses.

One of the first such consortia was organized in 1975 and named the University of Mid-America (UMA). UMA was established by nine midwestern universities, based upon a successful video-based program at the University of Nebraska. The idea was that each of the universities would produce courses that would be available to any student in the consortium (McNeil, 1980). UMA was discontinued in 1982 due to low enrollments, high video production costs, and loss of funding support. However, independent study courses emphasizing the use of video continued at most of the universities that formed the consortium.

The National University Teleconferencing Network (NUTN)

NUTN was conceived at a NUCEA meeting in Washington, D.C., in February 1982. J. O. Grantham, Director of University Extension at Oklahoma State University, took the lead in convening a planning conference the following month in Kansas City. Of the 70 member institutions of NUCEA, 40 participated and agreed to work together to plan and deliver educational programs by satellite. The network was established with 66 universities and the Smithsonian Institution as members, and with its base at Oklahoma State University. It moved to Old Dominion University in 1994. (For more background on NUTN, see Oberle, 1990.)

Among the factors contributing to the founding of NUTN are some of the same reasons for the rapid expansion of other forms of distance education in the 1980s: limited resources, both financial and human, declining enrollments, the information explosion, and fundamental changes in how American society was communicating. Success of the consortium was due to the flexibility and local autonomy it provided. Virtually all of the founding institutions believed that by supporting one campus to develop courses or one-time programs to be shared with the entire group, they could not only reduce costs but serve more people as well.

NUTN allowed its members to share their experience with the technology of satellite teleconferencing to everyone's advantage. They discovered that the technology worked fine and that the major challenges were program quality, managing production costs, effective marketing, and convincing university faculty and administrators of the value of teleconferences. It also needs to be noted that the NUTN model works because it fits very well with the free enterprise and entrepreneurial philosophy of most U.S. universities. A teleconference on a timely topic that is marketed well can attract an audience at hundreds of sites and generate substantial revenue for the originating institution.

National Technological University (NTU)

NTU is a consortium of an entirely different nature. Established in 1985 and based in Fort Collins, Colorado, it is an accredited university offering graduate and continuing education courses in engineering, and it awards its own degrees. However, NTU has no faculty or campus of its own; it relies on courses taught by faculty at major universities around the country. Initially, courses were provided from a pool of 24 universities, and today 45 participate. Courses are uplinked to NTU by satellite from the originating university and then redistributed by satellite by NTU.

The success of NTU can be attributed to the dedication and energy of its founder, Lionel Baldwin (himself an engineer), as well as the particular market niche it occupies. Engineering is a rapidly changing field, and engineers are critically dependent on knowing about new developments. Organizations are quite willing to pay a significant price to keep their engineers up to date, especially when such in-service training is provided in a manner that eliminates travel costs and time away from the job. Engineering professors are willing to participate because they receive financial renumeration for every NTU student who takes their courses. Furthermore, the form of television technology involved ("candid classrooms") requires no real change in their usual teaching methods.

Both NUTN and NTU illustrate some of the key elements of teleconference consortia and a new form of market-driven distance education that emerged in the United States and elsewhere. Because they represent a large pool of universities, they are able to offer a broad selection of courses to prospective clients (either individuals or organizations). Thus the consortium can provide a better range of courses than any single member can, no matter how big or established they are. Second, members of the consortium compete against each other to offer the best quality and most timely courses, introducing a competitive element at all levels (including individual professors and the courses they teach) that has been largely absent from the U.S. educational system. As a result, the needs of the customer (students, employees, companies) dictate which courses are in demand and hence marketable, not the often esoteric interest of academics.

The latter half of the 1980s and the early 1990s saw the emergence of many more distance education consortia based on satellite television, and also a large industry of "business TV" delivered by satellite. More will be said about this in the next chapter.

Two-way Videoconferencing

The consortia described above use one-way-video–two-way-audio communications. Participants at all sites see and hear the presenters from the originating site but can only address them by audio; participants cannot see other participants but can hear them.

One of the newest technologies to be used in distance education is two-way videoconferencing. There are several ways that videoconferencing can be delivered, and they fall into two main types. The older method has been in existence in digital format since the early 1980s and consists of teaching from one classroom to another, using special data communications technology for transmission at rates of T1 (1.5 mbps., or megabits per second) to 384 kbps (kilobits per second). The video signals are compressed by a device called a codec. A few years ago a codec was as large as a refrigerator, but today it can be fitted inside a personal computer. As a result, videoconferencing is now possible at transmission rates as low as 56 kbps and it is common now to provide instruction by this technology on an individual basis at a learner's desktop computer.

Frequently referred to as videotelephony, this technology is associated with ISDN, which provides for 128 kbps of data transmission for the same cost as a standard telephone call and is now available in most U.S. metropolitan areas. Fiber-optic telephone lines make two-way video possible at even higher data rates (45 mbps). Thus this latest technology allows for videoconferencing between small groups of learners and other groups, or between individual learners and their instructors, with the video displayed in a live window on the participant's personal computer.

There are still significant technical limitations to the number of sites that can be accommodated, the cost of equipment is still high, and the actual merits of being able to see the instructor or other students are usually overestimated. This technology, however, is likely to become increasingly important in distance education in the years ahead. Furthermore, videoconferencing is becoming a fundamental component of computer networks and multimedia, the third generation of distance education technology.

Computer Networks and Multimedia

Toward the end of World War II when it took a soldier three days to calculate a ballistic trajectory, a computer, ENIAC, was invented that would do the job in 20 seconds. A few years later the first computer with the capacity of storing a program, EDSAC, began operating in Great Britain. The microprocessor was invented by Intel in 1971, and the first personal computer, the Altair 8800, came onto the market in 1975. By 1989, according to the U.S. Bureau of the Census, 15 percent of all households in the United States had a personal computer and nearly half of all children had access to computers at home or in school. By the end of 1992 there were over 50,000 mainframe computers in the world, including nearly 1,000 supercomputers and over 137 million personal computers. The United States has six times as many computers as Japan, eight times as many as Germany, and ten times the United Kingdom, the next three largest users (Juliussen and Juliussen, 1993).

In education the computer is used as a stand-alone tool when a student reads text, listens to sound, and views pictures stored in a program that is stored on a disc, nowadays usually a CD-ROM disc. Students can pick their way through various paths of information, and this is sometimes referred to by computer enthusiasts as "interaction." (In a later chapter we will label this type of interaction "learner-content interaction.") However, such interaction does not in itself qualify a computer program as educational. For a program to be educational there must be a relationship between learners and teachers. Like other recorded materials, computer programs become part of distance education when they are linked by telecommunications technologies to provide interaction, either delayed or in real time, with an instructor.

Linking computers by telecommunications is achieved for both individual learners and for group learning. When it is for groups, it is usually referred to as audiographics. The term audiographics refers to a range of systems that send graphics through standard telephone lines and thus enhance an audioconference. The most common audiographics systems consist of a series of personal computers linked through the public telephone system. Peripherals that can be attached to the computers include tablets and light pens, cameras that transmit slow-scan pictures, and scanners for transmitting documents. When linked through a bridge, the computers at all sites allow students and teachers to interact in real time with the graphic and visual images as well as the audio messages.

Computer networks link up personal computers with the telephone system. The teacher can prepare instructional materials on his or her personal computer and transmit them to students anywhere in the world through the Internet, a network of mainframe computers. The teacher can then conduct a computer conference interaction in real time or asynchronously by E-mail and bulletin board. Students can communicate with each other and search for information in the world's databases. With ISDN and fiber-optic lines, as well as improvements in compression technologies, the technology now emerging consists of a convergence of computing, TV, printing, and telecommunications on a multimedia workstation that allows communication in all media, from home or work, on a one-to-one or one-to-many basis in real time. It might seem that our history has come full circle, since in many ways teaching and learning by this medium is surely an electronic-age correspondence course.

Summary

- Distance education in the United States emerged principally from nineteenth-century correspondence study. The nature of correspondence courses placed considerable responsibility on the learner, which gave rise to the term "independent study" to describe university correspondence courses.

- Charles Wedemeyer's work at the University of Wisconsin contributed to the development of a total systems approach to distance education. This was taken up in one of the most significant developments in distance education—the founding of the British Open University. The success of the Open University led to the establishment of similar total systems around the world, although, ironically, not in the United States.

- Neither broadcast television nor especially radio have been as successful in the United States as in other countries. In the past decade we have seen the evolution of satellite television consortia that offer courses developed by members to subscribers. NUTN and NTU are two of the most successful examples in the postsecondary domain; others are in the K-12 domain and in business television.

- The most recent technologies are based on combinations of computers and telecommunications; these are mainly computer conferencing, audiographic conferencing, and two-way videoconferencing.

The Scope of Distance Education

Almost every university or college, large corporation, or
school district in the United States is involved in some type
of distance education. This chapter provides an overview of the
types of courses provided by correspondence schools, open universities, teleconference consortia, schools, universities, corporations,
and the armed forces.

Preceding chapters have presented the basic concepts and the historical evolution of distance education. In this chapter we survey its current status in terms
of specific programs and institutions. Addresses for many of the organizations
mentioned are provided in Appendix A.

Correspondence

Even today there are probably more people in the United States studying at a
distance by correspondence than by other methods. Of these the largest number take courses from commercial institutions accredited by the Distance Education and Training Council (DETC). The DETC estimates that in any one year
more than 4 million Americans enroll in home study courses, and that 70 million have taken such courses since 1900, including such well-known figures as
Franklin D. Roosevelt, Walter P. Chrysler, Walter Cronkite, Barry Goldwater, and
Charles Schultz (Valore and Diehl, 1987). Most home study courses are provided by small, commercial schools, although some institutions (such as military schools, who are members of DETC) are publicly funded and have large
enrollments. There are over 100 schools accredited by the DETC, offering more
than 500 different courses, covering training of beauticians and truck drivers,

Figure 3.1 A 1942 Advertisement for a Home Study Course Offered by the National Radio Institute (Courtesy, DETC).

jewellers and gun repairers, cooks, hotel managers, and travel agents. Almost all these courses are in print media and distributed by mail.

Two of the most famous home study schools are the American School, founded in 1897 in Chicago and the International Correspondence Schools (ICS) in Scranton, Pennsylvania, which was founded in 1890. ICS (which is now owned by National Education Corp.) is one of the largest distance education institutions in the world, with more than 250,000 students. It offers more than 40 diploma programs in technical skills (electronics, auto mechanics), computers (PC repair, programming), and business (accounting, marketing), as well as associate degrees in business and engineering.

The U.S. military and other government agencies make extensive use of correspondence study in their training programs. For example, the U.S. Air Force's Extension Course Institute (ECI) has over 300,000 new enrollments per year in approximately 350 courses (Diehl, 1990). Courses offered by ECI cover almost every aspect of air force training, including specialized military subjects and career development skills.

Home study courses usually involve a low degree of interaction (later we will refer to this as dialog) with the instructor and other students. In many home study courses, there may be no contact with an instructor or fellow students; only an exam is taken when the student completes the course material and a grade is mailed back.

Independent Study

Independent study is the term used to describe correspondence courses administered by traditional colleges and universities. There are more than 70 universities offering such courses in the United States today. In most respects these courses are similar to those of the DETC, except that in the independent study course there is usually a higher level of interaction between instructors and students through the exchange of student assignments and tests. In addition to the standard study guides and texts, university independent study courses are more likely to include other media, such as audio- or videotapes, television broadcasts, and computer programs. Access to independent study courses for degrees is not as open as it is to commercial courses, since students must satisfy the entrance requirements of the university offering the courses.

University independent study courses may be offered separate from the on-campus courses or integrated with them. For example, Penn State operates one of the largest independent study programs in this country, serving almost 15,000 students annually with approximately 300 credit and noncredit courses. Many regular students on campus take the courses as a way of solving class scheduling problems or simply because they prefer this way of studying. No distinction is made in their transcripts between the grades awarded for courses taken in class and courses taken by independent study.

About half the universities provide high school courses (Feasley, 1983). The University of Nebraska-Lincoln has specialized in offering high school courses. In 1988 its Independent Study High School (ISHS) had over 12,000 course registrations. ISHS has granted more than 1,000 diplomas since it began. Other universities operating large independent study programs include Alaska, Brigham Young (Utah), Indiana, Iowa, Kansas, Michigan, Minnesota, Missouri, North Dakota, Ohio, South Carolina, Texas, and Wisconsin.

Most independent study programs have an open enrollment policy—that is, students can register and begin a course at any time. However, some institutions require students to wait until the beginning of the month or semester to begin a course. In some cases independent study courses follow the same schedule as regular classes. For example, the University of Arizona VideoCampus is a distance education unit that teaches by videotapes instead of print. Instead of instruction being written out, as in a regular correspondence course, videotapes are made of conventional classes and these are mailed out to distant learners. Students must complete the course assignments by the end of the semester in which it is offered. In addition to campus classes, the VideoCampus also offers videotaped courses produced by the Association for Media-Based Continuing Education for Engineers (AMCEE) and television broadcasts from NTU (see below).

The University of Idaho's Video Outreach Graduate Program provides videotapes for off-campus study, and the Northern Illinois Learning Resources Cooperative offers video-based courses at public libraries. In South Dakota a project called "Overnight" allows special groups such as the universities or the bar association to transmit video programs statewide during early morning hours for recording and then local use as videotape (Summer and Spicer, 1989).

Besides the correspondence courses offered by DETC schools and NUCEA Independent Study Division universities, courses are offered by a number of state education departments. Prominent among these secondary correspondence schools are those of Alaska and North Dakota.

Telecourses

The term telecourses covers those courses in which the primary communication technology is recorded video. These courses may be as simple as the University of Arizona VideoCampus mentioned above, or they may be produced with sophisticated instructional design and to very high production standards. Courses are distributed in a variety of ways, including by mail, as in the Arizona case, or through local cable television channels and ITFS networks. As noted in Chapter 2, the first significant effort in the telecourse area was the work of the Chicago community colleges, who started to offer an Associate of Arts degree by television in 1956.

Learning About Disaster Management

In November 1982 a group of international experts gathered in Madison, Wisconsin, to help create a center to serve the educational needs of disaster and emergency management professionals in the developing world. The advisory board was given the task of defining educational problems in disaster management, identifying course topics, and suggesting individuals who could address these topics. It provided preliminary outlines for 55 courses. The board also recommended that the courses be developed in distance education format, specifically correspondence study, in order to be cost-effective and convenient for delivery to individuals in developing countries.

The following year, the Disaster Management Center (DMC) was established at the University of Wisconsin-Madison, and work was begun on the courses. By 1988, 11 courses were available with over 1,500 individuals enrolled. Courses include Aim and Scope of Disaster Management; Disaster Preparedness; Damage and Needs Assessment; Emergency Health Management After Natural Disaster; Emergency Vector Control After Natural Disaster; Refugee Camp Planning; Famine Assessment and Relief. Each course consists of a textbook and a printed study guide, as well as tests which are mailed to the DMC for scoring. Most courses are available in both English and Spanish.

Since 1985 the DMC has supported the distance learning by conducting a series of workshops around the world. In addition to the printed study materials, videotapes, slide/tape materials, and instructor guides have been developed for the workshops. To date, over 1,800 individuals representing more than 150 organizations and 75 countries have participated in these workshops. The DMC has established relationships with many educational institutions worldwide that are involved in disaster and emergency management activities. This network of collaborating institutions works in both the development and administration of the distance learning courses and workshops.

When the course materials are being prepared, individuals with field experience are asked to share their expertise. More than 50 disaster management professionals in over 20 countries have been involved in the creation of these materials. Funding for the development of the distance learning courses has come from the U.S. Agency for International Development, the Pan-American Health Organization, the U.S. Department of State, and U.S.A. for Africa. Support for the workshops has come from a number of United Nations agencies. The independent studies program of the University of Wisconsin extension department is responsible for the printing and distribution of the courses as well as testing and grading.

SOURCE: Schramm, D. (1992). Disaster Management Center, University of Wisconsin-Madison. *Disasters, 16(4)*, 363–367.

Table 3-1   Sources of Telecourses in the United States

Coast Community College (CCC)
Dallas County Community College (DCCC)
Great Plains National (GPN)
Southern California Consortium
International University Consortium (IUC)
Kirkwood Community College
Maryland Instructional Television
Miami-Dade Community College (MDCC)
Milwaukee Area Community College
San Mateo County Community College
South Carolina ETV (SCETV)
University of Wisconsin Extension (UWEX)

Today, more than 200 college level television courses are produced by community colleges and universities; public broadcasting stations, among which one of the leaders is Maryland Public Television; and by members of the International University Consortium, a consortium of universities and colleges established for this specific purpose (Table 3-1). One of the leading consortia, the Southern California Consortium for Community College Television, includes 35 two-year colleges extending from Santa Barbara to San Diego and has been in existence for over 20 years. Most of these telecourse producers are linked in a voluntary association known as the Telecourse People and share in such activities as marketing and holding conferences for professional development of their faculty and staff.

In 1981 the publisher Walter Annenberg made a grant of $150 million to the Corporation for Public Broadcasting to be used for the improvement of higher education through telecommunications. One of the Annenberg/CPB Project's main contributions has been the provision of funds, typically in the $2 million to $3 million range, for the production of exemplary telecourses. Over 170 college-level credit courses have been produced (Annenberg/CPB Project, 1988). The Annenberg/CPB Project does not itself produce educational programs, but contracts with producers who compete for funding. The Southern California Consortium, led by Coastline Community College, was awarded $5 million to produce The Mechanical Universe. Such a course includes not only television programs, but textbooks, study guides, and faculty and administrator guides.

Courses to be produced under Annenberg/CPB grants announced in 1994 include *A World of Art* (to be produced by the art department of Oregon State University with station KOPB/Portland) an art appreciation course consisting of 10 half-hour videos, accompanying text, study and faculty guides, and CD-ROM ($1 million); and *Music of the World* (to be produced by the Educational Film Center [U.S], with ABC-Australia, Teleac of Holland, and UR, Sweden), an introductory music course with 12 half-hour programs, 12 one-hour audio modules, text, study and faculty guides ($800,000).

Courses are designed by teams of television and other media specialists, instructional designers, and content experts drawn from the contracting institution or consortium, and usually including experts from universities and colleges nationwide. Once produced, telecourses are bought by colleges and universities that provide their own instruction and student support either on campus or through their correspondence divisions and also give their own testing and credit.

Many telecourses are delivered by the Adult Learning Services (ALS) of the Public Broadcasting System (PBS) in cooperation with 190 public television stations and over 2,000 colleges around the country. About 60 percent of American colleges and universities licensed telecourses through the PBS in 1990; of the nation's public television stations, nearly 96 percent broadcast college-level telecourses. By 1992 more than 2 million students had enrolled in ALS courses, with about a quarter million now enrolling every year. A handbook published in 1994 by the Annenberg/CPB Project lists more than 150 nationally available television and audio courses and a list of PBS Adult Learning Services liasions in all states.

Open Universities

When the British Open University (BOU) was established in 1969, it was not the first university dedicated solely to distance learning. The right to such a title probably belongs to the University of South Africa, which began a nationwide distance education system soon after the end of World War II. In fact the British studied the South African experience as well as that of Australia, the U.S.S.R., Japan, and the United States as they prepared plans for their Open University in the late 1960s. Within a very few years, the BOU had proven itself to be so excellent and so successful that it transformed distance education, many would say higher education also, and became a model for many similar institutions around the world (Table 3-2).

With over 100,000 graduates since 1972 and more than 130,000 students taking courses every year, a full-time staff of 2,800 and a part-time staff of over 5,000 tutors and counselors, with 13 regional and 250 local learning centers across Britain, the OU is one of the most successful examples of a total system of distance education. One of the primary missions of the British Open University, which has been adopted by many others, but not all, is to open access to higher education and make it available to anyone who wants it, not just by offering courses at a distance but also by removing other constraints.

While not all open universities are the same, the majority adhere to most of the following general principles:

- Any person can enroll, regardless of previous education.
- Students can begin a course at any time.

Table 3-2   Open Universities

University of South Africa
British Open University, United Kingdom
Universidad Nacional de Educación a Distancia, Spain
Allama Iqbal Open University, Pakistan
Al Quds Open University, Jordan
Anadoulou University, Turkey
Andhra Pradesh Open University, India
Athabasca University, Canada
Central Broadcasting & Television University, China
Open Universiteit Heerlen, Netherlands
FernUniversität, Germany
Indira Gandhi National Open University, India
Kyongi Open University, Korea
National Open University, Taiwan
Open Polytechnic of New Zealand
Open University of Israel
Sukhothai Thammathirat Open University, Thailand
Universidad Estatal a Distancia, Costa Rica
Universidad Nacional Abierta, Venezuela
Universidade Aberta, Portugal
Universitas Terbuka, Indonesia
University of the Air, Japan

- Course study is done at a home or anywhere the student chooses.
- Course materials are developed by a team of experts.
- Tutoring is provided by other specialists.
- The enterprise is national in scope.
- The enterprise enrolls large numbers and enjoys economies of scale.

Of course, there are exceptions to each of these principles. For example, while the BOU admits anyone on a first-come-first-served basis, it imposes a lower age limit, and enrollment in a particular course may require prerequisites. BOU courses have fixed start dates and schedules that all students must meet. Some courses may insist on participation in local study groups or residential weeks. Purchased rather than original materials (such as texts or tapes) may be used. Tutoring may not be provided to all students or for all courses. In a few countries, the university may have only regional or provincial rather than national outreach.

Another characteristic of open universities is their commitment to the use of audio, visual, and computer media to supplement print in a very systematic way. For example, the BOU produces its courses in association with BBC television (initially, it was to be called the University of the Air). Audio- and videotapes are common components of open university courses, and many of these universities are currently exploring ways of using computer-based learning. However, as with independent study courses in the United States, print materials still provide the backbone of most open university courses. Print has been found to be most effective for communicating much of a university curriculum, and is generally preferred by students to audio and video media. Most open universities, and this is certainly true of the BOU, invest much money and time and human resources to ensure their printed materials are extremely well designed and well produced, to make them both very attractive to study from as well as pedagogically sound.

Although the United States does not currently have an open university, there are a number of institutions that share some similarities with the open universities. Empire State College (which is part of the State University of New York) offers associate and bachelor degrees, while having no campus or faculty of its own. Instead it relies on courses and faculty from other institutions. Students create their own individualized degree program and are assigned a faculty member (mentor) from a cooperating institution to work with. Empire State College was established in 1971 and enrolls over 6,000 students annually. Regents College of the University of the State of New York, Thomas A. Edison State College in New Jersey, and Governors State University in Illinois are similar in their "open" nature. These institutions are important because they offer a way of obtaining a college degree after learning in nontraditional ways, including distance education.

Nova University, founded in 1964 and based in Fort Lauderdale, Florida, offers graduate degrees (master and doctoral) through a system of regional learning centers and adjunct faculty. Students are assigned to groups called clusters that meet together for weekend seminars. A professional educator (usually a professor located at a university in the area) is assigned to coordinate the academic and administrative affairs for each cluster and serve as liasion between the students, faculty, and the university. Students may join clusters at one of three times of the year and must complete one seminar every three months. Walden University, which has its headquarters in Naples, Florida, offers doctoral programs in administration/management, health services, human services, and education. Walden uses procedures similar to Nova, organizing weekend regional sessions with adjunct faculty, along with three-week summer sessions at the University of Indiana, Bloomington. In 1994 Walden began to use a computer network to facilitate interaction with and among its students.

While institutions such as those mentioned above are not strictly engaged in distance education (since the main form of communication is in conventional face-to-face classes), they are of interest because they share several of the characteristics of open universities, including flexible enrollment/completion policies, lack of full-time teaching faculty or a central campus, and the practice of tutoring or mentoring. In some cases, they allow students to combine credits earned from a variety of different learning experiences (including corre-spondence study).

Verduin and Clark (1991) provide further discussion of such alternative institutions of higher learning in the context of distance education in the United States. For further description and discussion of open universities, see MacKen-zie, Postgate, and Scupham (1975) or Rumble and Harry (1982).

Satellite Television Networks

The use of satellites to deliver courses has become one of the most popular forms of distance education and training. A variety of networks and consortia have emerged to serve different student populations. Altogether it is estimated that there are over 60,000 receive sites in the United States. Unlike the other forms of distance education discussed so far in this chapter, satellite-based courses are usually delivered to students in groups according to a schedule determined by the instructor. Sometimes this form of television is referred to as "narrowcasting" to distinguish it from broadcast programs that can be received by the general public.

Business TV and Corporate Training

Many major corporations make extensive use of satellite transmission to con-duct training at their branch offices and plants around the country and world. The use by corporations of their own private satellite network is usually referred to as business television (BTV), and includes a range of functions besides training, such as product announcements and sales meetings. In most cases the programs are one-way broadcasts, but in some cases they become teleconferences by the addition of a two-way audio channel. Most programs originate from private television studios owned by the corporation, and they are received by means of a satellite dish outside local offices or plants. There are over 80 private BTV networks in the United States, some of which reach thou-sands of sites and millions of employees (Irwin, 1992).

The expenditures on American corporate training are estimated at over $40 billion per year, which is comparable to the total funds spent on university edu-cation. About half the Fortune 500 companies use some form of satellite tele-conferencing to deliver this continuing education. Typical is IBM's Interactive Satellite Education Network (ISEN). This was set up in 1983 and was comple-mented by a second operation called Corporate Educational Network (CENET) in 1987. It has been estimated (Lane, 1992b) that in the period 1989 to 1992 the savings for IBM in travel and other expenses of using the satellite networks amounted to over $15 million. The IBM system broadcasts 12 concurrent courses to 238 classrooms in 49 locations. Each day about 100 students view 1 of 9 courses with up to 3 courses offered at each location. The system allows one-way full-motion videopictures, high-quality two-way audio, and digital key-pad response units. The success of the system in this country has led to IBM

Classroom and control room used for broadcasting and receiving broadcasts by satellite video.

installing similar networks in Japan, Australia, the United Kingdom, France, and Germany.

Other corporations using satellite television include Kodak Corporation, which transmits twice-weekly, two-hour training programs, currently nationwide but with plans for an international network; Tandem Computers, broadcasting to 11 European countries as well as to 72 sites in North America; the AETNA Life and Casualty corporation; and Domino's Pizza, whose training director sends his mobile uplink to any store in the country where an employee has something to teach the rest. AT&T expanded from 5 teleconference sites in 1983 to 130 in 1987, and some 20,000 of their employees take teleconference courses each year.

Satellite television is a highly cost-effective way to provide employee training. Ostendorf (1988) reports a study conducted by Merrill Lynch in which offices that received television broadcasts had a 40 percent higher sales record than offices that did not get the programs. Porter (1990) describes the positive impact of televised courses at AETNA for business writing skills. When there is a new product, the capability of training the entire sales force at one time means more immediate sales and hence extra revenue. Most companies find that compared to the costs of travel for training, satellite television saves considerable money (Johnson, 1989).

Business TV programming accomplishes many other functions important to companies other than formal training courses. One of these is developing and maintaining company morale and employees' motivation. Federal Express, for example, produces a daily broadcast that goes to more than 800 company locations. These broadcasts provide details about current shipping operations or problems as well as focusing on examples of outstanding employee performance. It is common for the senior executives of companies to make regular appearances to explain policies and reinforce goals.

In addition to the private corporate networks, there are also more than 20 BTV consortia that serve specific industries or professions (Table 3-3). In most cases, these consortia maintain an administration to manage the network and serve as brokers for courses developed by members. Many of these courses are accredited, and their completion provides continuing education credits for participants. Some examples include:

- The American Management Association (AMA) offers a series of satellite conferences each year on topics of interest to their membership. Programs offered in 1993 included First Annual Conference for Working Women, Fifth Annual Multicultural Black Managers Forum, and Sixth Annual Secretaries Briefing.

- Executive Communications and the American Rehabilitation Education Network (AREN) are related companies, the first of which provides videoconferences for upper- and middle-level executives and the latter is a network for health-care professionals and administrators involved in medical rehabilitation. Executive Communications broadcasts a series of

Table 3-3   Examples of Business Television Networks

American Law Network (ALN)
American Rehabilitation Educational Network (AREN)
Automotive Satellite Television Network (ASTN)
Bankers-TV/CPA-TV
Continuing Legal Education Satellite Network (CLESN)
Emergency Education Network (EENET)
Financial Services Network (FSN)
Food Services Network (FSNET)
Hospital Satellite Network (HSN)
Law Enforcement Television Network (LETN)

videoconferences called *ManagemenTVision* to about 300 locations. AREN distributes programs to about 650 locations, examples of programs being "Empowering Staff Nurses Through Nursing Care Management" and "Computer Technology: Applications for Clinical Nursing Practice."

• EENET (Emergency Education Network) is the Federal Emergency Management Agency's satellite training system aimed at fire service and emergency management personnel. Programs broadcast in 1988 included "Hazardous Materials and Protective Clothing."

Department of Defense

There are numerous distance education programs involving satellite television in military settings. The Army Logistics Management College has offered one-way-video–two-way-audio programs on its Satellite Education Network (SEN) for several years to some 13,000 learners within the armed forces and government agencies. In 1994 it had 71 sites. The Air Technology Network (ATN) is operated by the Air Force Institute of Technology and currently reaches over 18,000 students at 69 sites across the United States. ATN offers courses primarily in engineering and logistics, and by the end of 1994, is supposed to be available to every air force base in the country. The navy operates the CNET Electronic Schoolhouse Network which downlinks classes to major naval training centers around the country. The Interservice distance learning network is called the Defense Information Systems Agency (DISA). DISA manages the Defense Commercial Telecommunications Network (DCTN), which uses the Telstar 4 satellite. ATN is the first user of DCTN.

In addition to these large nationwide networks, the armed forces are experimenting with two-way interactive videoconferencing systems that connect a smaller number of sites. For example, the army TNET system allows up to 16 sites to be linked together for the full transfer of video, audio, and data between all sites. This allows tactical communications equipment to be included as part of the videoconferencing infrastructure. The navy's video teletraining (VTT) system uses digital video compression to network 11 sites and 16 classrooms; it is available 24 hours a day and is in use for 10 hours a day. In 1994 a $3.4 million contract was awarded to expand VTT to 25 sites, including several in Japan, Guam, and Spain. The House Armed Services Committee FY defense authorization bill authorized $17 million to expand the army's Interactive Teletraining Network to a minimum of 120 site network for "worldwide training" (Barry and Runyan, 1994, p. 11).

Higher Education

The National University Teleconference Network (NUTN) has a membership of approximately 260 universities, community and junior colleges, vocational and technical institutes. Nearly every state is represented. NUTN courses consist of one or more teleconferences, with pictures delivered by satellite, and with interactions conducted with receiving sites by telephone. Most courses are continuing education courses. They are produced and transmitted by only a minority of members, around 25. One of these member institutions develops the teleconference on a topic of current interest, using expert presenters, and offers the programs to other institutions throughout the country. Other members provide reception facilities.

The typical program consists of a live video presentation transmitted by satellite, and an audio discussion and question period. Each receiving site pays a registration fee to the originating institution; these fees typically range from $200 to $500 per site. The NUTN administration helps members market the courses but does not get involved in their production or transmission, which is the responsibility of the originating site. NUTN also conducts some training activities.

Among NUTN's early successes was "Passion for Excellence," produced by Brigham Young University and viewed by 6000 participants at 60 sites. The "1985 World Food Day" program was received by 202 locations in all 50 states and in Canada. A program on micro-computer software produced by Oklahoma State University went to 86 sites and 3500 participants.

National Technological University (NTU)

As discussed in Chapter 2, the National Technological University (NTU) is a university accredited by Commission on Institutions of Higher Education of the North Central Association of Colleges and Schools. It offers its own master's degrees in ten different engineering fields, as well as a range of continuing education courses, also in engineering. Courses are offered in such subjects as Computer Engineering, Electrical Engineering, and Engineering Management. Programs are delivered by satellite video with audio feedback. In essence, NTU represents a large-scale training network using satellite television to deliver the expertise available at universities across the country to engineers in their workplace. NTU has no faculty or campus and uses satellite technology to transmit more than 400 courses taught by faculty at 45 major universities around the country.

NTU clients are not individual students, but organizations. Over 100 major corporations and government agencies subscribe to NTU and pay fees for the courses they want to receive. The organizations decide which employees will participate in NTU courses and arrange on-site facilities for watching the programs. In any one year more than 30,000 technical professionals participate in NTU's 1,400 hours of noncredit professional development short courses and workshops. Among corporations that receive or have received NTU programs across the whole corporation are AT&T, Digital Equipment Corporation, Eastman Kodak, Hewlett Packard, General Electric, Motorola, and IBM Corporation. In 1992 NTU replaced its analog satellite transmission technology with digital compressed video. This has allowed NTU to cut its transmission costs in half, saving more than $1 million a year, and triple its programming capacity.

Other Satellite Consortia

Besides the Adult Learning Service, which delivers telecourses, the Public Broadcasting Service (PBS) also operates the Adult Learning Satellite Services (ALSS). ALSS delivers a variety of satellite courses to colleges and universities, businesses, hospitals, and other organizations, based primarily on programs developed by PBS stations. One specialized offering of ALSS is the Business Channel, which focuses on courses relating to business skills and knowledge. In 1994 PBS began to operate six channels on the AT&T Telstar 401 satellite using compressed digital video technology to broadcast their own programming as well as that of other major providers such as NTU, SCOLA, and SERC.

A number of consortia provide programming in specific content areas or for certain audiences. For example, AG*SAT (Agricultural Satellite Corp) is a consortium that provides courses on agricultural topics to 32 colleges. The SCOLA (Satellite Communications for Learning) consortium distributes foreign language news broadcasts from 35 countries to member schools and cable systems. The Community College Satellite Network (CCSN) was set up in 1989 by the American Association of Community and Junior Colleges. HealthNet, operated by Boston University Medical School, carries continuing education courses for health-care professionals. The Black College Satellite Network (BCSN) broadcasts primarily from Howard University with programs aimed at 105 colleges located in 23 states and the District of Columbia.

Besides participating in consortial efforts, most universities and colleges use their satellite uplinking/downlinking resources to deliver their own programs. Examples include:

- The State University of New York (SUNY) uses its tracking satellite dish to downlink programs from a Russian satellite, repackages them, and uplinks to educational institutions in the state.
- Since September 1984 the Center for Regional and Continuing Education at California State University, Chico (CSU, Chico) has provided satellite-

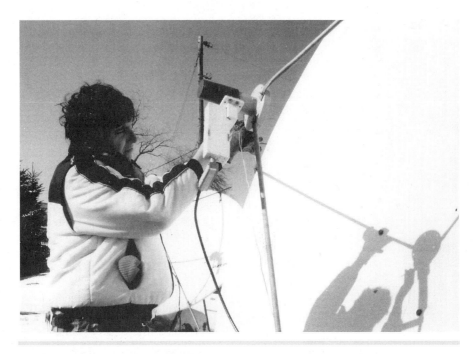

Besides participating in consortial efforts, most universities and colleges use their satellite uplinking/downlinking resources to deliver their own programs. Here an engineer makes adjustments to the antenna in preparation for downlinking a major national satellite conference.

delivered courses for the M.S. degree in computer science. Fifteen hours a week of live instruction are received by more than 20 corporate locations in 11 states. Companies include Hewlett-Packard, Texas Instruments, Alcoa Laboratories, and MCI.

- The Georgia Tech Satellite Literacy Project provides literacy training originating at Georgia Tech in Atlanta. Programs are transmitted to 75 classrooms at 63 sites. Students meet in groups for two evenings a week under the supervision of a qualified teacher who has access to the satellite teacher through an 800 number. The satellite broadcast comprises half of the two-hour session.

K-12 Schools

In 1987 the Federal Star Schools Program Assistance Act was passed by Congress authorizing a five-year budget of $100 million to promote the use of telecommunications for instruction in math, science, and foreign languages at the K-12 level. The program stipulated that funds be allocated to state-level partnerships and required matching funds from the participating states. Furthermore, half of the funding had to be used to benefit economically disadvantaged schools. The Star Schools program was administered by the Office of

Table 3-4   Star Schools Consortia

1988–1990
Midlands Consortium
TI-IN (Texas Interactive Instructional Network)
SERC (Satellite Education Resources Consortium)
TERC (Technical Education Research Center)

1990–1992
BCSN (Black College Satellite Network)
MCET (Massachusetts Corporation for Educational Telecommunications)
STEP (Satellite Telecommunications Educational Programming)
TEAMS (Telecommunication Education for Advances in Math and Science)

1992–1994
SERC (Satellite Education Resources Consortium)
BCSN (Black College Satellite Network)
MCET (Massachusetts Corporation for Educational Telecommunications)
STEP (Satellite Telecommunications Educational Programming)
TEAMS (Telecommunication Education for Advances in Math and Science)
IDEA (Iowa Distance Educational Alliance)
St. Lawrence Seaway Educational Consortium

Educational Research and Improvement in the federal Department of Education. In 1988 four consortia (Table 3-4) covering 45 states and reaching almost 3,000 schools received Star School grants.

The TI-IN Service broadcasts courses to high schools in 1,000 school districts in 29 states. From its studios in Texas, TI-IN sends nearly two dozen courses over the airwaves five days a week. The Arts and Sciences Teleconferencing Service, based at Oklahoma State University, began offering high school German in 1985 and has since added calculus, physics, history, and government. This first Star Schools project provided over 8,000 students with direct high school credit courses; 32,037 participated in science programs; and 720 teachers received college credit. Thirty-two high school courses offered included Japanese, German, Russian, and Spanish; math and science courses included calculus, statistics, physics, earth sciences, and biology.

In 1990 four new grants totalling $14,813,000 were given to consortia located in the northeastern and northwestern United States. In 1992 additional grants were given to the previous awardees, as well as a number of new groups. Each consortium involves a partnership of educational institutions, state/local educational agencies, and school systems. For example, the Midlands consortium brought together five major universities in Alabama, Kansas, Mississippi, and Oklahoma as well as the Missouri School Boards Association and the Missouri and Oklahoma State Departments of Education to serve over 200 schools. The Massachusetts Corporation for Educational Telecommunications (MCET) links together 1,300 schools in the state and 1,000 schools in surrounding states as well as 22 colleges and universities in New England.

The consortia have become major providers of distance education. For example, TI-IN broadcasts more that two dozen courses five days a week to more than 700 schools across 32 states; SERC delivers courses in mathematics, science, and foreign languages to secondary schools in 19 states. In addition to K-12 classes, the Star Schools programming also includes teacher-training courses and adult education. While most of the Star Schools consortia only provide programming to participating schools, in some cases equipment purchase (e.g., satellite dishes and televisions) was also supported. The Star Schools pro-·gram has had tremendous impact on the use of television for distance education in K-12 classrooms by getting equipment installed, programs developed, and providing teachers with training in using the technology (Martin, 1993; Worley, 1993).

In addition to the Star School consortia, many states have established their own satellite television efforts for school instruction. In 1985 Oklahoma started the Arts and Sciences Teleconferencing Service (ASTS) as a partnership of the Oklahoma State University and the state department of education. The initial offering of ASTS, a German language course, was very successful and is now distributed to hundreds of high schools around the country. At $1,700 per semester, this ASTS course was far cheaper than hiring a qualified German teacher. In Washington State, Educational Service District 101 began its Satellite Telecommunications Educational Programming (STEP) in 1986. STEP provides courses to over 100 subscribing schools, mostly in the state's rural areas. These courses include advanced senior English, Spanish II, Japanese, sociology, psychology, and pre-calculus.

Kentucky established the Kentucky Educational Television (KET) system in 1988 and installed satellite downlinks at every school in the state at a cost of $11.5 million. During the 1991–1992 school year, over 2,300 students were enrolled in KET math, foreign language, and science courses. Missouri created the Education Satellite Network (ESN) in 1987 to provide satellite programming to schools in the state. Other states that have established educational satellite networks with varying degrees of coverage include Alaska, where the Learn-Alaska network served 250 communities; Georgia, Indiana, Nebraska, Virginia, and Utah where one project delivers Spanish to more than two dozen schools. In some cases these statewide satellite networks have been woven together with existing ITFS and cable television systems to provide very extensive geographical coverage to schools and homes.

In the K-12 domain there have been several, often controversial, commercial initiatives. For example, Whittle Communications established Channel One, a daily news broadcast for high schools that attempts to present information in a context relevant to teenagers (see Chapter 4). CNN Newsroom is a daily,

GALAXY: An Experiment in Distance Education at the Elementary Level

The GALAXY classroom is a satellite learning network aimed at elementary school students (K-5). Begun in the spring of 1993, it links together 39 schools across the United States and 1 in Mexico. The nonprofit network was created by Hughes Aircraft Co. (who provide the satellite resources) with support from the National Science Foundation. The network uses a combination of technologies including video, computer, fax, and telephones to provide young children with a highly interactive learning experience. GALAXY uses VSAT (Very Small Aperture Terminals) technology for the digital transmission of video and data, and plans to use the DirecTV system beginning in 1994, a direct broadcast satellite (DBS) system using small and relatively inexpensive dishes.

To ensure that GALAXY learning activities are truly interactive, a new curriculum has been developed in science and language arts that takes advantage of the capabilities that new technologies offer. And the new curriculum seems to work; in the first year, students who were enrolled in the GALAXY language arts classes for grades 3–5 had higher overall test scores and greater gains in vocabulary skills than comparable students in traditional classes. The GALAXY broadcasts are intended to be springboards for discussions, debates, creating, asking questions, exploring, conducting experiments, and communicating with other students. The programming is produced by educational television stations regarded as leaders in the field, such as WGBH and WQED. All broadcasts include Spanish language soundtracks as well as closed captions for the hearing disabled.

The current pricing of GALAXY courses is $30 per student per year (all students in a grade must subscribe). Teacher training is available via the network for $150 per teacher. These prices compare very favorably with any other form of educational offering, including books or video materials.

commercial-free newsprogram designed for classroom use offered by Turner Broadcasting System. The Discovery Channel and the Learning Channel provide a variety of educational programs for children, some of which are specifically designed for certain skill areas and curricula. Mind Extension University (a subsidiary of Jones Cable) broadcasts high school and college courses through its cable system to schools and individual subscribers across the United States.

SCOLA (Satellite Communications for Learning) is a unique commercial service providing original-language foreign TV newsprograms (including translation and study guides) from over 35 countries via satellite to more than 100 schools around the country. Fees are based on the total number of students, ranging from 20 cents to $1.50 per student per year.

Computer Networks

Computer telecommunications (conferencing, electronic mail, bulletin board systems) are playing an increasingly important role in regional, national, and international distance education efforts. In some cases these efforts have resulted in unique courses that are quite different from other distance learning experiences.

A number of institutions offer complete degree programs via computer conferencing: the Online Campus of the New York Institute of Technology offers Bachelor of Science degrees; Connect Ed offers an MA in Technology and Society in conjunction with the New School for Social Reseach in New York; the International School of Information Management (Irvine, Calif.) offers MBA and MS degrees; and the University of Phoenix Online offers computer-based courses leading to award of its business and management degrees (see Lewis and Hedegaard, 1993).

The Electronic University Network (EUN) uses America Online, a commercial network, to provide access to a variety of undergraduate, graduate, and continuing education courses taught by accredited institutions. For example, EUN allows students to take BA and BS programs from Thomas Edison State College and Regents College and an MBA program offered by Heriot-Watt University in Scotland. In these programs all interaction among students and professors takes place via computer.

Many institutions include the use of computer conferencing as a component of their distance education programs. For example, the City University in Seattle, Washington, allows students to use electronic mail to interact with professors in its bachelor's and master's degree programs. Similarly, Mind Extension University (MEU) provides a computer bulletin board system for use by students in some of its television-based courses. The Rochester Institute of Technology (RIT) uses electronic mail and computer conferencing extensively in its Telecourse program. Nova University also makes use of computer networking in some of its graduate programs. Penn State's Certificate in Distance Education is taught to students in Europe and Mexico as well as the United States, and this international participation could not be possible without the extensive use of computer conferencing. Students send papers to the instructor and each other, receive weekly programs and follow-up discussions on issues raised in audioconferences, and prepare and present projects online. Computer conferencing is especially valued by persons using a second language, since it allows time for translation.

Computer networks are used by many high schools and elementary schools across the United States (Table 3-5). In recent years there has been tremendous

Table 3-5   **Examples of Computer Networks for K-12**

Academy One	National online cooperative for telecomputing activities (part of the Cleveland Freenet)
AT&T Learning Link	A curriculum-based program that involves learning circles at different schools
CORE	California Online Resources for Education links schools and state university system
FrEdMail	Low-cost telecommunications consortium that connect students and teachers worldwide
FIRN	Florida Information Resource Network connects 3,000 teachers and administrators
Kidsnet/Kidsphere	Global electronic discussion group for kids and their teachers
Kids Network	International computer network for science and geography activities run by the NGS & TERC
Newton	Bulletin board run by Argonne National Laboratory (U.S. Dept of Energy) for students and teachers
NASA Spacelink	Bulletin board run by Marshall Space Flight Center for students and teachers
SpecialNet	Online network for special education run by GTE
TENET	Texas Education Network links more than 15,000 teachers and administrators in that state

interest in the use of the Internet (a global electronic network or networks) at all levels of education. The nature and uses of computer-mediated communications in distance education programs is discussed further in Chapter 7.

Summary

As this chapter illustrates, there are many forms of distance education in the United States. Table 3-6 summarizes the main characteristics of the four major approaches discussed in terms of degree of interaction (i.e., contact with faculty and students), degree of flexibility (i.e., enrollment and completion of courses), level of learning, and primary media used.

- The two types of correspondence courses (home study and independent study) differ in all four attributes. Home study schools primarily offer print-based courses in vocational subjects with maximum scheduling flexibility and minimum interaction with instructors and other students. Independent study programs provide secondary and postsecondary courses with a moderate degree of interaction with instructors, moderate

Factory Workers Learn New Skills at Home With Computer Satellite Link

A novel computer-based experiment is bringing new knowledge and skills into the homes of factory workers in the Phoenix area. Called Project SALSA (Southwest Advanced Learning System for Adults), it marks the first time in the country that personal computers and satellite technologies have been teamed to bring adult literacy curriculum into people's homes.

Project SALSA was made possible because of an alliance among five high-technology companies and two colleges: Apple Computer, Inc.; Motorola, Inc.; US West; University Communications, Inc.; Businessland; Rio Salados Community College; and the University of Illinois.

Project SALSA employs sophisticated earth satellite and telecommunications technology to link personal computers in the home with a large library of interactive software located at the University of Illinois. Fifty-three employees of Motorola, Inc., at its Mesa and Tempe, Arizona, semiconductor plants are participating in the six-month pilot project using Macintosh SE computers provided by Apple Computer, Inc. The participants use the educational software at high-tech learning stations in their own homes, supplementing traditional classroom instruction.

SOURCE: *Ed, 5(2)*, Feb 1991, p. 14.

Table 3-6   Comparison of Distance Education Approaches

	Degree of Interaction	*Degree of Flexibility*	*Level of Learning*	*Primary Media*
Correspondence				
home study	Minimal	Moderate	Vocational	Print, video
independent study	Moderate	High	Secondary and postsecondary	Print, audio, computer
Open universities	Moderate	High	Postsecondary	Print, audio/visual
Satellite television	Low-high	Low	K-12, postsecondary	TV/Teleconferences
Networks	High	High	K-12, postsecondary	Computers

flexibility (enrollment and completion dates may be scheduled), and the possible use of audio- or computer conferencing.

- Open university programs typically offer postsecondary courses with a moderate level of interaction (especially with tutors), a high degree of flexibility, and likely use of audiovisual media. Satellite television consortia provide K-12 or postsecondary programs with a low level of flexibility (due to scheduling) and with levels of interaction that can range from low (broadcasts) to high (teleconferences with two-way audio or video).

- While this chapter has described the major categories of distance education in the United States, it is important to realize that there are many local and regional efforts not touched upon in this discussion. For example, there are numerous universities, colleges, and school systems across the country that make extensive use of audioconferencing, audiographics, and ITFS systems to provide instruction to their students (see OTA, 1989, for a summary).

- Many teachers and trainers are independently exploring the use of two-way interactive video- or computer-based learning in their courses. Indeed, within a single large institution or corporation, it is not unusual today to find a variety of different distance education initiatives occurring simultaneously. This pluralism defines distance education at all levels in the United States.

CHAPTER 4

Research on Effectiveness

Distance education is a field rich in opportunities for graduate student research. In this chapter we review some of the research, looking in particular at what the research says about the effectiveness of distance education. While there can be little doubt that distance education can be very effective in bringing about learning, there are many unanswered questions about how this happens and what to do to make it happen.

Many questions are asked about how effective distance education really is. Research has been done on some of these questions, but except for a few of them, much more research is needed. Some of the most common questions are

- What is the impact of distance education on (1) learner achievement and (2) learner attitudes, and how does this compare with traditional classroom instruction?
- What is the relative effectiveness of different communications technology for achieving communication between teachers and learners?
- Do particular types of learners find some technology to be more effective than others, and if so, what are the relationships?
- Which technologies are more effective for particular teaching processes, such as information-giving, compared with motivation or group discussion?
- Are some technologies more effective in teaching a particular subject than others?
- What course designs are more effective, what work less well, and what are the most effective organizational procedures to use when designing courses?

- What interaction strategies are most effective?
- Is distance education cost-effective and under what conditions?
- What educational policies at institutional, state, or national level are likely to be most effective for developing and supporting distance education?
- What theories are effective in explaining distance education and for generating research?

Some answers to these questions will be found throughout this book. However, we want to introduce these topics here in the form of questions and to review a few representative items of relevant research, to help students as a way of emphasising that much remains to be discovered about these issues. By approaching these questions in this way we hope that we can encourage students to understand that this is a field that provides many research opportunities.

The Effectiveness of Technologies

The single largest group of research studies in distance education focuses on the effectiveness of the communications technology. There are two main bodies of this technology-effectiveness research: descriptive case studies and learner achievement.

Descriptive Case Studies

First, there are a lot of simple descriptions of particular programs and how a teacher or an institution used one or more communications technologies to teach, usually from a classroom or studio, to one or more distant learners. These classes may be children in schools, university students, or adults in continuing education in universities, colleges, corporations, or the armed forces. Descriptive reports can be found about programs that use every kind of technology, including correspondence, audioteleconferencing, computer conferencing, audiographics, fiber-optic and microwave transmissions, cable television, satellite, and over-the-air television. In these reports the teachers or researchers are simply explaining their personal discovery of teaching at a distance, and the fact that they discovered that teaching through a communications medium could work.

This research is a bit like that of the anthropologists or geographers who find a new tribe or a new land and proceed to write descriptive "travelers' stories" about their discoveries. In the case of distance education, such stories are interesting when they describe an untested technology, which is rare, or a new way of using it, which is needed but also is unusual, or a population or content that has not been described already. Such anecdotal and case-study research points the way for research that is more controlled and systematic and that can therefore lead to results that can be generalized and applied to improve practice in the field.

Here are a few examples of descriptive case studies:

- In Iowa in 1987 the Master Gardener program in horticulture was presented by the Cooperative Extension Service by satellite to 16 locations.
- Deaton and Clark (1987) reported the use of a statewide telephone network and written programmed instruction used by the University of Montana Department of Social Work to provide courses for foster parents and social workers on the subject of foster care.
- Castleberry (1989) summarized developments in the federally funded Star Schools Program: TI-IN, the Midland Consortium, the Technical Education Research Center (TERC), and the Satellite Educational Resources Consortium (SERC).
- At the Nevada State Department of Human Resources (1990), the goal of Project NETWORC was to provide training in rural areas to individuals interested in working, or already working, with young children with special needs.
- Arias and Bellman (1990) described BESTNET (Binational English and Spanish Telecommunications Network), a project that used computer-mediated communication in universities in the United States and Mexico to teach minority students.
- Passaro et al. (1991) describes how ten state education agencies participated in a satellite teleconferencing project which trained 128 attorneys as "due process hearing officers."
- McElveen and Roberts (1992) report on a Louisiana project using audio-graphics to provide 13 high school courses to 113 schools serving 942 students.

This is just a small sample of hundreds of reports about the experiences of educators at all levels who are trying to use technology to teach at a distance.

Learner Achievement

One step in sophistication beyond these one-shot case descriptions are studies that compare the effectiveness of teaching in terms of learner achievement. Most often these studies compare the results of teaching and learning in a conventional classroom environment with teaching and learning in a distant environment. More recent studies compare learning outcomes in two or more distant environments. Occasionally in these studies, subjects are randomly assigned to the two treatments, which leads to more valid conclusions, but usually this experimental technique is not possible.

Comparing the achievement of learners (as measured by grades, test scores, retention, job performance) who are taught at a distance and those taught in face-to-face classes is a line of research going back more than 50 years. The usual finding in these comparison studies is that there are no significant differences between learning in the two different environments, regardless of the nature of the content, the educational level of the students, or the media involved. The following are some examples of these kind of studies:

- Boswell, Mocker, and Hamlin (1968) compared the results of distance teaching and face-to-face instruction in three classes of introductory college psychology. Pre- and post-test scores showed no significant differences in mastery of course content.

- Kruh (1983) reported the academic achievement of students in six university teleconference courses and students in similar courses taught in the traditional manner and concluded there was no difference.

- Kuramoto (1984) evaluated three alternative methods (face-to-face, teleconferencing, and correspondence study) in continuing nursing education and examined eight different measures including pre-/post-test scores and post-course use of course content. She concluded that all three methods were equally effective.

- After comparing the results of a course in behavioral and environmental management taught to university students by traditional lecture, lecture with videotape backup, group audioconference, independent study with audiotapes, group videoconference, and independent study with videotapes, Beare concluded that the different communications formats had little effect on student achievement or on how they evaluated the course (Beare, 1989).

- Another study at graduate level (Souder, 1993) compared the effectiveness of a course in management of technology taught by National Technological University (NTU) and the same course taught in conventional classrooms by the same instructor. Students took the same examinations. Souder found that "The NTU students performed the best" and concluded, "This study adds to the burgeoning evidence that distance learners should not be viewed as disadvantaged in their learning experiences" (p. 50).

- At high school level, Martin and Rainey (1993) compared the results of a course in anatomy and physiology taught to seven conventional classes with the results of teaching the same course to seven classes by videoconference. While there were no differences in the students' pre-test scores, there were significant differences in the post-test scores, in favor of the distance learners.

- Cheng, Lehman, and Armstrong (1991) describe a study of the effectiveness of computer-mediated communication (CMC) used in a graduate-level instructional computing course in Indiana. The study compared the results of in-service training of 25 teachers taking part on campus with 28 off-campus teachers who studied either by correspondence or by CMC. The study compared the three groups' achievements, time on tasks, and attitudes.

There is no evidence to suggest that classroom instruction is the optimum delivery method. Distance education is often more individualized and personal than face-to-face instruction.

Other examples of comparative effectiveness studies are comparison of audioconference and classroom teaching of adults participating in a cooperative extension class (Blackwood and Trent, 1968); comparison of university extension classes taught in a classroom and by audioteleconferencing (Puzzuoli, 1970); six undergraduate and graduate courses taught by audioteleconference compared with identical on-campus classes (Hoyt and Frye, 1972). Weingand (1984) analyzed differences in the performance of students in a graduate library science course taught both by teleconferencing and in the traditional classroom. Bruning et al. (1993) and Knott (1993) compare the performance of high school students in foreign languages courses taught in a classroom and by satellite television.

Research in the armed forces includes a comparison of audio and video teaching of U.S. Air Force students at remote sites in eight states (Christopher, 1982) and studies of interactive television in Army Reserve officer training (Keene and Cary, 1990; Partin and Atkins, 1984). Phelps et al. (1991) reported how part of an army resident course was converted for distance study via computer-mediated communication (CMC). Test scores, completion rates, student perceptions, and costs were compared to resident training, and results of instruction by CMC were found to be no different from that of resident instruction.

At the corporate level, Chute, Balthazar, and Poston (1989) compared two groups, one taught traditionally and one via teleconferencing (electronic conference board, two-way voice, and graphics). The groups were presented with

The Value of Distance Education Degrees

In 1994 the Distance Education & Training Council (formerly the National Home Study Council) surveyed graduates from ten member institutions to determine how these individuals felt about their distance learning experience. The sample involved 674 students who had received associate, bachelors' or masters' degrees. A follow-up survey was sent to employers of those individuals who responded to the survey.

Here are some results from both surveys:

1. Ninety-four percent of the students thought that the course material was sufficiently comprehensive to satisfy their needs.

2. Most students (67 percent) rated home study more difficult and challenging than traditional classroom instruction.

3. When students were asked to rate the ways they benefited by obtaining a degree, 75 percent selected "personal satisfaction," 65 percent selected "enjoyment of learning," and 62 percent selected "improve job skills."

4. Almost all students (96 percent) felt that the degree they earned was worth the effort.

5. When asked "To what extent do you think this degree program provided the knowledge, skills, and education you were seeking?", 61 percent chose "superior."

6. Ninety-five percent of the students said they would recommend the degree program to a friend.

7. Eighty percent said they would enroll in another degree program offered via distance study.

8. The majority of employers (94 percent) thought that the graduates compared favorably in skills, knowledge, and attitude with employees holding resident degrees.

9. When asked "Do you think this person performs better on the job because of the degree earned?", 81 percent responded yes.

10. Almost all employers (97 percent) said they would encourage others to enroll in distance education programs to increase their job competence.

SOURCE: Accredited Distance Study Degrees: Graduates and Employers Evaluate Their Worth. DETC, Washington, D.C. August 1994.

identical content and hours of instruction, and although the pre-test scores of the two groups were not significantly different, the post-test scores of the distant group were significantly higher than those of the face-to-face classroom group.

Valore and Diehl (1987, p. 3) summarized studies of the effectiveness of home study courses and concluded: "All of the research published since 1920 has indicated that correspondence students perform just as well as, and in most cases better than, their classroom counterparts."

Research is sometimes done to evaluate the effectiveness of a particular program in terms of how satisfied the learners were rather than how much they learned. For example, St. Pierre and Olsen (1991) undertook a study on students' perception of instructors and instructional effectiveness in terms of student satisfaction with the delivery of college credit correspondence courses.

Given the evidence of research illustrated by the above studies, it seems unreasonable to continue to ask if distance education courses can be as effective as conventional classroom instruction in terms of learner achievement measures. It seems more reasonable to conclude that (1) there is insufficient evidence to support the idea that classroom instruction is the optimum delivery method; (2) instruction at a distance can be as effective in bringing about learning as classroom instruction; (3) the absence of face-to-face contact is not in itself detrimental to the learning process; and (4) what makes any course good or poor is a consequence of how well it is designed, delivered, and conducted, not whether the students are face-to-face or at a distance.

Media Effectiveness

In most of the studies mentioned above, the question was which learning environment is more effective, and the dependent variable was the average score of groups of learners. This is a question that is not worth pursuing further. For any group of students, the environment in which learning occurs and the medium of communication between teacher and learner are not significant as predictors of achievement. Provided the medium is well-chosen and functioning effectively, it plays only a minor role in affecting learning outcomes, in general.

The more valuable questions to research are those concerning the characteristics of students within a group. We would like to know what types of students learn best in one environment, or from one medium, and what characterises those who learn better from the alternatives. Similarly, we may ask what are the types of information or other educational messages that can better be communicated by one medium than another. In other words, whether the students learn or not depends less on the medium than on the characteristics of the learners, and on numerous other variables of program design, instruction, and administration, as well as content variables.

From a practitioner's point of view, it is particularly important that we find out which students will benefit from expensive technologies and what teaching

Channel One: Controversy in the Classroom

Channel One is a commercial television news program offered free of charge to schools by Whittle Educational Network. The 12-minute program airs daily in approximately 12,000 middle and high schools around the country. Whittle provides a Ku-band satellite dish, color television monitors, and a VCR to each school which agrees to show the program. The program is normally shown before or after classes and during lunch periods so that it doesn't reduce classroom time. Each program provides highlights of national and world news from the perspective of teenagers as well as lifestyle items. The reporters and anchors are in their late teens, and an attempt has been made to select them from different ethnic groups.

In addition to the news coverage (10 minutes), the programs also include 2 minutes of public service announcements of direct interest to teenage viewers and commercial advertising targeted at this population. The inclusion of commercials has made Channel One very controversial—many teachers, administrators, and parents feel this is a corrupting influence in classrooms. Indeed, many school boards and districts have tried through legal means (unsuccessfully) to prevent Channel One from being aired in their schools.

A study by Johnston and Brzezinski (1992) that evaluated the first year of Channel One in 11 schools around the country found:

- Sixty percent of the teachers would recommend it to other teachers without any reservations.

- Students in all the schools watched the program at least three days a week, and in many schools students watched every program.

- Students reported that the lifestyle segments of the program were more interesting to them than the news segments.

- About half of the students felt that they learned something important from the programs most of the time.

- Overall, students who watched the programs did not score better on tests of current events, although there was considerable variation from school to school.

- Few teachers discussed the content of programs in their classes or integrated programs into their teaching activities.

The authors point out that even though the instructional impact of Channel One appears to have been negligible in the first year, changes to program design and classroom use could change this outcome in subsequent years. Furthermore, the program did have significant impact in some schools and some groups of students. For further discussion of Channel One outcomes, see Tiene (1993).

processes and what content, if any, are actually presented better by expensive as compared to cheaper technologies. At present it seems as if a lot of money is being spent on expensive communications technologies when our research suggests that most people can learn through simple technology when instruction is well designed and delivered. Perhaps we can test the different effects of investing a similar amount of money in the quality of course design in simple media compared to the same money invested in more expensive technology. For example, we might investigate the different results of spending money on more careful design of an audioconference network supported by good quality correspondence materials compared to the same money invested in the technology of an expensive satellite system.

Because which is the "best" medium will vary from student to student, a mixture of media is likely to be most effective for providing instruction to a large and varied student body, since this allows different types of students to find the combination that suits them best. A useful line of research is one into the synergistic effects of certain media—that is, the effectiveness of using one medium as a complement to another. As long as 20 years ago, Ahlm (1972) and Beijer (1972) investigated the effect of combining telephone tutoring to correspondence instruction (and in fact found little evidence to suggest that adding the second medium made much difference to learners' achievement). Lauzon (1992), arguing that in the learning process there is a need for multiple patterns of interaction, recommends the addition of computer conferencing to enhance computer-based instruction. Gunawardena (1992) advocates combining audiographic conferencing and computer-mediated communication. More work needs to be done in this area to find out the possible combinations of technologies and their interactions with different student types, content, and teaching processes.

Effective Course Design

Many research questions can be asked about the techniques of designing courses, including:

- How can academic content be most effectively structured and presented for study by the distant learners?
- How do we communicate various teaching processes? For example, how can we design our distance education courses to obtain each student's maximum participation in interaction with the instructor and with other students?
- How is a study guide to be laid out, a television program to be scripted, or an audioconference to be structured to obtain maximum results in student understanding?
- What learning objectives may best be achieved by televised or teleconferenced programs; what may be achieved by printed materials? What

kinds of printed materials are effective? How can you effectively link the printed materials with the electronic, and each of these with a local tutor?

- What are the most effective methods to ensure feedback about learner progress within the distance education course?
- How can we provide for the different pace at which students learn?
- What are effective instruments for the summative evaluation of learning?
- What are the most cost-effective methods of producing and distributing course materials?
- What are the procedures by which media are chosen by distance teaching organizations? By whom are they selected, and by what criteria? What training, if any, is given to the administrators and other decision makers who make these selections?

Examples of Course Design Studies

Among the hundreds of studies of the effectiveness of different aspects of course design are the following:

- Rekkedal (1983) studied the effects of sending letters of encouragement to correspondence students and the effect of reducing delays in feedback from the tutor.
- Holstein (1992) describes a method for suffusing the flexibility of speech into student manuals for correspondence courses. The goal of this effort is creation of a text that transcends time and space by engaging readers in "conversation" with the author.
- Coldeway (1988) compared the completion and cost-effectiveness of self-paced learning with that paced by the distance teaching organization (paced students completed sooner and at lower costs). Shale (1987) also discusses the concept of pacing as it relates to the following variables: academic standards, activity scheduling, student independence, student interaction, the effective use of media, course materials, learning methods, motivation, drop-out rate, and cost-effectiveness.
- Parker and Monson (1980) say that teleconference course design should provide a good learning environment, with feelings of rapport between teacher and students; provide good interaction between instructor and learners and among learners themselves; provide a variety of ways of enhancing a presentation; give opportunity for verbal and written feedback through questionnaires, interviews, or group reports.
- Hezekiah (1986) looked for these key characteristics in a credit course for nurses. She offered nine recommendations for improving the effectiveness of the instructional design, the most important of which was that administrators should accept that planning and implementing tele-

conference courses requires greater expenditures of faculty time and effort than they give to traditional courses.

Course Development Methods

The two main approaches to the development of distance education courses and materials—the course team model and the author-editor model—will be discussed in Chapter 6. There are numerous questions about their effectiveness, especially the course team model. For example:

- How much specialization is really needed in a course team?
- What should be the relative roles of the content expert and the television or other media producer?
- How do you best organize and control the work of specialists?
- Are such teams really cost-efficient?

The surprising thing is that while there are strongly held opinions on this subject, no institution has actually undertaken a comparison of the two main approaches. It seems reasonable to hypothesize that the development of desktop publishing techniques and networking by personal computers should have made many course team procedures redundant.

On the issue of who is most effective in designing courses, Downing (1984), in his 1983 survey of fourteen states, found that the schools relied on a variety of sources, including national consortia, university units, or independent vendors, but used their own teachers very little.

Media Selection

The process of deciding what to teach in print, recorded audio, recorded video, interactive audio, video, audiographic, or computer conference—that is, selecting a medium of communication—will have a major impact on the effectiveness of a program. Dutton and Lievrouw (1982) caution that, since media differ in their suitability for different educational tasks, media selection must be "content-driven rather than technology-driven" (p. 113). This means that consideration of instructional content, of the need for student involvement, and the particular learning outcomes desired should provide the basis for technology choices. Dutton and Lievrow compare media on the basis of the kind of communication provided (one-way, reactive, two-way), ease of modification, expense, complexity, and learning taxonomies (cognitive, affective, psychomotor).

Wagner and Reddy (1987) echo this caution against "hardware-driven" design decisions and present a discussion of the transmission characteristics that make for greater effectiveness of the principal modes of teleconferenced delivery: audioconferencing (effective for discussions of abstract concepts); audiographic teleconferencing (combination of verbal messages and visual materials is effective for both abstract and concrete learning experiences); videoteleconferencing (permits both audio and visual interaction, thereby enhancing learner "satisfaction"); computer conferencing (allows convenient transmission of text or graphics).

Norenburg and Lundblad (1987) contend that effective selection of medium in a given situation depends on the objectives of the organization, initial cost, personnel, users, anticipated use, level of interactivity desired, technological infrastructure already in place, legal considerations, topographical context, equipment compatibility, governmental and school jurisdictions, business service areas, and cost of operation. These authors developed two planning matrices to help distance education planners make effective choices in their educational and management decisions. Matrix 1 presents general, learner, teacher, and pedagogical considerations for each technology; Matrix 2 presents technology costs, advantages, and limitations.

This research reminds us that media, to be effective, must be selected for specific content and pedagogical purposes. The goal for researchers must be the further testing, and building on work like that of Wagner and Reddy, Dutton and Lievrow, and Norenburg and Lundblad, to assemble a body of knowledge that helps practitioners make effective selections so they can assemble multimedia programs that take advantage of the strengths of each medium.

Teaching Strategies

There are many unresearched questions about how to be an effective distance teacher, such as:

- What are the skills and techniques needed to be effective in interacting with learners by correspondence? by audioconference? by computer conference? by satellite teleconference? on tape?
- Are there skills that are generic to all the above, and if so, what are they?
- How should we train students in these skills?
- Are all teachers capable of becoming proficient and effective with any medium, or are some individuals more suited to certain media?

With a focus on teaching in small rural schools by means of live, satellite-transmitted television courses, Barker and Patrick (1988) used a content analysis design to calculate the frequency of the following teaching techniques: instructor-initiated interaction, student-initiated interaction, wait time, level of questioning, advance organizers, statements of expectations for students, review, praise, and corrective feedback.

On the basis of his years of experience as an instructor who teaches credit courses by means of computer, Boston (1992) compares the interactive potential of this medium and with that of traditional delivery and cites the unique skills needed for instructors to be effective. Gunawardena (1992) likewise explains the faculty roles needed to effectively teach by audiographics.

From existing research it is already clear that teaching by correspondence or electronic technologies is an art that is different from the art of broadcasting or even of conducting a teleconference meeting of business persons, or conducting interaction in a classroom. The key to being effective is that the teacher takes full advantage of the interactive nature of the media and resists the temptation to lecture, which is better done through the recorded medium. The instructor brings learners frequently, indeed almost continously, into action by asking questions, encouraging student presentations, getting students to talk to each other, and in other ways involving them fully in the teaching-learning process. However, further research, especially of an experimental kind, is urgently needed concerning these techniques of facilitating interaction.

Another important area of research is into the effectiveness of on-site facilitators. A study by Moore, Burton, and Dodl (1991) suggested that local facilitators are critical to the effectiveness of television-based distance education. However, other studies indicate that with a very skillful distance instructor, faciliators may not be essential. For example, Russell (1991) examined the effects of the receive-site facilitators' knowledge and practices on student achievement in a satellite distance education course. No significant relationship was found between students' semester grades and either the facilitators' knowledge about the satellite delivery system or their attempts to enhance student interaction with the distance teacher and the course content.

Clearly, there is more need for research into the work of site facilitators. Until future research suggests exactly when and for what purposes, for which learners and what content such helpers may be needed, prudence would suggest they are provided whenever possible. They must be trained to aid the distant instructor and not replace the instructor's role, but they can provide assistance to learners at their sites and help in individualizing content.

We discuss teacher training further in Chapters 7 and 11.

Cost-Effectiveness

The research questions of primary interest to educational administrators are about how to organize resources of people and capital in ways that will produce good results at the lowest cost.

A number of different positions have been taken regarding the cost-effectiveness of distance education. The view that the use of telecommunications requires extremely expensive capital investment is countered by the alternative opinion that technology is less expensive than conventional, labor intensive, methods. The middle position is that most telecommunications systems are expensive but may be cost-effective in delivering effective instruction of high quality, especially in areas that would otherwise lack the instruction, when used intensively, and also extensively with large numbers of students.

Examples of Cost-Effectiveness Studies

Studies of the cost-effectiveness of distance education include the following:

- The cost of delivering continuing education via audioteleconferencing was examined by Showalter (1983). It was calculated that during the project he evaluated, if the instruction had not been provided at a distance, 282 consultants would have traveled 519,958 miles to deliver 991 hours of face-to-face instruction. The estimated cost for this travel was $156,271. The actual cost of teleconferencing was $69,635, and the savings of $86,636 represented a 55 percent cost benefit.

- In a study at AT&T, the productivity loss of attending conventional training was factored into a cost-benefit analysis (Chute, Hulik, and Palmer, 1987). Estimated savings from travel, meals, and lodging were $500 per student per course, for a total savings of $1,588,000. Avoidance of nonproductive time for students (estimated at six hours per student) saved an additional $457,300. The company incurred teletraining costs of $234,900. Total cost benefits realized were $1,810,400 for one year.

- In a national survey on the cost effectiveness of distance education in schools, responses were received representing 34 classes serving 812 students in 47 schools. Equipment start-up costs ranged from $3,000 for one type of audiographics system to $60,000 for microwave-based television. Transmission costs ranged from $75 to $966 per course per month. In 15 classes, the cost per student for the distance delivery system was shown to be lower than with a live teacher but the cost effectiveness was high because in most cases the courses would not have been offered in the traditional format because there were no local teachers in the subject (Ellertson, Wydra, and Jolley, 1987).

- Rule, DeWulf, and Stowitschek (1988) describe a three-year federally funded demonstration project aimed at providing in-service training via videoteleconferencing supported by an electronic mail system. During Year One, in which only one site was used, costs for teletraining and face-to-face training were almost identical ($29,246 vs. $29,863). During the next two years when additional sites were added and system charges decreased, teletraining resulted in major cost savings: the costs were $30,718 vs. 62,077 for Year Two and $18,148 vs. $55,404 for Year Three.

- Phelps et al. (1991) examined the cost-effectiveness of computer conferencing in two U.S. Army Reserve courses (engineering and leadership). They compared the costs and learning outcomes of officers who took the courses via computer with groups who took the same courses in a classroom setting. While the content of both versions was the same, extensive changes were made to the course to make it suitable for computer conferencing and distance learning. There were no significant differences in student test scores between the two versions. The costs of converting and delivering the distance learning version of the course were comparable to the costs of providing the classroom version ($289,600 versus $288,200); however, the repeat costs of the distance learning version were less (43 percent after five iterations). The more often the course was given, the greater its cost-effectiveness.

- Lockheed Space Operations Company's Technical Training Department provides certification classes to personnel at other National Aeronautics and Space Administration (NASA) Centers using the Kennedy Space Center's Video Teleconferencing System (ViTS). The ViTS system uses two-way compressed video and two-way audio between participating sites. Fifteen distance learning classes were offered during 1992, resulting in a savings of approximately $50,000 in travel expenses (Hosley and Randolph, 1993).

- In Project NETWORC, the Nevada State Department of Human Resources, in cooperation with the department of Instructional Media Services of the University of Nevada, Reno (1990), set out to develop a cost-effective model for providing pre-service and in-service training in rural areas to individuals interested in working, or already working, with young children with special needs. The project used one-way video and two-way audio, printed curriculum guides, and supplemental videotapes. Student evaluations were extremely positive. The average cost of providing a Project NETWORC course in a rural site was approximately $8,000 compared to $18,360 for a continuing education course with a comparable level of instructor-student interaction.

- In a successful application of audiographics in Alaska, it was estimated (Fredrickson, 1990) that the cost of each site is between $3,000 and $8,500, depending on the equipment chosen, which compares with $15,000 to $25,000 to use satellites or to hire teachers to teach at each site.

Foreign experience confirms that distance education can be extremely effective and extremely cost-effective, the proviso being that to be highly cost-effective it must be delivered on a large scale in order to amortize the costs of the investment in technology and design time. Wagner (1977) showed that the unit cost per student at the British Open University (BOU) was about one-third of that at the conventional universities, and the cost per graduate was about one-half. Similar studies have been done of the cost-effectiveness of at least three other distance teaching institutions. Snowden and Daniel (1980) analyzed the cost-effectiveness of Athabasca University in Canada; Rumble analyzed the Universidad Estatal a Distancia, Costa Rica (1981), and the Universidad Nacional Abierta in Venezuela (1982).

Economies of Scale

Distance education is rarely both good and cost effective unless it is done on a fairly large scale. This is because heavy investment is required to produce programs by publishing, broadcasting, and other media-related activities, so significant costs have to be incurred in the preparation of teaching materials before any students are enrolled and regardless of how many students are to be enrolled. The fixed costs of a distance education system tend to be higher than those of the conventional university, while the variable or direct cost per student is usually much lower. In distance education, the more students take the course, the lower are the average costs of the course. This is what is meant by economy of scale. There are greater economies of scale with recorded media than with real-time interactive media. Laidlaw and Layard (1974) showed that the threshold at which the BOU became more efficient than the average campus-based university was 21,691 students. In general, conventional teaching methods are cheaper for low numbers of students, whereas distance teaching is more cost-effective for higher numbers of students.

One entity that can, and has, achieved economy of scale in distance education is the U.S. Department of Defense. For example, cost avoidance derived from U.S. Navy training courses and conferences conducted on their Video Teletraining (VTT) network from FY89 through FY94 was $7,154,000 in travel costs and per diem alone. Cost-avoidance figures for training totaled $4,386,000 for the same period (CNET Briefing, 1994). And the U.S. Air Force satellite training system yielded a $5,000,000 cost avoidance (1992–1993) in delivering their Acquisition Planning and Analysis course via a distance learning mode. Also travel time avoidance yielded 30 person-years, and student throughput increased from 300 to 3,000 (Westfall, 1994; Barry and Runyan, 1995).

Cost Elements

While distance education provided by distance education institutions is highly cost-effective, the position for distance education programs, units, and consortia is less clear. A determination of whether a particular course is cost-effective is usually based on several considerations, including the cost of distance delivery compared to traditional delivery, potential savings due to lowered travel expenses or the hiring of fewer teachers, and the possibility of increased enrollments of students. It has been suggested that the following elements should be included in any evaluation of costs: determination of overall costs, component costs, and per student costs; determination of the cost of alternative delivery methods; a record of all cost data, including "already paid for" costs; and a relating of costs to educational gains (Batey and Cowell, 1986). More difficult to quantify is the "value-added" aspects of distance education such as convenience and educational opportunities that would not otherwise be available.

Research on Policy

While quite a lot of research has been done on the effectiveness of media, course design techniques, and instruction, very little has been done to find out what are effective policies or what are the effective mechanisms for making policy at either national, state, or institutional level. Of course, policies are made and are described in reports and other documents, but they are not often subjected to academic analysis, and the process by which they are arrived at is even less scrutinized.

Questions about Effective Policy

The most important policy issues in this field concern the process by which decisions are made to establish distance education institutions, programs, and even courses, and perhaps more interestingly, the reasons a policy to establish distance education is *not* developed in many states and institutions. Why are so many states and institutions willing to adopt distance education at the program level, but not to develop full distance teaching institutions or a statewide system?

Other policy issues include: What government regulations are necessary to control distance education? What is the role of the state in deciding or giving approval for new curricula or curricular changes? What are the certification and accreditation implications for instructors, institutions, and students? In what ways should cooperation among institutions, states, and nations be promoted?

In 1989 the Office of Technology Assessment (a research facility for the U.S. Congress) produced a descriptive report about distance education entitled "Linking for Learning." The report was almost entirely focused on the use of telecommunications in the K-12 schools, and it was intended to serve as background information for policy formation by the Congress and government agencies. It stated that the following four factors would affect the growth and development of distance education in the schools: (1) telecommunications policy and regulations, (2) research and evaluation studies, (3) teacher preparation and training, and (4) the degree of federal and state funding.

An attempt to systematically gather information about the policies of the states regarding the use of distance education in the schools was made by England (1991), who gathered information in answer to the following questions:

- What was the state's policy regarding use of telecommunications in the schools?
- Was a statewide system being planned?
- Was there a special department at state level that attended to policy regarding distance education?
- Is funding provided by the state?
- What are the state's policies regarding the certification (licensing) of teachers who teach by means of electronic media?
- Are teachers from other states permitted to teach in the state by means of electronic media?

The implications raised by these questions about policy are discussed further in Chapters 9 and 11.

Conclusion: Theory and Research

The weight of evidence that can be gathered from the literature points overwhelmingly to the conclusion that teaching and studying at a distance, especially that which uses interactive electronic telecommunications media, is effective when effectiveness is measured by the achievement of learning, by the attitudes of students, and by cost effectiveness.

To this optimistic conclusion it is necessary to append several reservations. First, the sheer weight of opinion in the literature should not allow us to overestimate its significance, since much of what is written is based on anecdotal evidence offered by persons and institutions with vested interests in the techniques being evaluated or in the very programs they are evaluating. Furthermore, the research has often been undertaken by teachers or university faculty with extremely limited resources, and as a result, the methodology of many of the research designs is weak. In many large institutions where more resources are available, there is a preoccupation with so-called "institutional research" which aims at solving a particular problem of that institution or evaluating a particular course. It is usually unrelated to any theoretical framework, and this means it has little or no general value. Even where the research is done in research universities, it is usually undertaken by persons with an interest in technology, but little or no knowledge of distance education theory.

This lack of theoretical framework is a serious problem and calls into question the effectiveness of a lot of the distance education research. Unless they set their research in a theoretical context, researchers are unlikely to ask the important questions, and they will fail to link their questions to what other researchers have revealed. In turn, the results of their research are less mean-

Table 4-1   Variables That Determine the Effectiveness of Distance Education Courses

- Number of students at learning site (individuals, small groups, large groups)
- Length of class/course (hours, days, weeks, months)
- Reasons for student taking class/course (required, personal development, certification)
- Prior educational background of student (especially experience with self-study or distance education)
- Nature of instructional strategies used (lecture, discussion/debate, problem-solving activities)
- Kind of learning involved (concepts, skills, attitudes)
- Type of pacing (student determined, teacher defined, completion dates)
- Amount and type of interaction/learner feedback provided
- Role of tutors/site facilitators (low to high course involvement)
- Preparation and experience of instructors and administrators (minimal to extensive)
- Extent of learner support provided (minimal to extensive)

ingful to other researchers, who might more easily build on their work if it was set in a coherent theoretical context.

It should be apparent from the review of literature in this chapter that there is an immediate and vital need to develop a more sophisticated and integrated program of research based on theory, that will explore beyond the primary setting and give the power to predict and control general variables in the distance education environment. Table 4-1 lists some of the variables that have been shown to influence the effectiveness or outcomes of distance education courses (without taking into consideration media factors). While the theoretical frameworks to be discussed later in Chapter 10 do address certain of these variables, many are not covered by any existing theories. Furthermore, there are no theories that deal with the interactions or interrelationships of variables in terms of the effectiveness of distance learning programs. This is why we need to apply a systems model to the theory as well as the practice of distance education.

Summary

- The single largest group of research studies in distance education focuses on the effectiveness of the communications media.

- There are a lot of simple program descriptions about the effectiveness of a teacher or an institution that used one or more communications technologies.

- Other studies compare the effectiveness of teaching in one medium with that of another. Most often these studies compare the effectiveness of teaching in a conventional classroom with teaching through an electronic technology. More recent studies compare learning outcomes in two or more distant learning settings.

- There is need for more research to find out what is the most effective medium for different types of students and what media are most effective for different types of distance teaching strategy and content.

- Other areas of research about effectiveness include effective media selection, effectiveness of different aspects of course design, effectiveness of various teaching strategies, cost effectiveness, and effective policies and policy making.

- Research is ineffective when it is not set in a theoretical framework: Researchers are not able to build on the work of others, they are less likely to identify the really significant questions, and their results are of limited generalizability.

CHAPTER 5

Technologies and Media

We have already encountered the most important of the communications technologies in Chapters 2 and 3, which cover the history and scope of distance education. In this chapter we will discuss these technologies a bit more, and in particular, will introduce some of the pedagogical characteristics that make each valuable. This subject will be continued in Chapter 6 when we discuss course design and development. In a total systems approach, designers use a rich combination of most, if not all, the media so that the learner benefits from the pedagogical strengths of each medium.

Because communication is so central to distance education, there are many important issues with respect to the use of technology and media in distance education courses. In this chapter we will introduce just three:

1. What are the characteristics of different communication technologies and media, and how have they been used in distance education?
2. Which communications media are the best choice for a given course or program?
3. How should media be combined for maximum effectiveness?

Print

Print is undoubtedly the most common medium used in distance education. Print takes such forms as textbooks, books of readings or reprints, manuals, course notes, and study guides. Print materials are relatively inexpensive to develop and can be distributed easily via the public mail or private delivery services. The skills of writing and illustration as well as the production capabilities of printing or duplication are widely available. Students and teachers are very familiar with printed materials and are likely to have a good understanding of how to manipulate them and make the most of them. Furthermore, print materials are highly portable, and they do not easily deteriorate or break, which makes them dependable and convenient to use.

In distance education, instruction that is based mainly on printed media is called correspondence study, home study, or independent study (Pittman, 1990). The most basic characteristic of correspondence study is that it is not only the presentation of information by the teacher that is done in print, but the interaction is by text also, though it is likely to be typed or even handwritten rather than printed. Such instruction is always individual and is always private. It allows students to study at their own pace and in their own time. The interaction by mail is of course slow, but in fact this appeals to more reflective and less emotional, more rational students, and it makes print the medium of choice for many students, especially adults.

Besides correspondence instruction, print is used in some form by almost all distance education courses, regardless of what other media they employ. The most common and most important form of print used in such courses is the study guide. Study guides are used to provide an organization and a structure for the course and to integrate any instruction delivered by other media. For example, courses produced by Annenberg/CPB Project funds, though they use video or other electronic media substantially, are usually built around a printed student's guide and a printed instructor's guide. In foreign distance teaching institutions, including the British Open University, course teams pay a great deal of attention to the printed study guides, which form an anchor for the other media and are generally the medium most favored by the students.

Study Guides

The study guide should do more than merely present subject matter. It should contain directions and guidance for the students in their study of the content and provide a structure for interaction between learners and instructors, whether by correspondence or by teleconference. There is no medium better than the study guide for communicating the instructors' goals and objectives and their general approach and philosophy about the subject. They can give opinions and advice concerning pathways through the subject, about how much time to spend on a particular topic or exercise. As every teacher knows, the logical order or structure in the content in any field is not necessarily the appropriate psychological order for its study. Textbooks are invariably designed to comply with the logic and structure of the discipline. The author of the study guide must break free from the structure of the content and the structure of the text and construct devices and techniques that assist the student to master the content.

The study guide should be written in a style that reflects the writers' concern for their students. While the study guide is of course more impersonal than face-to-face teaching, or the teaching that occurs in writing between correspondence instructors and individual learners, the study guide should attempt to be friendly, encouraging, and supportive. It should be remembered that this is neither an academic paper nor a learned text, but a form of teaching. Therefore, the writer's personality should be expressed, and the concern and interest in the learner should show through.

Newspapers and Newsletters

One interesting way of using print for distance education in the workplace is the publication of newsletters. While people may be too busy or unwilling to take formal courses, they are likely to read a newsletter on a regular basis, particularly if it includes information that is useful. It is also possible to create a structured course around newspapers, journals, or magazines. For example, the School of Education at the University of Connecticut teamed up with *Technology & Learning* magazine to offer a professional development course for teachers about technology in schools. Participants established their own local learning group consisting of at least three people with a designated leader. Course activities were based on articles in each issue of the magazine, and each group met once a month to discuss its members' work.

Design Principles

The design of print materials can significantly affect their instructional effectiveness (Davis, 1990; Hartley, 1978; Moore, 1987). Table 5-1 lists some principles for effective text design. Reading level and simplicity of writing style are two critical factors. The layout of the text (i.e., typography and page design) can make a significant difference in the usability of print materials. Modularization (i.e., breaking ideas up into small "chunks" or distinct instructional components) is also an important aspect of improving understanding from text. Jonassen (1982, 1985) provides an overview of research about print. Duffy and Waller (1985) provide guidelines for the design of effective text materials. Rowntree (1981, 1986) presents principles for the design of instructional texts in the context of self-study learning.

Preparation Time

Well-designed print materials can take considerable time to prepare. For example, the kinds of study guides used in large-scale distance education courses offered by open universities and telecourse producers (e.g., PBS/CPB) often involve the work of large design teams and take many months or years to develop. Materials must be collected from subject matter experts, written, and edited; graphics must be created, copyright releases obtained, designs tested out, etc. This stands in contrast to the hastily assembled collections of articles or notes that may be sent out to students by professors in teleconference settings at program levels of distance education. So the quality of print materials

Table 5-1   **Some Principles for Text Design**

Principles for Writing Sentences
Use the active voice.
Use personal pronouns.
Avoid nouns created from verbs; use action verbs.
Avoid deletion of connecting words.
Write short sentences.
Do not insert excess information in a sentence.
List conditions separately.
Keep equivalent items parallel.
Avoid unnecessary and difficult words.
Unstring noun strings.
Avoid multiple negatives.

Principles for Organizing Text
Put sentences and paragraphs in logical order.
Give an overview of the main ideas of the text.
Use informative headings.
Provide a table of contents.

Typographic Principles
Use highlighting techniques, but don't overuse them.
Use 8-10 point type for text.
Avoid lines of text that are too long or too short.
Use white space in margins and between sections.
Use ragged right margins.
Avoid using all caps.

Graphic Principles
Use illustrations, tables, and graphs to supplement text.
Use rules (lines) to separate sections or columns.

SOURCE: Felker et al., (1981). *Guidelines for Document Design-ers.* Washington, D.C. : American Institutes for Research.

can vary considerably with the type and level of distance education in which they are used.

Impact of Electronic Publishing

Electronic desktop publishing technology has had a tremendous impact on the efficiency and quality of producing print materials (see Misanchuk, 1992). Before the advent of personal computers, an author's manuscript was typeset, meaning that a master copy of the page was created and printing plates were

The layout of the text (i.e. typography and page design) can make significant difference to the usability of print materials. Here an editor discusses study guide design with the graphic artist.

made. This process required the work of typesetters, illustrators, and design and layout artists. Publishing in this way usually takes several months, and printing takes several weeks, if not months, from the time of handing over the manuscript.

When the process is done electronically, text, illustrations, diagrams, pictures can all be created and revised much faster and then either sent to a printer or output on an office laser printer. Such desktop publishing (DTP) using word processing and page-layout software makes it possible for anyone with a personal computer to produce text materials. Documents can be transmitted via telecommunications, making it much easier for authors and editors to interact with each other. Indeed, it is technically very simple to deliver text materials directly to the student in online form, eliminating the need for print entirely. However, to date, most people prefer to read large amounts of information in printed format rather than on a computer display. Over time, this preference may change. Desktop publishing also makes it possible to produce small quantities of documents for courses with limited enrollments or in which the subject changes a lot.

Many study guides and other printed materials are prepared too cheaply and too carelessly, as add-ons to an electronically transmitted program, with the result that they are unattractive and uninteresting. These shortcomings are not limitations of the printed media per se, but of the way in which educators use them. Improvements need to focus on training educators and organizing them to use print better as a teaching medium.

Audio- and Videocassettes

Over the past two decades, audio- and videotapes have come to play an increasingly important role as media for distance education. With the widespread availability of audio- and videocassette players (VCRs), both technologies have become very convenient and cost-effective ways to disseminate instructional materials. Audiocassette players are highly portable and hence allow people to study where they wish. Most people have VCRs in their homes, making home study with videotape materials quite feasible. Furthermore, audio- and videocassettes are relatively easy and inexpensive to distribute via mail or delivery services.

Usage and Effectiveness

At the British Open University, the introduction of audiocassettes is often said to be the most important technological innovation in its 20-year history, in terms of the numbers of students and courses affected and the impact on learning. Audio delivered on cassette is the most widely used medium after print. Each year the BOU mails more than 750,000 hours of audiocassette teaching material (Bates, 1990b).

Audio- or videotapes should seldom if ever be used for carrying lectures, though in the United States they frequently are. In a total system, such direct transmission of information is better done in print. Audio or video can communicate content, but of types that cannot be communicated by print. The use of audio or video can also improve the motivational aspects of a distance learning program. Audio can be used to provide narrative or dramatic examples (see Table 5-2). Video is a very powerful medium in terms of capturing attention and conveying a lot of information quickly. Because of its capability to show people interacting, video is a good medium for teaching interpersonal skills. It is also a good medium for teaching any kind of procedure since it can show the sequence and actions involved.

Both audio and video can be used to present the views of experts, which increases the credibility and interest of the materials. Audio and video are also especially effective at conveying attitudinal or emotional aspects of a subject, something which it is difficult to do with other media. Spitzer, Bauwens, and Quast (1989), McMahill (1993), and Stone (1988) discuss the effects of using video in college-level distance learning.

Table 5-2   Teaching Functions of Audiotapes

Talking students through parts of the printed material (analyzing the argument in a text; explaining formulae and equations, illustrations, graphs, diagrams, maps, technical drawings, statistical tables)

Talking about real objects that need to be observed (e.g., rock samples, reproductions of paintings, metal fatigue in home experiments)

Talking students through practical procedures, such as computer operation, so that their hands are free for the practical work

Analyzing human interactions (e.g., decision making, conduct of meetings). The text explains what is happening on the tape.

Collecting the views and experiences of specialists and experts, or personal experiences

Providing aural experiences: music, foreign speech, sounds of natural phenomena or human events, such as the inauguration of a president

SOURCE: Based on A.W. Bates (ed.), *Media and Technology in European Distance Education,* Heerlen, Netherlands. European Association of Distance Teaching Universities.

Course Materials

There are thousands of commercially available audio- and videotapes that might be integrated into distance education courses. A large percentage of correspondence (especially home study) and open university course materials include audiotape segments. The Annenberg/CPB Project funded a series of undergraduate courses on such subjects as American history, music, and nutrition, consisting of a study guide and audiotapes.

Many organizations have created distance learning programs based primarily on videotapes. For example, the Association for Media-Based Continuing Education for Engineers (AMCEE) offers hundreds of engineering courses, each course consisting of a set of videotaped lectures. Most of the PBS/CPB telecourses are available in videotape format (see Levine, 1992). Many large corporations provide much of their employee and customer training in the form of videotape materials.

Production

Producing audio- or videotape materials is generally expensive and involves specialized skills (e.g., editing). Unless the subject matter is an interview or presentation (or a naturally occurring event), a script will be needed. Even with modern tape recorders and camcorders, experienced audio/video technicians are needed to obtain good quality audio or video. Professional talent such as an announcer or actor may be needed. Editing facilities and equipment are likely to be needed to produce the final tapes. While these considerations are not

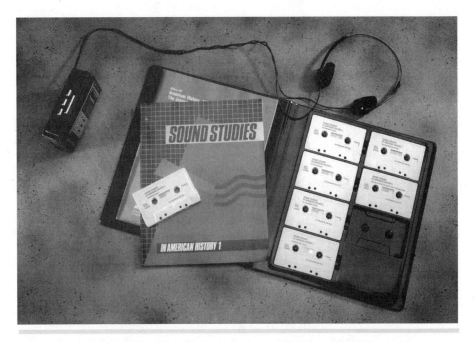

With a good study guide, audiocassettes are a valuable teaching medium. These audio tapes were produced by a multi-institutional course team funded by the Annenberg/CPB Project.

obstacles to the production of audiovisual materials, they do increase the time and money required to create such materials.

The emerging generation of digital audio and video editing software for personal computers has made the production of audiovisual materials much easier and faster (analogous to the impact of electronic desktop publishing on print production). These programs make it possible to do special effects and sequences that previously required very expensive equipment. Furthermore, they make it possible to integrate audio and video into multimedia programs (see discussion below).

Radio and Television

The broadcast media of radio and television have been used for educational purposes for many years (Saettler, 1990; Schramm, 1977; Zigerell, 1991), and there is ample evidence that instructional television can be effective (e.g., Chung, 1991; Egan et al., 1992; Lochte, 1992; Porter, 1990; Whittington, 1987). With the emergence of satellite networks (see Chapter 3), instructional television has become very popular at all levels of education (see Gilbert, Temple, and Underwood, 1991).

We need to keep in mind a distinction between broadcast television that is available to anyone with a television receiver, a cable outlet, or a direct broadcast satellite (DBS) antenna, and what is sometimes referred to as "narrowcast" television, which are programs like those transmitted by private channels such as the National University Teleconference Network, or Business TV channels (see Figure 5-1). These programs can only be received by sites that have paid licenses or are otherwise authorized to receive them. Among other differences, programs for general broadcasting are usually of much higher "production values," meaning there are more location shots, more drama, music, editing, scripting, and studio production.

As explained in Chapter 2, there is a long history of teaching by broadcast radio and television. The British Open University was one of the first institutions to use radio and television extensively in distance education programs. Radio has been used extensively for distance education in developing countries (Tilson, 1994) and was used on a limited basis in the United States during the 1930s and 1940s (see Saettler, 1990), but was supplanted by television. PBS/CPB has used the public broadcasting system for the delivery of telecourses primarily at the college level since 1981. By the end of the 1980s, over 1,500 colleges in cooperation with almost 300 PBS stations had enrolled more than a million students in telecourses (see Levine, 1992). In addition, many state and regional consortia offer telecourses of their own.

Strengths and Uses of Broadcasting

Broadcast and narrowcast radio and television have the advantages of "immediacy." They can be used to give up-to-the-minute reports about the subject matter of a course. They can be used for talks, phone-ins, and discussions. If programs are broadcast in association with a study guide and written assigments, broadcast programs help keep students on track. They help distant learners perceive that they are part of a community of people involved in the same issues. Broadcast programs are seen and heard by the general public, and therefore can be a recruiting instrument, since potential students can hear about issues that are discussed in the courses. Broadcasting helps create the image of the distance teaching institution in the general public. Radio has the advantage of being a very flexible medium, allowing swift updating of material at low production costs. Television has the disadvantage that to be good, it has to be expensive.

Instructional Television Fixed Service (ITFS)

ITFS involves the use of microwave transmission (with a range of about 25 miles) and special antennae to receive the signal. Because ITFS is a relatively inexpensive form of distribution, it quickly became a popular form of transmission of teaching over small areas. Many colleges and school systems have developed regional education programs using ITFS. An ITFS studio is similar to

Figure 5.1   Different Forms of Television Transmission

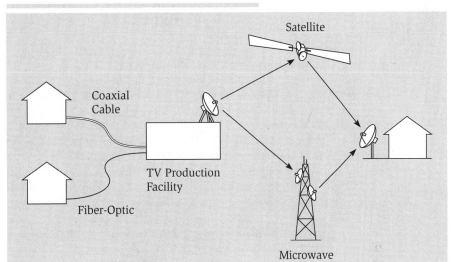

a general broadcasting studio, though perhaps smaller and less complex. The materials presented are usually pre-recorded or copied material. Increasingly, teachers present lessons and conduct discussion by telephone. A network of receive sites at schools, training centers, or off-campus classrooms is established where students meet to take rather conventionally taught classes. Usually, a telephone bridge is used so that students can have audio contact with the instructor during the program to ask or answer questions.

In some cases the ITFS transmission feeds into a cable system which redistributes the programs to people at home or in their workplace. Being an over-the-air transmission technology, ITFS suffers the same problems of frequency crowding and interference as other over-the-air systems. ITFS can communicate programs recorded from, or fed from, a satellite downlink, as well as provide a means for teachers in a limited geographic locality to present the same kind of programs as satellites deliver more widely.

Cable Television (CATV)

Cable television (CATV) involves the distribution of television signals through a coaxial or fiber-optic cable connected directly to the viewer's television set. The majority of U.S. homes have cable television service provided by one of the hundreds of cable companies. Because most cable companies are required by law to provide educational programming, cable channels are a popular medium for distance education. While such programming is usually provided by local schools and colleges, it is possible to deliver national programs via cable

Hawaii: Instructional Television Across the Islands

Hawaii presents a unique opportunity for distance education: the use of technology to tie together the five major islands that comprise the state. This is accomplished by the Hawaii Interactive Television System (HITS), a partnership of the Hawaii Department of Education, the University of Hawaii, and the Hawaii Public Broadcasting Authority (KHET). HITS is an interactive closed-circuit television network that consists of four outgoing channels from Oahu to each of the other islands and a single channel from each island back to Oahu. The system involves point-to-point microwave, ITFS, cable, and satellite links to connect classrooms on each of the university's campuses and the KHET complex at the main campus on Oahu.

Many university classes are broadcast live to the campuses on other islands, and directly to students' homes when cable is used. While the university is responsible for programming, the Hawaii Public Broadcasting authority is responsible for assuring reliable television transmission and the state is responsible for installing and maintaining all transmission equipment. Besides producing its own programs, the university also supports the production of classes for the Department of Education, including in-service training for teachers. In addition, HITS is interconnected to Skybridge, a two-way video network operated by the Maui Community College for educational broadcasting to residents of Maui.

The UH-Manoa campus has a Ku-band satellite uplink that allows it to deliver live video programs to the continental United States. While each UH campus manages local programming, the Office of Information Technology (OIT) provides coordination for all systemwide programs and liasion with the Hawaii Public Broadcasting Authority and the Department of Education. Each semester, OIT prepares a master ITV schedule which is based on user demand, state needs, the willingness and capability of university departments to deliver courses, and the ability of campuses to support ITV courses.

In addition to these activities, other technologies such as audiographics, two-way videoconferencing, and computer networks are used for distance education in Hawaii. For example, each public school in the state has a still-frame videophone (Mitsubishi Lumaphone) that allows teachers and children to interact with those in other schools, as well as with the continental United States and Japan, via ordinary telephone lines. Schools also participate in national computer networks such as the National Geographic Kids Network and AT&T Learning Network.

For further discussion of HITS and distance education in Hawaii, see the December 1992 issue of *Ed* (a USDLA publication).

The Hewlett-Packard ITE–NET

In the fast-paced world of business, good training is often seen as a competitive edge. This is especially true in the computer field where technology changes quickly and there is always a small window of opportunity for a new product. If a company can provide timely and effective training to its employees and customers, it creates a strong advantage in the marketplace. Hewlett-Packard is using distance education to achieve that kind of advantage. It has invested more than $1.5 million to create the HP Interactive Technology Network (ITE-Net), a teaching facility headquartered in Cupertino, California.

The ITE-Net facility consists of a "teleclassroom" equipped with seven television cameras, a touch-activated master console, and a control room staffed by television production specialists. Using satellite uplinks, classes are broadcast to more than 100 sites in the United States and Europe. Every student at each site has a response keypad that allows him or her to respond to questions asked by the instructor during a presentation. This makes it possible for all students to participate fully in classes as well as providing the instructor with instantaneous feedback.

ITE-Net is used primarily for sales and engineering training on HP products. For example, every month about 300 field technical engineers receive up-to-date information on HP and competitive products. The savings in travel expenses alone easily justify the costs of creating and running the ITE-Net system. Furthermore, because of the high level of interactivity made possible by the response units, training provided by ITE-Net is a very effective learning experience for both students and instructors.

SOURCE: ASTD *Technical & Skills Training*, May/June 1993.

television. For example, Mind Extension University (MEU), which is operated by Jones Intercable, offers undergraduate and graduate programs on over 200 of its cable affiliates across the United States. Students can watch the programs at home and use the telephone to call in questions or comments. It is also possible for organizations to install coaxial cable in their own buildings for closed-circuit transmission of television programs. CATV is no longer just coaxial cable, since most systems are gradually being converted to fiber-optic cable. Many schools, companies, and colleges have closed-circuit systems in their facilities which are used to distribute internally produced programs or outside broadcasts.

Direct Broadcast Satellites (DBS)

In addition to the satellite networks discussed in Chapter 2, there is another form of satellite technology that is becoming increasingly common that could significantly impact distance education in the future. Direct broadcast satellites use a smaller and less expensive satellite dish (about 1 to 2 feet in diameter) that makes it feasible for students to directly receive programs at their home or office. DBS technology (e.g., the Galaxy system mentioned in Chapter 3) is in limited use at the present time but is likely to become commonplace within this decade.

Teleconferencing

Teleconferencing describes the interaction of students and instructors via some form of telecommunications technology. There are four different types of tele-conferencing: audio, audiographics, video, and computer.

Audioconferencing

Audioconferencing is the most common and least expensive form of teleconferencing. All participants in an audioconference are connected via a telephone call. Individual participants can use their regular telephones while groups can use a speakerphone or specially designed sets of speakers and push-to-talk microphones. In order for all participants to be able to interact with each other, a "bridge" is used that connects all lines together (like an old-fashioned party line). This bridge may be provided by a telephone company or the organization conducting the teleconference.

The University of Wisconsin-Madison Extension has made the most extensive use of audioconferencing in this country. In 1966 it created the Education Telephone Network (ETN) as a means of extending the campus to the entire state. The system is used to deliver dozens of credit and noncredit courses each semester, often in conjunction with television broadcasts. At its peak in 1980, ETN served 32,000 students and connected over 200 sites in 100 towns and cities across Wisconsin. The primary use of ETN is for continuing professional education, especially in the health-care field. The ETN service is supplemented by WisLine, an audioconference call-in service that can link up to 68 phone lines simultaneously. In addition to these audioconferencing services, the university also runs WisView, an audiographics system that is installed at 21 sites across the state as well as numerous corporate locations.

Parker (1984) describes some of the technical and educational issues associated with audioconferencing. Garrison (1990) examines the benefits and effectiveness of audioconferencing. Schaffer (1990) discusses faculty training and course design for audioconferences based on experiences at the University of Wyoming. Sponder (1990) discusses the use of audioconferencing in rural Alaska, with particular focus on its use by Native American students. Cookson, Quigley, and Borland (1994) surveyed the policies and practices associated with the use of audioconferencing for graduate instruction at seven major universities.

Teleconferencing for Continuing Medical Education

While teleconferencing has been employed in all disciplines and subject domains, it has been particularly popular in the health care field as a means of providing continuing medical education. Almost all health care professionals are required to take courses regularly to stay up-to-date with new developments in medicine. Distance education meets the needs of many health-care workers who are too busy to take the time to attend traditional classes. Furthermore, expertise on certain diseases or treatments is often very scarce; telecommunications can be used to disseminate such expertise to a wide audience in a timely manner. The use of videoconferencing is especially valuable in medical education because it allows new procedures and equipment to be demonstrated as well as patient case studies. Anderson (1992) provides a historical overview of the use of teleconferencing in the health-care industry. Hartigan and St. John (1980) discuss the use of satellite teleconferencing to provide AIDS training in third world countries. Kuramoto (1984) and Major and Shane (1992) describe the use of teleconferencing for nursing education.

Emerging multimedia and network technology promises to increase the role of distance education in the health care domain. Of particular importance are the capabilities to remotely deliver high resolution images of x-rays and other lab results in digital form, and to permit face-to-face interaction between medical experts and patients via videoconferencing. Schnepf et al. (1995) describe the HDDL (High-Definition Distance Learning) project at the University of Minnesota that involves the use of multimedia networks to deliver medical lectures to radiology residents at hospitals in the Minnesota area. The system allows for interactive lectures and discussions, including the simultaneous presentation of video, audio, and digital slides. The Georgia Statewide Academic and Medical System (GSAMS) is a videoconferencing system that connects approximately 50 different health-care sites in the state (along with over 100 other educational institutions) for medical education and telemedicine. In the coming decades, we can expect to see such regional and national networks proliferate.

Audiographics

Audiographics systems involve the use of computer or facsimile technology to transmit visual images to support instruction by voice over telephone lines. Facsimile-based systems transmit physical copies of documents to all sites. Electronic blackboards can also be used; they transmit anything written or drawn at one site to television monitors at the others. There are many computer-based systems that allow the transmission of graphics, programs, and data. Each site sees anything drawn on the computer screen (using a graphics tablet) as well as hearing the audio. Some of these systems also include a digitizing camera that produces an image of anything placed in front of it, including drawings,

Use of audiographics to teach technical Japanese at the University of Wisconsin (Courtesy, ICS/UW Extension. Photo: Bruce Fritz).

objects, and people's faces. Audiographics systems are well suited to courses that involve a lot of illustrations or notational information (e.g., formula, equations). For this reason, they have been especially popular in the teaching of science and engineering classes.

At the University of Wisconsin-Madison, audiographics is used to teach technical Japanese courses, which involves a lot of handwritten *kanji* and pronounciation practice (see Smith, 1992). Art and music courses are often taught via audiographics. McGreal (1993) describes an interesting application of a computer-based audiographics system in Ontario secondary schools: Representatives of museums and galleries take students on "electronic tours" of their institutions by showing photographic slides that have been digitized as computer graphics. In addition to asking questions at any time, students can point to things on the screen that they want to know more about. Gilcher and Johnstone (1989) conducted a critical analysis of the use of audiographic systems at nine different educational institutions and provide guidelines for successful projects. Different aspects of audiographics are discussed by Gardner, Rudolph, and Della-Piana (1987); Gunawardena (1992); Idrus (1992); Knapczyk (1990); and Smith (1992).

Two-way Videoconferencing

Two-way videoconferencing can be transmitted via satellite or cable, or it can be accomplished by means of "slow-scan" or compressed video. Slow-scan video involves transmitting a picture every 20 to 30 seconds and uses standard telephone lines, making it as cost-effective as audio- or audiographics conferencing. Compressed video can be full-motion (30 frames per second) but often involves a lower resolution picture (10–15 frames per second). Compressed video requires expensive digital telephone lines and the use of a device called a codec (compression decoder) at each end. Since codecs cost $20,000 to $30,000 each, this makes the initial costs of videoconferencing rather expensive. However, new forms of codecs that fit into personal computers are now appearing on the market selling for $3,000 to $5,000 each. Telephone companies also sell "videophones" which can also be used for face-to-face interaction.

Two-way television allows the student and instructor to interact face-to-face and is the closest match to traditional classroom instruction. Students and instructors typically like distance education courses delivered by videoconferencing, although equipment reliability, camera placement, and instructor/student behavior can significantly affect its success (e.g., Rifkind, 1992).

Massoumian (1989) discusses some of the key factors affecting the success of two-way television. For further discussion of videoconferencing technology, see Portway and Lane (1992).

Computer Conferencing

Computer conferencing allows students and instructors to interact via a computer network. They can send messages to each other (called electronic mail, or E-mail) as well as transfer data files (i.e., assignments, bibliographies, project reports, readings, etc.). While a computer conference can take place "live" (synchronous), most interaction is spread out over time (asynchronous) allowing people to send or read messages when they want. When people sign on to the system, it displays all the messages sent to them since the last time they were on. It is possible to sign on to a network from any computer that is connected to a telephone line by a device called a modem (modulator-demodulator).

The instructional characteristics of computer conferencing include the following:

- It combines discipline of writing and flexibility of conversation. Being required to formulate ideas in such a way that they can be communicated in writing is important in most educational programs.
- It can be a powerful tool for group communication and for cooperative learning. For example, turn-taking tends to be more equally distributed in CMC discussions, and inputs are often more thoughfully composed because of the text-based nature of the medium.
- A written record is maintained of discussions which can run continuously over a given period.
- CMC is ideal in courses aimed at professionals in which there is strong emphasis on the contributions which students can make from their own personal experience.

- Inputs to a course of study can be made by visiting "electronic lecturers" that would be impossible by any other means.

Computer conferencing has become widely used in education in the past decade (see Harasim, 1990; Mason and Kaye, 1989; Waggoner, 1992). Coombs (1990) discusses its significance for handicapped learners. Boston (1992), Hansen et al. (1993), Paulsen (1992b), and Wells (1992) provide descriptions of specific projects involving computer conferencing. Lauzon (1992) discusses the integration of computer conferencing with computer-based instruction. Ryan (1992) analyzes the impact of cultural differences in international computer conferences.

Computer-Based Instruction

Computer-based instruction refers to instructional programs that the student uses alone on a personal computer, the program being provided on a floppy disc. This contrasts with computer conferencing in which the computer is used with its modem and the telephone line to link the student with other students and the instructor. Since the advent of the personal computer in the 1980s, computer-based instructional materials have become widely used in education (e.g., Cannings and Finkel, 1993; Kearsley, Hunter, and Furlong, 1992; OTA, 1988).

However, until recently, computer-based materials have not been common in distance education courses. Apart from the fact that they are expensive to develop, the primary consideration has been the availability of computers in people's homes or offices. Furthermore, there are a number of different types of computers, and materials need to be provided in different versions for each type of machine. One of the strengths of computer-based instruction is that it can provide a type of interactive learning experience, what in Chapter 8 is described as learner-content interaction. However, past programs have relied heavily on simple drill and tutorial formats that resulted in materials that are boring and failed to challenge learners. (Ironically, computer games are quite the opposite.)

Newer instructional programs embody more sophisticated learning strategies such as inquiry, simulation, or collaboration and are more successful. In addition, new methods for organizing information, such as hypertext/hypermedia, are being used which provide powerful learning and teaching tools (e.g., Berk and Devlin, 1991; Jonassen, 1989; Jonassen and Mandl, 1990). In the workplace a great deal of emphasis has been placed on providing so called Electronic Performance Support Systems (EPSS) which make job-related information immediately available to the employee and hence minimize the amount of formal training required (see Gery, 1990; Raybould, 1990).

The latest forms of computer-based instruction use CD-ROM for multimedia presentations (Gayeski, 1993; Schwier and Misanchuk, 1993). CD-ROM is a digital form of the familiar audio CDs that can store text, graphics, sound, and video. Approximately 600–800 megabytes of information can be stored on a sin-

When Is a Computer a TV?

One interesting development in computer technology is a circuit board that contains a television tuner. Once this board is installed in a personal computer, the computer can receive and display television broadcasts—turning itself into a television. Ford Motor Company has made use of this trick to bring instructional television to its engineers in the workplace. The courses are taught by professors at nearby Wayne State University; Ford engineers access these classes by turning on their IBM PS/2 computers equipped with the TV boards. The engineers watch the class on their machine and can simultaneously use software to take notes, perform calculations, or search for information. A headset is used to listen to the programs to avoid disturbing co-workers. In addition, they can use the keypad to signal that they have a question or to provide a response to a question asked by the professor. In addition to the television broadcasts, the courses involve telephone conferences and the use of electronic mail for interaction among participants and professors.

SOURCE: ASTD *Technical & Skills Training,* October 1993.

gle CD-ROM disc. Most newer computers come with CD-ROM drives built in. CD-ROM seems to have much promise as a medium for distance education since it can provide very effective presentations and is a very cost-effective way to distribute information.

Media Selection

From the preceding discussion, it should be clear that there are a large number of technological and media options available for the delivery of distance learning courses. How do you select the best medium or mixture of media for a specific course or program? First of all, we must keep in mind that each medium has its strengths and weaknesses (Table 5-3), and these should be matched to the nature of the learning setting. Print has the virtues of being relatively inexpensive to develop and distribute and is very reliable. It carries large volumes of information very efficiently, and the student can read the material whenever and as often as desired. However, it is difficult for the instructor to write in print in ways that stimulate the learners to keep a high level of involvement.

For some students, especially less well educated, print can become a passive medium, and presentations then can become boring. Interaction depends on correspondence, which is too slow for most students. Computer-based instruction provides a high volume of text as well as audio and video media and is attractive to students who may find it hard to be motivated by printed mate-

Table 5-3   **Strengths and Weaknesses of Different Media**

	Strengths	*Weaknesses*
Print	inexpensive reliable dense information learner-controlled use	passive
Audio/video	dynamic vicarious experience visually/conceptually dense information learner-controlled use	development time/cost
Radio/television	dynamic pacing immediacy mass distribution	development time/costs real-time use
Teleconferencing	interactive immediacy participative	complexity unreliability real-time use
Computers	multimedia dynamic	equipment required development time/costs

rials. However, it requires the availability of appropriate computers and is usually expensive and time consuming to create.

Audio- and videocassettes can present information in a dynamic and stimulating manner, and students can control their use, but good programs can be expensive and time consuming to prepare. Radio and television are also dynamic media because they give immediate up-to-the-minute information, and they provide mass distribution; typically, they involve expensive and time-consuming program development costs and very high distribution costs. Teleconferencing provides good interactive capability but involves the use of complex and sometimes unreliable equipment (although audioconferencing is usually quite simple, cheap, and dependable).

When course designers are considering which medium to use to achieve a particular teaching goal, or what combination of media to use, they should keep in mind Rowntree's (1981) advice—to make choices in light of the functions they are to perform in the learning situation. Our selection will be determined in part by whether the messages we are trying to communicate are aimed at

- engaging the student's motivation;
- recalling earlier learning;
- providing new learning stimuli;
- activating the student's responses;
- giving speedy feedback to the student; and/or
- encouraging appropriate practice.

Media Selection Procedures

This summary of the general strengths and weaknesses of different categories of media indicates some selection considerations. For example, if development time and budgets are very limited, print and teleconferencing are better choices than audio/video, radio/television, or computer-based instruction. On the other hand, if motivation of the students is a serious concern (which it often is in distance education), introducing the use of the more dynamic and interactive media would be of primary interest. In some settings, the reliability and simplicity of the delivery system might be a major factor, in which case print would be favored and teleconferencing would not.

If teleconferencing is desired, it is usually unwise to select the video technologies until full consideration has been given to audio, computer, and audiographics, since the former are more expensive, need more preparation, more technical support, and greater sophistication on the part of the instructor. Of course, these generalizations about different categories of media have to be examined for a particular learning situation in a specific distance education system.

Media selection models (see Heinich, Molenda, and Russell, 1985; Lane, 1992; Reiser and Gagne, 1983; Romiszowski, 1974) provide a procedure for choosing one medium over another for entire programs or a specific course. The main steps in most media selection models are as follows:

1. Identify the media attributes required by the instructional objectives or learning activities.
2. Identify the student characteristics which suggest or preclude certain media.
3. Identify characteristics of the learning environment which favor or preclude certain media.
4. Identify economic or organizational factors which may affect the feasibility of certain media.

The first step specifies that the nature of the learning involved as specified in the instructional objectives or learning activities should be the starting place for chosing the media to be used. For example, if the learning involves an auditory stimulus or response (such as reading or foreign language instruction), then a medium with sound capability is necessary. The second step involves the identification of any student characteristics that might be relevant. For example, if the students are known to be poor readers, emphasis on audiovisual media would seem appropriate, whereas it would be silly to send information on a tape to graduate students who are perfectly capable of reading such information in text. The third step is to examine the learning environment in terms of media suitability. Some media are better for learning at home, others for learning with other students at learning centers, others more suitable for learning at work, etc. The last step is to assess economic or organizational factors such as the available budget or past/existing use of particular media.

The procedures just described, when applied in conjunction with understanding of the strengths and weaknesses of the different technologies, provide some rough guidelines that can be used to make decisions about the most appropriate media for a given distance education program or course. However, what matters eventually is not so much what media are employed, but *how* they are actually used. The effectiveness of any medium does not depend so much on the characteristic of the medium but on the quality of the course design, each lesson design, and the quality of the interaction that the instructor is capable of. Effective use of a medium depends on having ample experience with it in distance learning applications. Even media that we are very familar with, such as print or television, require special adaptations in order to work well in distance learning settings. This is why it is so important to have media expertise as part of the distance learning development team.

Media Integration

So far in this chapter, we have discussed each type of medium separately. However, in most distance education programs and courses, a combination of media are used. No single medium is likely to address all the learning requirements across a full course or program, the needs of different learners, or the variations in learning environments that are likely to occur in a distance education program. Another reason to have multiple media is to provide redundancy and flexibility. Should there be a problem with the distribution of one medium, the other media can compensate. For example, a program that uses broadcast television in conjunction with computer conferencing can rely on either medium to deliver information if one fails. Videotapes are a good backup for students who miss a television program. Fax can substitute for certain aspects of teleconferencing if necessary. Captioning a videotape or television broadcast is a good idea not only to make the information accessible to the hearing impaired but also to provide a safety factor if the sound is poor or lost.

Perhaps most important of all, using a mixture of media allows for differences in student learning styles or capabilities. Some students prefer the reflective thinking style associated with print, whereas others thrive on the impulsive live dialog in a teleconference. In short, the more media alternatives provided, the more effective the distance education course is likely to be for a wider range of students.

Decisions about Multiple Media

Unfortunately, each medium added to a course or program increases the development time and costs, as well as the complexity for the learner and the administration of the course or program. Thus some measure of parsimony must be practiced in selecting the number and type of media to be used. Before experimenting with a new medium, consideration should be given to media that are already in use to see if they are sufficient. It is suprising how many organizations have invested in expensive technologies like satellite channels or desktop video without ever trying to achieve educational and training goals by means of the telephones already on their desks, or by means of printed materials that could be produced by a competent designer on the office computers.

The extent of use is another consideration: Is the medium likely to be used a number of times in a course or across different courses? On the other hand, the requirements of a particular learning segment or group of learners may be so compelling that something new is justified, even though it has not been used before or is only needed for one aspect of a course or program. When integrating a number of different media into a single course, one of the most important design considerations is to ensure that the media work together. There is always the possibility that learners will get "lost" when they go from one media component to another. For this reason, it is highly desirable to provide the learner with a course "map" (usually part of the study guide) that depicts the different media used and how they relate to each other.

In addition, it is a good idea to have each medium include directions on where to go next. For example, the study guide might recommend that the learner listen to an audiotape before reading a chapter in the textbook; at the end of the tape segment, instructions would be provided on the tape to next read the chapter. Of course, there is no guarantee that students will follow the recommendations, although tests, quizzes, and assignments can be used to enforce a learning sequence if this is necessary.

Summary

In this chapter, we have discussed the various delivery media available for distance education.

- Almost all distance education courses use some form of print, such as study guides, textbooks, or manuals. Audio- and videocassettes are also commonly used, especially in correspondence courses. A number of different forms of television are found in distance education, including broadcast, ITFS, CATV, and DBS. Teleconferencing (audio, audiographics, video, and computer) is also widely used. On the other hand, computer-based instruction is not extensively used in distance education at present, although new forms that involve multimedia and CD-ROM may become more popular in the future.

- There is no "right" or "wrong" technology for distance education. Each medium and each technology for delivering it has its own strengths and weaknesses. One of the worst mistakes an organization or an instructor can make is to become dogmatically committed to delivery by a single medium. The media selection process should be undertaken for each course and each program, since they all have different requirements depending on the objectives, learners, and learning environment.

- A decision about what technologies and media to employ should weigh many factors. Furthermore, a combination of media should be selected to meet the diversity of the subject matter and learners' needs, as well as to provide redundancy and flexibility.

- How a medium is used is more important than what particular technologies are selected. This indicates the significance of the design and implementation considerations discussed in subsequent chapters.

Further discussion about the use of technology in distance education can be found in Bates (1984, 1988, 1990b), OTA (1989), and Kearsley (1985). The design of study guides is discussed in greater detail in Chapter 6.

Course Design and Development

The courses and other programs offered in distance education are as varied in their content and the sophistication of their design as the range of institutions that produce them. Any institution that provides distance education must organize and manage the work of both academics and media specialists as they generate ideas and strategies and develop them into courses. The content must be structured in a form suitable for distance learning, and methods of evaluation must be designed. Printed and recorded materials must be produced and distributed, and where real-time interaction is part of the course, it must be planned and organized.

Many questions must be addressed in the design and development of a distance education course or program, including:

- What content should be included or left out?
- What is the best way to sequence and organize the material?
- What are the best media to use to present the material?
- What kind of teaching strategies should be employed?
- How can learning be measured most appropriately?
- What feedback should students receive about their progress?
- What methods should be used to create the materials?

The design and development methods used will depend on the nature of the course, its learners, the content, and especially on the level of the distance education organization as defined in Chapter 1. For example, a program-level course created by a single instructor for delivery by Instructional Television Fixed Service (ITFS) to a number of local sites will have less sophisticated design than a telecourse created by a multi-institutional team for national broadcast—even though both involve the same medium (television).

The chapter begins with a description of a particular approach that is widely used at all levels—Instructional Systems Design (ISD). Then we examine the nature of course development teams, the design of study guides, preparing audioconferences, planning a teleconference, and message design for computer conferences. We conclude the chapter with a discussion of evaluation and a summary of general design principles.

Instructional Systems Design

Instructional Systems Design (ISD) consists of some recognized standard procedures that are used to develop well-structured instructional materials. ISD emerged after World War II, with its origins in part in the pressure for more efficient training techniques that were generated by the war. It is a product of several theoretical perspectives on learning and teaching, frameworks that include systems theory, behavioral psychology, and communications and information theory (see Dick and Carey, 1985; Richey, 1986). The fundamental principle of the ISD approach is that all aspects of learning and instruction should be defined behaviorally, so that what the student is expected to learn can be measured, and teaching can concentrate on the student's observable performance.

Stages of Development

Figure 6-1 illustrates the basic model that underlies most ISD approaches. The central idea is that the development of instruction can be divided into a number of phases, or stages, each of which involves certain procedures. In the analysis phase, the most important activity for the teacher or teaching organization is to conduct some form of task or job analysis to identify the specific skills that are involved in the task or job. Another step in the analysis stage is to identify the characteristics of the learners and the learning environment and to find out what these students need to learn in order to perform the desired skills at the desired level.

In the design stage, the goals and objectives of the instructional program are articulated in very specific terms, as well as the structure and format of the course. If the course is based on the concept of criterion-referenced testing (i.e., mastery learning), test items matching the objectives can be created in the design stage (even though the content has not been developed yet). Media selection can also be made in the design stage based on the objectives and information on needs collected in the analysis phase.

During the development stage, instructional materials, such as films, study guides, books, audiotapes and teleconference outlines, are created, produced, and tested. Teachers and staff may also be trained during this stage. In the implementation phase, students register; instructional materials are delivered, and instructors/tutors interact with students. Evaluation activities involve the

Figure 6.1   Model of the Instructional Systems Design (ISD) Process

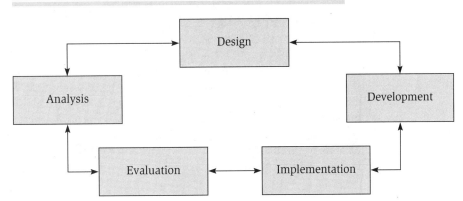

testing and grading of students and the assessment of instructional effectiveness of the course and materials. This last step usually leads to revision of courses and materials in readiness for their next use.

A Planned Approach

One important characteristic of the ISD approach is its emphasis on planning. Each stage normally involves planning some product that must be delivered in order that later steps in the ISD process can move forward. For example, in the design phase, it is usual to develop a specific set of objectives that then leads to the development of an evaluation plan that outlines how the course will be assessed and how learning will be measured. Planning the teaching strategies, such as how information will be presented and what learners will be expected to do, cannot begin until the objectives and evaluation plan have been prepared. This shows in another way how the different stages of course design are linked together into a system.

A Continuous Process

The five phases, or stages, are shown as an ongoing cycle since instructional development is normally a continuous process with considerable overlap of the activities in one stage with those in others. For example, even though the activities associated with the stage of analysis are normally conducted at the beginning of a development effort, they could be done at any time if there is a question or problem about the validity of the instructional needs, the learners, or the learning environment. Evaluation of one course, or part of the course, is very closely related to the analysis of need for a subsequent course.

The extent to which some or all of the procedures are followed in a given phase depends on the commitment of the teaching institution to the ISD approach and the extent to which the institution is actually organized to support an ISD approach. It is very difficult for an individual teacher to follow the model except superficially. Open universities, large corporations, and the U.S. Department of Defense tend to employ ISD approaches more extensively and more intensively than do traditional universities or home study schools. This is partly a result of the training that is given employees of those institutions, partly the greater funding they often have, partly their orientation to producing specific, short-term results, and partly the way that such organizations are organized to support a total systems approach to education and training.

For further discussion of ISD and instructional design principles, see Briggs, Gustafson, and Tillman (1991); Gagne, Briggs, and Wagner (1988); or Leshin, Pollock, and Reigeluth (1992).

The Development Team

On several previous occasions we have suggested that designing and teaching a distance education course should, and typically does, involve a team effort. The size of the team may be small, with as few as 2 individuals (the author-editor model) or may be a large group of 20 or more people (the course team model). The size and nature of the team depends on the scale of the course as well as the nature and level of the distance education institution involved.

The Author-Editor Model

The author-editor model is common in independent study programs in which a subject matter expert writes the draft of the study guide and an editor (or editorial staff) produces the final document. The course development process involves getting reviews from other experts and perhaps potential students, obtaining copyright clearances, designing page layout, proofreading, making corrections, and printing or duplicating (see Wright, 1988).

Although the author-editor approach developed as the favored way of producing correspondence courses, an analogous model exists in program-level teleconferencing where a content expert provides the content and works with media specialists who operate the television, telecommunications, or computer systems used.

What is strikingly missing in these arrangements, usually, is an instructional designer and many good features of the instructional design approach. It usually rests with the editorial staff to exert influence on the author to produce learning objectives, evaluation criteria, and teaching strategies, which some content specialists are willing and able to do and others are not.

A content expert, for example, is likely to set objectives in terms of what content will be presented rather than what learners will be required to know. Content experts invariably present a volume of material in excess of what a student can learn in the time available. An instructional designer first calculates the time available, then tailors the content accordingly. Sometimes an editor can achieve these ends, but in real life editors are outranked by authors, and the author's will usually prevails. A course team provides checks and balances against the vanity of the content specialist that the author-editor model does not have. On the other hand, the author-editor model is certainly cheaper and invariably produces quicker results than a course team.

The Course Team Model

The British Open University (BOU) pioneered the team approach to course design and provides the best examples of this model.

Each course is designed and produced by a team which might consist of as many as 20 or more people, each of whom is a specialist. At the design stage of the ISD process a group of academics, content specialists in a subject area, writes outlines of what should be taught in their particular specialities and engages in extensive discussions regarding the objectives and content of each unit and module of the course. These outlines and objectives are debated not only by the academics and others but by the whole team, including producers, editors, and external consultants. Eventually, after three separate drafts have been presented, a study guide on that subject emerges.

As well as taking responsibility for the study guide in their specialty areas, the academics assemble books of readings, make audio- and videotapes, and design tests and supplemental materials, all with the assistance and guidance of specialists in these tasks. These technical experts include editors, graphics designers, radio and television producers, instructional designers, and librarians, even a specialist photolibrarian. A senior academic chairs the team and an administrator is responsible for ensuring that each task in the development schedule (which often lasts one to two years) is completed on time. Discussions of the BOU course team model are provided by Crick (1980), Nichodemus (1984), and Tight (1985).

The development process in a course team is a very complex business, with many tasks to be accomplished by different people. Decisions must be made about teaching strategies, such as what proportion of time is to be spent on readings versus audio or video materials. Photographs or artwork may need to be commissioned. Audio and television components must be scripted, and produced, and carefully integrated with the printed study guide, and even the planning of study center tutorial meetings. Copyright clearance must be obtained for material from secondary sources (Pisacreta, 1993), for which purpose the BOU maintains a separate copyright office. Guidelines for tutors about assignments and exams must be prepared. A great deal of detailed planning and much creative work goes into every component to ensure that it fits together with the entire course "package" but also meets the specific objectives it was intended for.

Consensus forms the basis of a team development model. From the first exploratory meetings of experts and practitioners in the field to define the objectives and content, the process depends on many formal and informal meetings, a lot of telephone and E-mail consultation, and a great deal of argument. In the team's regular meetings to review each component of the course as it is designed, arguments are fierce regarding what content to include, and especially what is to be left out, with subject experts defending their own territory against their rivals. Criticism of the draft material is also intense. Each draft is commented on by the course team as well as external readers. The materials are written and rewritten to take into account the various criticisms and must be approved by the whole team before finally being produced for student use. Finally, meetings are held in the field with representatives of students, tutors, and employers to ensure that the course materials are appropriate.

Strengths and Weaknesses

Both the author-editor and course team approaches to the development and delivery of distance education have their strengths and weaknesses. The author-editor model is very cost-effective because it involves minimal human resources and results in the quick development and modification of courses. However, neither the instructor nor editor is an instructional design expert. Furthermore, the content and teaching strategies derive from the knowledge and experience of a single expert. In contrast, the course team model brings together instructional design experts as well as a number of content experts. The resulting course materials are usually much more complete and effective. Furthermore, the course team approach tends to emphasize the use of multiple media in a course, whereas the author-editor model typically results in teaching being delivered by a single medium with perhaps minimal support from another. The course team approach, however, is very labor-intensive and therefore expensive, and it involves a lengthy development period.

To be successful in a team environment, an individual needs to relinquish some decision-making control to others, respect the skills and knowledge of others, and be willing to compromise. Communication is essential to successful teamwork, and team members need to have a cooperative attitude.

Furthermore, planning and advance preparation are essential qualities of team efforts because sufficient time must be allowed for all members to carry out their duties. Following procedures and policies established by the group is also very important in order for work to flow smoothly. For example, if a standard format is established for a study guide, all course writers must prepare their material in that format, otherwise editing and layout of the guide become complicated. Table 6-1 lists some of the major activities and personnel involved in producing an instructional television program. The instructor needs to interact with many (but not all) members of the television team. Of course, in a large-scale operation, this team could be bigger and have more members. Interaction with a team usually involves many meetings—something most teachers are not very enthusiastic about.

Clearly, to succeed in most forms of distance education it is necessary for the instructor to be a "team player." Teachers who lack the personality attributes and work habits appropriate for teamwork will likely have difficulty with

Table 6-1   **Teamwork in Producing Instructional Television Programs**

Creation of script	Instructor(s), scriptwriter, producer
Preparation of graphics	Instructor(s), graphics designer
Preparation of set	Producer, lighting director, technicans
Video preproduction	Producer, editor, production assistant
Broadcast	Instructor(s), director, engineers, camera crew
Site support	Administrative assistant, site coordinators

distance education. Learning how to work as part of a team (and the underlying interpersonal and communication skills) could be an important aspect of teacher preparation for distance education.

The author-editor approach is the only one that makes economic sense if courses have very small enrollments or short lifetimes, while the course team approach is justified for courses with large enrollments and long-term use. To obtain the benefits of the team approach at a cost-effective level, it is necessary for administrators to organize the presentation of courses to larger populations and thus to obtain economies of scale that make the team approach viable. (See the discussion of the systems approach in Chapter 1.)

In the United States, ad hoc course teams of specialists from several different institutions have been assembled by the International University Consortium, as well as for the development of Annenberg/CPB telecourses (see Chapter 3). Holmberg and Bakshi (1992) discuss the details of how a course team worked in a specific course at Athabasca University in Canada.

Designing the Study Guide

Almost all distance education courses involve a printed study guide which provides the backbone of the course and a framework for the other materials to rest on. Much of the analysis, explanation, and discussion that an instructor might make in a face-to-face setting needs to be put into the study guide.

A typical study guide contains the following:

1. An introduction to the course and a statement of the goals and objectives

2. A substantial presentation of information relevant to each objective, with the instructor's commentary and discussion, the associated reading(s), other media, and written assignments

3. Directions for work to do with the course text and any other materials provided, including suggestions regarding what to give priority to

4. Directions and advice regarding the preparation and submission of written and other assignments

To help maintain students' interest, the study guide must be visually attractive and well-organized.

5. An annotated bibliography and suggestions for practical work of other activity outside the course

6. An explanation of the grading scheme and other course requirements

7. Suggestions for how to apply good study techniques

8. A set of self-testing questions to be answered or issues to be discussed for purpose of self-evaluation

9. A schedule of when specific lessons or activities are to be conducted or completed, and advice about how to use the time allotted for study

10. Information about how and when to contact a tutor or counselor

The study guide is quite different from a textbook or book of readings. These are intended primarily to communicate information; the study guide is intended to communicate teaching. It has sometimes been referred to as "a tutorial in text."

Here are some of the considerations involved in the design of a study guide (see Rowntree, 1986 or Duchastel, 1988 for further details).

Creating Lessons or Units

The information and activities that are communicated in distance learning materials should be organized into self-contained lessons or units. One of the reasons a person studies from a distance learning program rather than under-takes the study alone is that the program provides a structure of the content and the learning process. (See the importance of this in distance education theory in Chapter 10.)

The place to start is to lay out how the team will utilize the number of study hours the student is to devote to the subject. For example, if the course is 150 hours in length and there are 15 weeks for its completion, each unit may be calculated to take the student 10 hours. Then the amount of reading, writ-ing, viewing, listening, practicing, and testing can be calculated within this time budget.

Each unit might correspond to a single instructional objective and include some form of evaluation activity that allows the students to check the extent to which they have understood the material. Some teams try to break each unit into 15-to-20-minute segments of study. In this way, a lesson may correspond to what would be done in a 90-minute classroom session, but consist of six separate activities. For one period the students may read the study guide; then they are told to make some notes; then to listen to an audiotape; next to do a self-test; finally to read the study guide again. In distance education courses that involve teleconferences, each unit of the study guide may correspond to a separate teleconference.

There are many reasons to break the course down into a series of units and short lesson segments. For one thing, it makes it easier for the student to fit study into the normal, very active, adult lifestyle. Covering three segments of a unit may use up exactly the time of a daily railroad commute or the time that is available waiting for a child to return from day- care. Short segments not only help the student to organize the content but also make information easier to learn and remember. Students also find such a structure helps them evaluate and integrate as they go along. In addition, the short segments allow students to stop when they want to, providing a sense of closure and progress. It is also easier to identify student problems when the material is divided in this way, since they can be localized to a specific objective or learning activity.

Although some academic purists may express the view that breaking the course material into many small units makes it "choppy" or disconnected, doing so actually increases the chances that the student will be able to under-stand the material, integrate it into existing cognitive structures, and so com-plete the course. Instructional designers should aim to obtain a synthesis of content across the units and segments by discussing the relationships among content in the introduction to each unit, and also in summaries, as well as by designing evaluation activities that require the student to make such compar-isons and linkages.

Writing Style

While all authors have their own writing styles, it is important that a study guide be written in a conversational rather than a literary or scholarly tone. This means using the first person rather than the third and using a simple vocabu-

A course writer consults the photograph librarian to find suitable illustrative material for the study guide.

lary. The study guide is meant to substitute for the normal discussions that occur between an instructor and the student in a classroom or instructor's office, and the language should reflect this. Ideally, instructors can project their personalities in the study guide, so the students have a sense of being "taught" by a specific individual even though they are learning at a distance.

To a certain extent, the content of what is included in the study guide will determine the appropriate tone. Clarifiying difficult concepts, presenting personal anecdotes or examples, commenting about points of disagreement with the text or readings, or raising questions for students to think about—all help to establish a more conversational atmosphere in the study guide.

Layout

Just as the experienced classroom teacher has a repertoire of techniques for drawing attention to certain points, to planting questions or ideas in the students' minds, for provoking and for bringing synthesis and closure, so all these must be accomplished by the teacher at a distance. One of the techniques for doing this is the creative positioning of text and graphics on the printed page.

One of the primary responsibilities of the editor (or editing team) is to ensure that the layout of the study guide maximizes student learning. This means employing the kinds of techniques and principles discussed with reference to print media in Chapter 4. Probably the most important factor is allowing ample "white space" in the document so it is visually attractive and avoids overloading the learner with too much information at one time. White space literally gives the student "space to think."

In the same way, choice of typefaces, indentation, graphics, and headings all play pedagogical roles in the study guide. Use of color may be important in producing an attractive and interesting document. Since this introduces an extra cost factor into the printing and duplication budget, it may not be affordable to many providers. It will not be necessary for many subjects, but where it is needed, such as in a course about the history of art, it should be used. Expenditure on color still pictures will be cheaper than making a television film and should help the students accomplish the learning objectives just as well.

NUCEA Standards

Each year the Independent Study Division of the National University Continuing Education Association (NUCEA) conducts a national competition for study guides. A committee judges the study guides according to well-defined criteria (Table 6-2), and the best guides receive awards. These same criteria are often used as guidelines by independent study course developers.

Table 6-2   **NUCEA Evaluation Criteria**

Course preface

Introduction, overview, general
  Objectives
  Explanation of course procedures and grading
  Attention to student concerns
  Studying suggestions
  Biographical sketch of author/instructor

Lessons
  Well-formulated objectives
  Clear description of assignments
  Supplemental commentary
  Self-evaluation exercises
  Appropriate workload
  Variety of learning experiences

Communication
  Good writing style
  Layout and organization
  Use of media

Preparing an Audioconference

Audioconferencing is a popular medium in program-level distance education since it can be used with a minimum of technical assistance and is cheaper than other forms of teleconference. Audioconferencing can also be used as part of a multimedia delivery system in a distance teaching institution. In Chapter 7 we will discuss some of the critical aspects of conducting a successful audioconference. We suggest that the following three types of materials be prepared when designing such an event.

Outline Segments and Activities

An audioconference must have a structure that is more open than that of a radio program and probably more open than a videoconference. However, while there may appear to be considerable freedom to participate from the point of view of the students in the conference, the instructor should have a very firm understanding at all times of where the students are in the sequence of planned events and where they are going next.

One of the most important preparation steps is to prepare an outline or script of the audioconference that identifies the segments and student activities. In most programs a typical segment is likely to be about 10 to 15 minutes in length and correspond to a specific objective. Such segments correspond to the segments in study guides, as discussed above, except that the material in the audio segment consists of comments, questions, or ideas intended to promote discussion. It could involve an interview (live or taped), panel, debate, role-playing, brainstorming, or simply a short introduction by the instructor. It should never consist of simple reading from notes or a text, except perhaps for quotes or excerpts. A very valuable approach is to organize students to make brief presentations of assignments or their own projects. Any form of discussion is fine as long as it encourages participation and interaction. Table 6-3 is a typical outline used in a graduate-level training program. This is used by groups of sophisticated distance learners who have had a lot of experience in working together in this way, so the program structure is less specific than might be used with less experienced learners.

Study Guide and Other Media

A second preparatory step for an audioconference is the creation and distribution of a study guide, readings, and other recorded materials. While audioconferences provide the means for elaboration, explanation, and exchange of ideas, they cannot provide the density and depth of information that can be communicated by a textbook or other readings. It will still be necessary to provide a study guide that gives the background information necessary to understand the content and to participate in the discussions. Study guides for use in courses taught by audioconference may not be as comprehensive as those intended for

Table 6-3   Outline of a Three-hour Audioconference

Pennsylvania State University
American Center for the Study of Distance Education

Course Title: Teleconferencing in distance education: Third session
Jan. 28, 1995: (All times are EST and approximate.)

9:00:   Call in and welcome to all Mexican, Finnish, Estonian, and U.S. participants.

9:30:   Instructor introduces today's theme—site facilitation and site facilitator responsibilities.

9:45–10:15:   Local site discussion: From your reading and also your practical experience, what do you consider to be the most important responsibilities of a site coordinator?

Make a group list of TWO technical responsibilities and TWO administrative responsibilities.

10:15–10:45:   General discussion: Five-minute discussion with each site.

10:45–11:15:   Make a group list of TWO pedagogical responsibilities. Please discuss, with focus on the media as listed below (though there are many more similarities than differences with regard to the media).

11:15–12:00:   General discussion: Each site report and the interaction with me or the class that follows will be limited to FIVE MINUTES. This should allow for at least two reports per site. Choose a spokesperson, but be prepared to join in the five–minute interaction with your site.

Sites will report as follows:

1. UNAM (audioconferencing)

2. Vera Cruz (audioconferencing)

3. Turku (audiographic conferencing)

4. Lahti/Helsinki/Tallin (audiographic conferencing)

5. University Park (videoconferencing)

6. Pennsylvania (Library, Monroville, and Altoona groups) (computer conferencing; i.e., the role of the moderator not the instructor)

12:00 (approximately): Lunch

correspondence study, but they still need to contain the same principal elements and serve the same purposes.

Class Roster

A third step is for the instructor to prepare a class roster with background information about each student that can be referred to easily during an audioconference. This allows the instructor to ask specific students questions related to their interests or experience and makes the audioconference a more personal learning activity. Ideally, this class roster can be distributed to all students as well to facilitate interaction. (See Table 7-1 for an example of a class roster.)

Planning a Satellite Teleconference

Satellite teleconferences represent a special form of distance education because each one is usually conducted as a one-time-only effort, even though an organization may offer many teleconferences. Each teleconference is usually self-contained and has open enrollment (i.e., there are no prerequisites). A typical teleconference is one to three hours in duration, originates from a single site, and is broadcast to many locations nationally or internationally, with the pictures going to the sites and audio communication from the sites to the transmitting station. Most successful teleconferences involve a local component (e.g., panel of local experts or small group discussion sessions) which helps participants apply the content of the program to their immediate setting.

Components of a Satellite Teleconference

Here are the major components of a well-organized satellite teleconference:

1. **Program announcement** This provides details on the originator, date and time of transmission, satellite bands, rationale, objectives, intended audience, content outline, credentials of presenters and their topics, registration fees, restrictions on taping or reuse, and cancellation policy. Site coordinators and prospective participants should receive the announcement at least six months before the date of the teleconference. In addition, site coordinators should be provided with posters, a press release, and a promotional videotape to help them market the teleconference locally.

2. **Local site and experts identified** Site coordinator identifies the location for the teleconference and local experts who are willing to participate. He or she also arranges for technical support, needed equipment, facilities, and catering.

3. **Preregistration/registration** Participants must usually preregister for the teleconference and be provided with details about the location, agenda, background on the experts, and relevant readings. Typically, participants receive packages of materials when they register. On-site registration should begin well before the teleconference starts (e.g., one to two hours).

4. **Preconference activity** Before the teleconference begins, participants should have an opportunity to meet each other as well as the local experts. This meeting may take the form of an informal "coffee hour" or formal presentations by the local experts in a panel format.

5. **Test period** In the hour before the teleconference, technicians check out the satellite signal as well as the television monitors, speakers, and microphones (or fax) to be used for questions.

6. Interaction During the teleconference, there will usually be opportunities for participants at each site to ask questions. Questioning may be managed by the local site coordinator or directly by the originating site. Participants may ask their questions directly or give them in written form to the site coordinator to ask or to fax. The instructor in charge at the originating site should prepare questions for both experts and the audience so that discussion can be stimulated if necessary. If there are transmission problems during the conference (the satellite link may occasionally be lost or interrupted), the moderator should ask the local experts to comment or handle questions until the problems are resolved.

7. Post-conference activity After the teleconference is over, the local experts may be asked to comment or answer questions. Another possibility is that participants break into working groups and discuss specific issues or strategies. Alternatively, the teleconference may be followed by a lunch or dinner to allow informal discussions to take place.

8. Wrap-up and evaluation The moderator should summarize the main points of the teleconference and any themes that emerged in the postconference discussions. An evaluation questionnaire should be completed by all participants in order to assess the effectiveness and value of the teleconference.

Design and Development Activities

A satellite teleconference is a more structured event with less interaction (what in Chapter 10 will be called dialog) than either an audio-, audiographic, or two-way videoconference. A satellite teleconference is more of a presentation event than an interactive event. The above description of the major components of a teleconference helps to identify some of the major design and development activities:

1. Locating and preparing site coordinators Good site coordinators can make or break a teleconference. In many organizations and institutions, this is an official job responsibility (though probably not full-time). In other cases, someone will be designated or will volunteer for the role on an ad hoc basis. Since it must be assumed that the site coordinator may not have much experience, it is important to provide detailed guidelines (checklists are ideal) for tasks that they should perform, and their progress in following these guidelines should be checked by telephone. (More will be said about the role of teleconference coordinators in Chapter 7.)

2. Selecting the teleconference presenter and moderator Good presenters are usually well-known experts in their field but also have the kind of dynamic personality that projects well via television. Once the presenters have been selected, it is necessary to get them to provide material for graphics, videotaped segments, and the participants' package.

The moderator should have content expertise as well as television and satellite teleconferencing experience. The moderator must manage the presenters, deal with participants' questions and any discussion that occurs, as well as follow the instructions of the director or producer. If interaction is considered important in a particular program, then it is the moderator's job to ask the questions and stimulate the discussion.

3. Preparing the satellite teleconference announcement and participant materials The teleconference announcement plays a critical role in attracting participants and establishing their expectations about the content. Participant materials (presenter biographies, readings, bibliography, resource lists) ensure that participants have all the necessary reference material to prepare themselves for the teleconference. In order to distribute them to the sites in a timely fashion, it is necessary to prepare them well in advance. This means finalizing all details of the satellite teleconference quite early (typically six to nine months before the teleconference date).

4. Rehearsal A well-executed satellite teleconference is a very complicated undertaking, and it must be rehearsed if everything is to go smoothly. The moderator should go through the complete script with the producer/director and practice each segment. Presenters should run through their segments a number of times so they are comfortable with the timing, camera angles, and use of graphics and videotapes. Panel discussions and call-in questions should also be practiced—they will not be exactly the same during the teleconference, but the general nature will be the same.

Computer Conferencing

While some educational institutions conduct entire courses by computer conference, the best use of this form of teleconference is when it is integrated into a program that also utilizes other technologies (Bates, 1990a). There is considerable evidence that the asynchronous nature of the computer conference makes it an excellent complement to the audioconference, which should also be linked to recorded materials such as a study guide, video- and audiotapes. In an appropriate configuration of media, the computer conference is very valuable. It is especially appreciated by people learning in a second language and by students whose learning style is more reflective than those who excel in the give-and-take of a classroom.

Most computer conferencing systems allow participants to correspond by E-mail; to share common discussion space in the form of bulletin boards, which may have separate areas for special interest groups; to archive conference files; and to allow (usually very limited) synchronous communication (see Berge and Collins, 1993).

This range of communication options provides an environment that includes the benefits of conversation (both real-time and delayed); the reviewing of conference discussions; and the storage, retrieval, searching, and distribution of documents. Some computer-conference systems also provide capabilities for group decision making and the editing by many persons of a single document file. A particularly useful software program called LISTSERV (available on most Internet hosts) enables an instructor and students in a course to communicate by E-mail exclusively among the members of the course. The primary advantage of LISTSERV in distance education is its cross-platform compatibility, meaning that students are not required to learn how to access another machine or program at a different site. Asynchronous, LISTSERV-based computer conferencing offers several unique capabilities as an interactive medium.

Discussions started during class time can be continued, unconstrained by allotted airtime and without the costs incurred by long distance telephone connections. Students who can access their E-mail accounts from their homes can work at whatever hour suits them. Students who speak English as a second language can take their time to read, with dictionary in hand if necessary, and compose their replies. Participants can be geographically dispersed and still receive messages almost instantly. If students are online at the same time at locations sometimes many thousands of miles apart, it can often appear as if they were conducting a synchronous conversation, with the delay only in the composition and transmission of each note. All students can retrieve documents such as reading assignments, resource documents, and transcripts of previous discussions from the LISTSERV archives. A paper contributed by a guest lecturer to a class conference can be sent to each individual's mailbox to ensure that students would each have their own copy, which they may or may not choose to print out. LISTSERV also maintains a database archive of all distributed messages, which can be made available for analysis (Berge, 1995).

Design of Computer Conferences

Whether used at the program level of distance education or incorporated into a total systems design, the crux of a computer conference is the nature of the messages that are exchanged among the instructor (or moderator) and students. Here are some considerations regarding message design:

- Each message should be about a single idea or issue; don't use the same message to cover many different points. Having one message for each point helps keep messages short, which is desirable for reading on a computer screen, and makes it easier to understand and follow up on.

- Conduct a computer conference like other teleconferences by asking good questions. As respondents answer your question, always restate it or restate the issue being addressed so that other recipients can figure out what the message is about. Some systems allow you to annotate the original message with comments; this is ideal.

- Take the time to provide a meaningful subject header to a message. This helps to prepare the recipient for the content of the message.

- Periodically provide summary messages that restate the major points made in a series of messages. This helps to minimize the fragmentation and chaos that are common in computer conferences.

- Be careful to distinguish personal replies containing feedback for specific individuals from public comments intended for the entire group. Never give a "public flogging," no matter how tempting this may be.

- Every message should be acknowledged so the sender knows the message was received. Some systems automatically indicate receipt.

- Each student should receive personal feedback on assignments that identifies the strength and weakness of their answer. It is also desirable to post a public message after an assignment is completed that summarizes the strengths and weaknesses of all responses.

- Never be sarcastic or insulting in messages; negative comments have more force when made in written messages than verbally in person or over the telephone.

- While there is typically limited opportunity for good visual design in current computer message systems (because the computer uses a single typeface, typestyle, and font size), spaces and lines can be used to break up paragraphs or sections of a message and hence improve its readability. However, tabs and any type of formating (e.g., underlining, italics, bold) should be avoided, since these features are not likely to display properly across different systems.

Public Versus Private Messages

One issue that comes up in most computer conferences is whether assignments should be sent as private messages to the instructor or posted as public messages for all students to see. The advantages of the former approach is that every student has to prepare a personal response; in the latter method, students can read and perhaps build upon other people's answers. This also results in many messages for students to read (which could be beneficial). One method is to have all assignments sent as private messages to the instructor, who can copy them to a file that is publicly accessible. This allows students to examine each other's answers after the assignment is due.

It is highly desirable to have students work in teams on assignments and projects. To do this it is necessary to assign students to groups (either randomly or on the basis of common interests) and specify which student is responsible for submitting the final response. Students need to be reminded to keep all their discussion in a subconference and to use private messages when possible to avoid "cluttering up" the conference area. Teamwork on an electronic network is complex and requires a lot of organization. New kinds of software (called "groupware") are being developed to facilitate on-line collaboration.

For further discussion about the design and implementation of computer conferences, see Berge and Collins (1995), Eisley (1992), Harasim (1990, 1993), Hiltz and Turoff (1993), or Lewis and Hegegaard (1993).

Creating Student Involvement

Regardless of what form of distance education is being designed, one element that is always critical is student involvement. In a teleconference-based course this is usually achieved by creating opportunities for participation in the discussion of the subject, perhaps some part of the presentation of the project, and interaction with an instructor and other students. More structured activities such as quizzes or simulations can also be used. Students need to be given a chance to ask (or answer) questions or share their views about a topic being discussed. This kind of activity can be organized in a print or video telecourse by the addition of a teleconference or by setting up student groups at local sites. Whatever the form of communications technology used, however, such participation is not likely to happen unless it is deliberately planned and the instructor/moderator encourages it.

In recorded materials such as the printed study guide or audio-/videotapes, the student should be presented with questions or problems to respond to at the end of each unit or throughout the presentation. Such items can be multiple choice or open-ended questions, with the answers discussed after the practice section. While some students will skip these self-evaluations, most will take advantage of the opportunity to check their understanding of the material. These sections can also be the basis for discussions with tutors or formal assignments to be handed in.

Any time students have to hand in assignments or respond to questions, they should receive feedback, from the instructor, moderator, or tutor. If students do not receive feedback, they will fail to develop a sense of participation in the course or program. While many students can tolerate some delay, most people like feedback to be immediate, and few people find one-way communication with no feedback to be satisfying. While there are many aspects to providing feedback (Howard, 1987), in general it should be prompt, focused, and constructive. Lack of sufficient relevant feedback is one of the most common sources of dissatisfaction and frustration for distance learners.

Self-directed Learning

The ability to undertake all or most of the design of one's own learning, to evaluate performance, and to make adjustments accordingly are the attributes of being a self-directed learner. Distance education is easier for people who have an ability to direct their own learning than it is for people who are dependent on an extraordinary degree of direction, encouragement, and feedback. Some students, adult as well as children, are heavily dependent on the emotional support of a teacher and are unable to learn on their own. Others are highly independent and self-directed. Most people fall somewhere in between. Distance education materials must be designed to encourage and support self-directed learning as well as provide the degree of support needed by people at different stages of self-directedness. This range of ability to be self-directed, to exercise "learner autonomy," is a key concept in distance learning and is discussed further in Chapter 10. The most important thing to remember is that more autonomous, self-directed learners need less interaction with an instructor and need less structured materials than people who are less capable at directing their learning.

People who are good self-directed learners are able to formulate their own learning objectives, identify resources that will help them achieve their objectives, chose appropriate methods of achieving the objectives, and test and evaluate their performance.

Wherever possible, distance education materials and courses should be designed to involve students in these activities and to help them become better at them. It must always be taken into account that students vary in their ability to practice self-directed learning, depending on their personality characteristics and previous learning experiences. (See Candy, 1991; Coldeway and Spencer, 1982; Piskurich, 1993.)

Evaluation

One of the weakest elements in the design and development of many distance education programs is failure to routinely assess the effectiveness of their materials and media. Evaluation should be practiced continuously through the design, development, and implementation cycles to ensure that things work as anticipated and intended.

Data Collection Methods

Many methods can be used to collect data for the purpose of evaluation, including observation of students, questionnaires and interviews, protocol analysis, online monitoring, prototypes, and focus groups.

Simple *observation of students* participating in a teleconference or using self-study materials is one of the easiest (yet often best) ways to determine how well the instruction works. If students are showing lack of interest or seem confused at certain points in a program, it indicates a potential problem that needs attention.

Questionnaires and interviews are other simple methods of discovering how well a program is working—in most cases, if you ask them, students will be quite candid about problems they are having or will tell you what they dislike about a course. *Protocol analysis* is a technique that asks students to "think aloud" while they are learning. It is useful for uncovering problems that cannot be directly observed or would be forgotten by the time a student answered a questionnaire. For example, it is possible to sit with a handful of students as they work through a study guide or watch a videotape and have them stop every five minutes and tell you their reactions to the material. An alternative to this is the "in-text questionnaire" technique, which consists of questions integrated into a text at the time of development that are answered by the students to tell the designers about specific elements in the design.

Online monitoring refers to the process of recording the exact responses students make while interacting through a computer or during a teleconference. Such data can be used to provide a very detailed analysis of student response patterns for a certain component or portion of a program or lesson. Research work aimed at course improvement as well as basic understanding about distance teaching is conducted at Penn State University using this technique (see Chapter 10).

Most of the evaluation techniques mentioned so far require that course materials or a program exists. However, as explained earlier, it is often desirable to evaluate design alternatives before any major development begins. This is especially true in a distance education institution or unit where the production run of course materials may run into several thousands, and the cost of revision might be hundreds of thousands of dollars.

Prototyping refers to the creation of a sample lesson or program that can be used to test out design ideas. Prototypes can be created early in the design process and tested with a small sample of the intended learners. Prototypes can be tested by individual learners or in *focus groups*. A small group of the intended learners are assembled and a program idea is described to them verbally or visually. They are then asked to discuss their reaction to the idea. Note that neither prototypes nor focus groups yield perfectly reliable data; however, they often identify major flaws or serious problems, and these can be corrected before the course is developed further.

Measures

There are many different types of variables that can be evaluated. The easiest variable to measure is usage of course elements. The questions can be asked about what materials or what programs were used most frequently and most favorably; who used them; when were they used; where were they used; how much were they used? Since most distance learning is voluntary, usage is one of the most meaningful measures because it indicates that students found the materials or program useful and worth completing. On the other hand, usage data does not shed any light on the instructional effectiveness of a program or materials.

The measurement of student satisfaction is very common. It is easy to ask students to complete a questionnaire rating various aspects of a course or program and/or indicating their degree of satisfaction in other ways. While the value of such data should not be underestimated since dissatisfied students are not likely to remain students for very long, it is not always highly reliable or valid data. This may be because the questionnaires have not been well constructed or tested, or because the circumstances under which the data were gathered were unsatisfactory. For example, questionnaires are often distributed by the instructor at the end of a course, and the students' responses may be more emotional than objective. This kind of data does not measure learning effectiveness, although students may describe their impressions or their opinions about how much they learned.

Students may have liked the program but not learned what was intended, or perhaps could have learned it more efficiently and effectively if it had been presented in some other way. To evaluate learning, it is necessary to measure changes in retention, comprehension or errors, changes in levels of skill, or perhaps attitudinal changes. Retention is assessed by asking students to remember information or demonstrate skills some time after the initial learning activity. Comprehension can be examined during the learning activity and requires the student to explain or apply the information presented. The number (or nature) of errors made on a test or a task is another immediate measure of learning.

Each of the different techniques and measures just discussed has its strengths and weaknesses. Experts in evaluation usually recommend that more than one technique and several measures be used in order to obtain a complete picture of how well a course or program is working. They also usually recommend that evaluation efforts be conducted by a neutral party— that is, someone who is not part of the design or development team and has a relatively objective position. However, most experts also agree that any form of evaluation is better than none—and the more, the better!

For further discussion of evaluation methodology relevant to distance education, see Flagg (1990), Gooler (1979), Harrison et al. (1990), Heinzen and Alberico (1990), Shaeffer and Farr (1993), or Thorpe (1988).

General Design Principles

Although there are different design considerations associated with the various types of distance education, it is possible to identify some general principles that apply to all of them:

1. **Good structure** The organization of the course and materials must be well defined and clear to the student; there must be internal consistency among the different parts of the course. Students should at all times know what they are trying to learn, what is expected of them to achieve the learning, and when they have arrived at the goal. It is easy to become lost as a distant learner, and good design always takes care that this does not happen.

2. **Clear objectives** If a course has clear objectives, the task of the instructors in identifying suitable learning experiences becomes fairly easy; evaluation is easy also. Students and tutors know exactly what is expected of them. The right selection and application of technology is more likely.

3. **Small units** The content of the course and the way the materials are organized and presented should be broken down and presented in small units. These may correspond to a single instructional objective or learning activity.

4. **Planned participation** Opportunities for interaction, through student activities or exercises, are embedded throughout the course and materials.

5. Completeness The course materials or program must contain extensive commentary or examples like those that would be provided, often extemporaneously, in a traditional classroom setting.

6. Repetition Important ideas should be repeated periodically (especially in summaries) to provide reinforcement and to compensate for distractions and memory limitations.

7. Synthesis Important ideas expressed in the materials or contributed by students should be woven together (especially in summaries).

8. Stimulation Through the use of interesting formats, content, or guests, course materials need to capture and hold the attention of students.

9. Variety Information should be presented in a number of different formats and different media to appeal to varying interests and backgrounds of the students.

10. Open-ended Assignments, examples, and problems should be open-ended so they allow the students to adapt the content to their own interests or situation.

11. Feedback Students should receive regular feedback on their assignments or progress in the course.

12. Continuous evaluation The effectiveness of the materials, media, and instructional methods should be routinely assessed using a variety of methods.

In distance education at the program level as defined in Chapter 1, it is normally not possible to satisfy all of these design considerations because of time and budget limitations. However, the more factors addressed, the more effective the course is likely to be. In distance education institutions there is enough money and specialist personnel to attend to all the design features, which is part of the explanation for the ability of institutions to develop higher quality courses.

Summary

This chapter has discussed a number of different facets of designing and developing distance education courses:

- Instructional Systems Design (ISD) is a widely accepted set of procedures and processes for the development of instructional programs.

- There are two quite different development approaches (i.e., author-editor versus course team); each approach has its strengths and weaknesses.

- The major design characteristics of study guides include organization of the content into units, a relatively informal writing style, and good document layout.

- Different factors are important in preparing an audioconference, planning a satellite teleconference, and designing computer conferences.

- Getting student participation is a challenge for all forms of distance learning.

- Evaluation considerations include data collection techniques, measurement variables, prototyping, and use of multiple methods.

One common thread throughout the chapter is the need for significant periods of time and numbers of personnel to be committed to planning. This is before the actual production of course materials and long before the first students are enrolled. Whether the communications format is, for example, independent study or a satellite teleconference, or a combination of both, there are many tasks that must be carried out long before any course is delivered. A major challenge in distance education is knowing what design tasks need to done and ensuring that there is adequate time to do them. One of the greatest tests of effective management is to release the up-front resources needed for these design efforts, on which the success of the course or program will depend.

CHAPTER 7

Teaching and Tutoring

In the previous chapter we have already introduced ideas about the roles of instructors in teaching the distant learner. In this chapter we begin by looking more closely at the concept of interaction, and we discuss the different roles of the distance teacher as one who presents information for learners to interact with; one who interacts with individual students to guide their learning; and one who organizes interaction among learners to help them create, apply, and test their knowledge. As has been seen, in a total system these roles are played by different specialists. Facilitating interaction in a total system is a specialization sometimes called tutoring. The chapter includes brief discussions about the role of site coordinators, managing tests and assignments, and the question of teacher training.

The nature of teaching and the role of the instructor in distance education differs from the traditional classroom. The extent to which it differs depends on whether one is teaching in a distance education institution, unit, consortium, or program, as defined in Chapter 1. In a distance teaching institution that has adopted a total systems approach, specialist tutors give their attention to assisting small numbers of students to interact with content that is designed and presented by other specialists. In distance teaching programs, responsibility for both presentation and guidance usually rests with a single instructor. In a distance teaching unit, such instructors are assisted by designers, producers, and production staff to varying degrees, depending on the size of the unit and its importance in the parent body. In a consortium, teaching varies according to whether the consortium is made up of programs, units, or institutions, and their quality.

How Distance Teaching Differs

Whatever the level of distance teaching organization, many factors make teaching a distance education course different from teaching in a traditional classroom. From the instructor's point of view, the most obvious difference is that you probably will not see how students react to what you are saying or doing (unless you happen to be using two-way interactive television). If you are using some form of audioconferencing, you may get immediate verbal feedback if you are able to organize it within the structure of the course sessions. If you are teaching via some form of correspondence study, recorded audio or video, or computer network, it is likely there will be a substantial delay in the flow of communication between you and your students. For this reason alone, distance teaching is a greater challenge for less experienced instructors; those with more experience are more able to anticipate student responses and plan how to deal with them.

A second factor making distance teaching a challenge for most teachers is the fact that the effectiveness of your teaching is highly dependent on how well you can use the technology involved. This means that you must not only understand the limitations and the potential of each piece of technology (and in some cases, how to operate it) but also know the teaching techniques associated with successful use of that technology. For example, if you are teaching via television, you should be aware of how to "behave" on-camera. Similarly, if you are using audioconferencing, audiographic, or computer conferencing, you need to learn what techniques work well in these media. When teaching in a correspondence course, you need to understand how to effectively communicate in writing, and not just writing, but writing of a particular kind that will be "instructive."

Teachers in distance education courses need to pay a lot of attention to students' feelings, especially their motivation. Students are likely to be more anxious about taking a course at a distance than a conventional course, and at the same time find it difficult to express their anxiety to a distant teacher. The distant teacher will find it difficult to identify these and other emotions without much practice. In many programs, students don't have the peer support of classmates or the routine of physically attending classes, and this may affect their motivation to learn. The instructor must therefore think of ways of providing the structure and motivational support that will help the student to persist with the study.

Students are at their most vulnerable at the beginning of the distance learning course, and instructors must try especially hard to be encouraging, to give them confidence, and to give them opportunity to test the unfamiliar approach, including giving them a chance to use the technology when that is appropriate. Above all instructors must get the students actively involved in the process. Having students participate actively as soon as possible is important because it not only helps break the ice but also sets the tone of future work. Active participation in some forms of distance education is more difficult to organize than it might be in a classroom. There may be fewer chances for students to ask questions or make comments, and the opportunity to construct knowledge in the company of others may not arise very often. Students are likely to have acquired a view of the communications media they must use as learners that leads them to expect to adopt passive roles rather than to be active. If the instructor takes care to get the students actively involved from the beginning, they will almost certainly overcome their fears and become excited about and motivated by the new freedom they enjoy as distance learners.

Yet another factor distinguishing teaching at a distance from conventional teaching, especially when courses are taught by units, consortia, and institutions, is the relationship of the person in direct interaction with the students and the rest of the members of the team who design and develop the course. In a traditional classroom teaching is an individual endeavor, whereas in distance education instructors usually work closely with a number of different people in the development and delivery of the course. For example, collaboration with technical specialists such as television production or computer support staff is likely if these media are used; if print materials are used, an editor will probably be involved.

Most distance education courses have a course manager who handles administrative details. Finally, most distance education institutions rely on tutors to perform many of the functions normally carried out by instructors in traditional classroom learning or in distance teaching programs. Even in the most simple program, where an instructor teaches a face-to-face class in a traditional way and simultaneously teaches one or more distant groups by a simple medium such as the audioconference, there will be coordinators at distant sites who make up the instructional team.

More will be said in this chapter about these different ways in which teaching at a distance is different from traditional classroom teaching. Of course, you should not expect to learn how to teach at a distance from this book. Each medium has its own skills, and different skills are needed in each of the levels of distance education as we have defined them. To explain these skills would require at least one book dedicated to that purpose alone. However, it is hoped that this chapter will alert you to some of the many opportunities to develop new teaching techniques and will also help you see that there are many variables of teaching that ought to be researched in your term papers, theses, and dissertations.

Three Types of Interaction

It seems that everybody in distance education talks about interaction. To help us understand some foundations of teaching at a distance, we think it would be helpful to look closer at the concept of interaction and in particular to distinquish three types of interaction that have to be practiced by distance teachers: learner-content interaction, learner-instructor interaction, and learner-learner interaction.

Reflections of a Correspondence Teacher

I have been teaching Jewish studies in the School of Religion at the University of Iowa for twenty-two years. For the past decade or so I have offered several guided correspondence courses through the Division of Continuing Education.

Just as I had been brought up short in my initial attempts as a classroom teacher, so too with my first efforts in correspondence courses. For instance, the first assignment in "Quest" asks the student to submit an outline of the book of Ecclesiastes. I had in mind a summary which would consist of a systematic listing of the book's most obvious features. It quickly became apparent to me that most students not only did not follow my argument but that many did not know what I expected in terms of an outline. I received mail-in assignments ranging from a few casual observations to virtual paraphrases. In the classroom, when this material is assigned, it is checked for conflicting interpretations by me and/or graduate teaching assistants, and we are able to respond immediately to questions about our expectations. In one way or another the same problem, i.e., my failure to communicate with sufficent clarity, surfaced repeatedly. It is a truism that the success of a correspondence course depends upon the instructor's ability to communicate what is expected of the student with as much exactitude as possible.

One more point. My correspondence courses have attracted both the best and worst of students. Some students appear to take correspondence courses as an end run around what they perceive to be a more difficult campus hurdle. They are almost always mistaken, I believe, because of the great difficulty many of today's students have in reading with care and writing with clarity. There are also students, often non-traditional ones, who exhibit a depth of understanding that is breathtaking. One of the best students I have ever encountered in any setting, a housewife in Los Angeles, took the Holocaust course and displayed such intellectual acuity, curiosity, and integrity that I was left grasping for words of sufficent power to praise her. Were it not for my correspondence courses I never would have encountered this woman and others like her.

Source: Holstein (1992, p. 22–33)

1. Learner-content Interaction

The first type of interaction that the teacher must bring about, or assist, is the interaction the student has with the subject matter that is presented for study. This interaction of student with content is a defining characteristic of education. Education is a process of planned learning assisted by a teacher or teaching institution. Every learner has to construct knowledge through a process of personally accommodating information into previously existing cognitive structures. It is interacting with content that results in these changes in the learner's understanding, what we sometimes call a change in perspective, when the

The most fundamental form of interaction in distance education courses is learner-content interaction in which the student becomes involved with the subject matter.

learners construct their own knowledge. One of the main purposes of distance teaching is presenting the content needed for this process.

Since time immemorial, texts have been offered as a means of teaching. In medieval times virtually all texts were meant to teach, not merely inform, and certainly not entertain. In the nineteenth century the use of print for teaching was advanced by the invention of home study guides that accompanied a text, providing explanations of it and directions for its study. There was very little interaction with instructors or other students, but students expected to spend a great deal of time interacting with the subject matter as presented in the textual materials. In more recent times learners interact with content presented in radio and television broadcasts and by electronic recordings on audio- or videotape, and computer software, with interactive multimedia (videodisc, CD-ROM) being the most advanced technology for content interaction invented so far (Dede, 1990).

2. Learner-instructor Interaction

The second type of interaction, regarded as essential by most learners and as highly desirable by most educators, is interaction between the learner and an instructor. After the content has been presented, whether it is information, demonstration of skill, or modeling certain attitudes and values, the instructors

Where interaction between learner and a distant teacher is possible through correspondence or teleconference, the learner is able to draw on the experience of a
professional instructor. Here the instructor teaches by computer conference.

assist the students in interacting with it. To do this, they try to stimulate or at
least maintain the students' interest in the subject and their motivation to learn.
Next they try to organize the students' application of what they are learning,
either by practicing the skills they have seen demonstrated or by manipulating
information and ideas that have been presented. Instructors organize formal
and informal testing and evaluation to ascertain if the learner is making
progress and to help decide whether to change strategies. Finally, instructors
provide counsel, support, and encouragement to each learner, though the
extent and nature of this support varies according to the educational level of the
learners, the teacher's personality and philosophy, and other situational and
organizational factors.

Where interaction between learner and a distant teacher is possible through
correspondence or teleconference, the learner is able to draw on the experience
of a professional instructor while interacting with the content in whatever manner is most effective for that particular individual learner. This individualization of instruction is a long-recognized advantage of correspondence instruction. When the correspondence instructor sits with a set of student papers,
there is no class, but instead the instructor enters a silent dialogue with each
individual. While each student and the instructor are attending to a common
piece of content, usually in a set text but quite likely on audio- or videotape,
each student's response to the presentation is different, and so the response by
the instructor to each student is different too.

To some students a misunderstanding is explained, to others elaborations are given, to others simplifications; to one analogies are drawn, to another supplementary readings suggested. The instructor is especially valuable in responding to the learners' application of new knowledge. Whatever self-directed learners may do alone when interacting with the content presented, they are vulnerable at the point of application since they do not know enough about the subject to be sure they are applying it correctly, or as intensively or extensively as is possible or desirable, or that there are potential areas of application they are not aware of.

3. Learner-learner Interaction

It is the third form of interaction that is a relatively new dimension for teachers in distance education. This is inter-learner interaction, interaction between one learner and other learners, alone or in group settings, with or without the real-time presence of an instructor.

After it became a goal of modern governments to provide education for all citizens, the only economical way of doing it was to organize students into classes. Even though there are now means of communicating with learners besides having a class, the class is still the main way that students are organized. This is partly because teachers and administrators can think of no other way of organizing students, and partly because in the short term—though not in the long term—it is the cheapest way of delivering the teaching acts of stimulation, presentation, application, evaluation, and student support.

However, learner-learner interaction among members of a group is sometimes desirable for pedagogical reasons. For example, Phillips, Santoro, and Kuehn (1989) used computer conferencing and recorded video technologies to train students in effective group functioning. Here is an example of content that makes it necessary for students to experience group interaction as a strategy for learning. One could study the presentation of principles of group leadership and group membership alone, or in interaction with an instructor, but at the point of application and evaluation the availability of a group of fellow learners becomes invaluable for learner and instructor alike. Interestingly, Phillips and his colleagues were on a conventional campus and came to use a distance learning technique after they discovered that in face-to-face classrooms they could not effectively facilitate interaction among members of an undergraduate class that was very large. These educators used the E-mail and computer conferencing to give their students both the advantages of individual interaction with the instructor as in a classic tutorial, and at the same time, the advantages of interaction with their peer group.

Apart from teaching interaction itself, when else is inter-learner group interaction between students highly desirable? The answer to this question depends largely on the circumstances of the learners and their age, experience, and level of learner autonomy. Many younger learners are likely to find inter-group interaction to be stimulating and motivating, though this may not be so important for many adult and advanced learners, who tend to be more self-motivated. Group settings are useful for some types of content presentations, especially when students can be organized into project teams and given responsibility for making presentations to their peers. Generally, inter-learner discussions are extremely valuable as a way of helping students to think out the content that has been presented and to test it in exchanges with their peers.

A session plan for an audio-/computer conference course was presented in Chapter 6. Later in that course the nine groups of students take turns making content presentations to their peers. Each presentation lasts for an hour. This is followed by discussion and analysis in small break-out groups at each site, and then by feedback and a general discussion session. This process is successful because of the level of self-management that adult graduate students are capable of, and it not only acknowledges and encourages the development of their expertise but also tests it and teaches important principles regarding the nature of knowledge and the role of the student and scholar as maker of knowledge.

Importance of All Forms of Interaction

Distance education organizations need to design and organize courses to ensure that there is each type of interaction and that they provide the type of interaction that is most suitable for the various teaching tasks for different subject areas for learners at different stages of development. The main weakness of many distance education programs is their commitment to a particular communications medium, and when there is only one medium, it is probable that only one kind of interaction is done well.

While correspondence can give good learner-content interaction and good, though slow, learner-instructor interaction, it gives no learner-learner interaction. Audio, audiographic, and videoteleconference groups give excellent inter-learner interaction but are not very good for individualized instructor-learner interaction and are frequently misused for instructor's content presentations that could be done better by print or recorded media. In the time saved from making content presentations, the teleconference could stimulate and facilitate the inter-learner interaction that has been difficult or impossible to achieve in distance education until now.

In short, it is most desirable for distance educators to use all three kinds of interaction.

New Ways of Teaching: Participation Versus Presentation

For most instructors, teaching at a distance involves the use of different skills than they use in a conventional classroom. Their role as teachers changes significantly—in particular, the balance between presenting content information and organizing the students' interaction with that information. In distance education institutions—that is, in total systems—subject matter is prepared, organized, and presented by people who are *not* the same teachers who interact with the learners. The sole work of teachers, called tutors in these institutions, is to interact with students on the basis of content prepared by other people.

In distance teaching units and programs, the teacher who conducts the interaction may be the same individual who prepares and presents the content, but even here the emphasis in teaching is on the interaction with students. Most of the subject matter should be presented through a recorded medium, such as print, audio- or videotape, or computer, while the distant teacher becomes a facilitator whose main job is to help students to interact with the content as well as with him-/herself and with other learners if that is technically possible.

The single most important skill that all distance educators must develop is to make their students active participants in their educational program. It is not too difficult to present information over a distance, but getting people to participate and making learning active at a distance is much harder.

Some specific techniques that may be used in teleconferencing include asking questions (either directed or rhetorical), presenting problems or issues for analysis, asking students to share their experiences, and group discussions or group self-evaluations.

To a certain extent, the choice of techniques will be shaped by the delivery media used. However, interactive teaching is really a "mental set" that requires teachers to think about inducing knowledge rather than instilling it, to asking questions rather than giving answers, to focusing on student participation rather than the teacher's presentation of information.

One important side effect of increasing the degree of participation and inter-learner interaction is that it affords more opportunity for social interaction among students and teachers, and students enjoy and appreciate this. As Hackman and Walker (1990, p. 7) report:

> Instructors who employed strategies for enhancing social presence such as encouraging involvement, offering individual feedback, and promoting interpersonal relationships were viewed more favorably. Specifically, offering individual attention and encouragement to off-campus students and using vocal variety were the most important factors in promoting distance learning."

In other words, increasing the level of participation in a class supports motivation as well as learning.

Presentations Are Not Teaching

Some of the most common causes of failure in distance education result from decision makers being unaware of the multidimensional nature of distance teaching and consequently neglecting one or more of its constituent activities. We often notice a sometimes cavalier neglect of what should occur before and after the delivery of teaching materials to the learner. This comes from an oversimple view of teaching that views teaching as merely the presentation of information. Whether the primary communication medium is print, audio, or videotape recordings, broadcasts or teleconferences, there is often an imbalance between the time and effort devoted to experts' presentations of information and the arrangements made for the learner to interact with the content thus presented, and the instructor-learner interaction and learner-learner interaction.

Consider this example: In a fairly typical 2-hour satellite videoconference, a presenter was interviewed for 30 minutes by a moderator, and this was followed by a 15-minute pretaped interview with another expert. After a return to the first two experts for a further 25 minutes and presentation of pretaped case study, the experts talked yet again for 20 minutes. Learners were given 15 minutes to put questions to the presenters, and this was the limit of the interaction. An evaluation report gave details about the opening music, animated graphics, upholstered chairs, and the plants on the sets. The main criticisms concerned the speakers' clothing, and the general conclusion was that the conference was "highly professional."

Of course it is very desirable that when a presentation must be made, it is made in the most excellent and professional manner. However, presentations are not in themselves teaching; they are only part of the transaction between learner and teacher that we call teaching. Simply making a video presentation is no more teaching than it would be to send the students a book through the mail. As well as presentations of information, at least as much attention should have been devoted to finding out each individual's need and motivation for learning; giving each individual the opportunity for testing and practicing new knowledge, and for receiving evaluation of the results of such practice. If there is any one secret to good teaching, it is summed up in the word "activity." Since the number of people in a live satellite conference is usually large, much of the activity needs to be organized at local sites; however, more satellite-delivered group learner-learner interaction would be possible if less time was devoted to the presentations.

Learner Autonomy and Group Interdependence

Learner autonomy refers to the potential of distant learners to participate in the determination of their learning objectives, the implementation of their programs of study, and the evaluation of their learning. This is a view that is somewhat different from traditional views about the distant learner, based on the ideas of behavioral psychology. In the behavioral view, distant learners are beyond the immediate environment of the teacher; the main problem of distance education is how to optimally control them. As we have seen, instructors attempt to identify their goals in very specific behavioral terms, to prescribe a regime of presentation, practice, and reward, and to test and measure achievement of all students according to the precise standards built into the objectives. The challenge for the educator is to produce a perfect set of objectives, techniques, and testing devices, one that will fit every learner, in large numbers, at a distance, so that no one would deviate, no one would fall between the cracks.

While there are many useful design techniques in this behavioral approach, we also need to take into account the idiosyncrasies and independence of learners and think of ways of working with these as a valuable resource rather than a distracting nuisance. In place of a model in which passive subjects, the learners, are trained by irresistibly elegant instructional tools, we should try to conceptualize distance education as a more open partnership of teachers and self-directing learners in which individual learners decide, conduct, and control much of the learning process.

Adult learners have different capacities for making decisions regarding their own learning. Designers of distance education programs should take into account those abilities and work with them. The ability of a learner to develop a personal learning plan in some ways different from others, or the ability to find resources for study in one's own work or community environment, or the ability to decide for oneself when progress was satisfactory should not be treated as extraneous and regrettable noise in a smooth-running, instructor-controlled system, but rather should be seen as powerful energy to be engaged by the instructional designers.

Further, learner autonomy should be a goal of distance education. We should consider it good for learners to be self-directing and try to devise ways of encouraging and supporting them. That does not mean that all learners are self-directing, but since each has an ability and a potential to be self-directing, the educational program should attempt to identify and build on their abilities. There is no doubt that it is even more difficult to devise a program that supports learners' self-direction than it is to produce one that controls.

With the emergence of teleconference technologies, a new and exciting challenge for instructional designers is how to develop and engage the interdependence of individuals in distant groups, how to develop the interdependence of groups within a total system, and how to develop the autonomy of the distant group. The problems concern curriculum, instruction, and interpersonal dynamics. The curriculum problem is how to bring the local interests and needs as well as the local knowledge that lies at each distant site into the content to be taught. The instructional problem is how to involve each distant site in determining objectives and implementing them.

A good strategy is to devise local group projects. A local group in a teleconference can decide on a topic or task for presentation to the other groups—that is, the virtual "class." In teaching research, for example, each group can decide on a research question to develop locally and present to the "class." In teaching design each group can design a module that they "teach" to the rest of the "class." Simple though this sounds, a great deal of care must go into managing the process as distant groups struggle, sometimes flounder, and eventually become organized to accomplish their goals.

The likelihood of a local site becoming a successful learning group is primarily a result of the personalities, the learner autonomy of the members of the group and the interpersonal dynamics within the local group. Given identical assignments, some groups respond with an extraordinarily high degree of competence, commitment, energy, and creativity while others do not. The former give time far in excess of what should be expected, are task-oriented, productive, and continue to communicate informally by E-mail and in other ways, seeming to have fun working together. In successful groups there seems to be a high degree of interdependence of relatively autonomous individuals.

In many groups the interdependent members cluster around an informal leader. These leaders seem to act as local chairpersons, guiding discussion and decision-making in an environment characterized by a high degree of participation, division of labor, and collaboration. Sometimes there are no particular leaders, but members of groups devise ways to share leadership responsibilities. Being relatively autonomous learners, the members of the successful group are likely to have sufficient understanding of the instructional process to be good collaborators with the distant instructor. Where problems occur it seems that someone wants a leadership role and is rejected, or two or more people compete for leadership, or the level of autonomy of all or most of the group members is so low that no one is able to lead the decision-making process. If there are individuals who have difficulty in collaborating with others, or instead of accepting informal local leadership look for control from the distant instructor, the situation might become volatile.

The Instructor's Role

The interdependence of the instructor's role and that of the learners is nowhere more evident than in the working of local study groups. The distant instructor can do everything possible to design and encourage an environment that allows for productive activities locally, but in the end it will be the responsibility of students to make the environment work for themselves.

In a teleconference most of the talking should come from the students. The role of the instructor is to induce inter-learner interaction among the participants, keep the discussion on track, and make sure that all students get involved. There have been a few research studies that attempt to identify good teleconference practices.

Audioconferencing

Guidelines that can be used for beginners to audioconferencing have been developed by the Instructional Communications Systems group at the University of Wisconsin-Madison. They suggest that teachers should learn four major strategies:

1. **Humanizing** the creation of an environment that emphasizes the importance of the individual and which overcomes the sense of distance by generating a feeling of group rapport. This can be achieved by using students' names, providing pictures of participants, making visits to remote sites, and asking for personal experiences and opinions during class.

2. **Participation** ensuring that there is a high level of interaction and dialog in an audio class. This is facilitated by posing questions, group prob-

Professor Michael G. Moore conducts a class of nine sites and 100 students, by audioconference.

lem-solving activities, participant presentations, and role-playing exercises.

3. **Message style** presenting information in such a way that it will be easily understood and remembered. Good techniques include providing overviews, using repetition and summaries, presenting variety, and relying on print materials for communicating detailed information.

4. **Feedback** getting information about the effectiveness of learning and teaching. Feedback can be obtained by direct questions, assignments, quizzes, polls, and questionnaires.

A manual for audioconferencing developed by the Rochester Institute of Technology focuses on two areas that teachers need to study. The first of these consists of technical tips for using the equipment, and the second consists of instructional techniques. Technical tips explain how the telephone bridge works and how to set up and operate the special types of telephones typically used in audioconferences. Instructional techniques include

- preparing a detailed outline or script for the conference listing all topics, questions, and activities;
- using a student roster;

- addressing questions to specific participants;
- summarizing periodically and at the end of the conference; and
- follow-up procedures for students needing help after the session.

Bronstein, Gill, and Koneman (1982) provided the following guidelines for audioteleconference teaching:

- Be prompt in coming on the line because it is essential that the program start on time.
- Use a natural style of delivery; speak slowly and enunciate clearly.
- Maintain spontaneity; avoid reading from a script.
- Use visuals effectively and verbalize appropriate guideposts.
- Use frequent change of pace or stimuli to maintain interest.
- Make frequent attempts to draw participants into discussions.
- Always refer to participants by name.

Boone and Bassett (1983) identified the following specific oral communication skills:

- good pronunciation and articulation
- good fluency, inflection, and pausing
- good rate and volume of speech
- giving positive feedback statements
- asking conversational questions
- making compliments and appreciation statements
- using anecdotes
- allowing adequate response time
- controlling duration of oral statements

In a follow-up study, Boone (1984) analyzed tape recordings of actual audioconferences and identified the following as important:

- ability to provide structure (uses authority; controls verbal traffic)
- ability to provide socioemotional support (e.g., integrates late group member; encourages humor)
- ability to establish a democratic atmosphere (shares authority; asks for participation)
- ability to create a sense of shared space (describes environment; creates a sense of shared history, when possible)
- ability to model appropriate behavior (models conciseness)
- ability to clarify (asks for confirmation; seeks common definition of terms)
- ability to repair sessions threatening to go awry (explains absence of group member; repairs interruptions)

- ability to set an appropriate pace (asks for conciseness; directs questions to a limited audience)

Haaland and Newby (1984) asked students for their opinions, and they said that good teleconference teachers

- used students' names,
- set out clear statements of purpose,
- made use of printed material,
- encouraged discussion, and
- did not speak in a monotone.

A Class Roster

As suggested in Chapter 6, the instructor of a teleconference should prepare a class roster with background information about each student. During the fast exchanges of the conference, it allows the instructor to ask particular students questions related to their interests or experience and makes the audioconference a more personal learning activity. Ideally, this class roster can be distributed to all students as well, as a way of helping them get to know each other. Table 7-1 is a roster showing names of students in one group. In this particular class students agreed to give themselves nicknames. This is a device that helps students quickly recognize each other. The voices take on different personalities when there is a distinctive characteristic attached to it, such as "pin-ball wizard"!

Audiographics

The technology of audiographic teaching is much more demanding than that of audioconferencing, and preliminary training is essential for anyone wanting to use this technology. Training may be provided by vendors of audiographic systems in the form of demonstrations of how the equipment can be used and provision of "hands-on" practice sessions. Vendors are not very good at providing training in teaching techniques, and most teachers are on their own when they wish to use audiographics for instruction. The University of Wisconsin-Madison Extension and Penn State's American Center for Study of Distance Education offer training to their own faculty and students.

As with other teleconference technologies, it is challenging for the audiographic instructor to get students actively engaged in the class. Graphics are much better for presenting information than for creating it. However, teachers can be trained to develop techniques that assist students at different sites to collaborate in gathering and organizing information on the graphics screen. Instructors must also learn how to put students at ease with the equipment, since most people have never used anything like a graphics tablet. One technique to overcome this reluctance is to have everyone sign in at the beginning

Table 7-1   A Typical Site Roster

American Center for Study of Distance Education
Course Title: Introduction to Distance Education

Anne S., Projects coordinator and mother
Jose S., Doctoral student in higher ed, from Puerto Rico, "connected to the sea"
Jyhemi J., From Taiwan, masters in instructional systems, "self-talker"
Carole K., Doctoral student in adult education, "pin-ball wizard"
Ted F., Mid-career academic, developmental psychologist, "actor"
Becky B., Nurse educator, "domestic goddess"
Patricia G., Media studies, Mexican, "international goddess"
Shelley C., Doctoral student in instructional systems, "calculated risk-taker"
Hasan A., Doctoral student in adult education, "swimming photographer"
Margaret K., Manager for center for distance education, "musician (cello)"
Yu-Bi C., From Taiwan, doctoral student in adult education, "pen-twister"
Shawn J., Doctoral student in adult education, "teacher/mother"
Chris D., admissions counselor, "father"
Joe L., Teacher and instructional designer, "the thinker"
Susanne S., Air force officer and dietitian, "the quilter"
Tammy E., Teacher and mother, "the baker"
David P., Student and financial aid officer, "expectant father"
Fred M., Pastor and doctoral student, "dynamic motorcyclist"
Kelley C., Television programmer, "the traveler"

of class using the tablet. Another strategy is to ask participants to draw a diagram to illustrate a concept being discussed. Students can also be directed to draw a question mark on the screen when they have a question, this being the equivalent of raising the hand in a traditional classroom.

It is probably a good idea to teach faculty how to use a graphics editor to create or modify slides, although a distance teaching organization should provide a graphics artist to prepare the slides for instructors, and so save faculty preparation time as well as ensure higher quality visuals. Because instructors and students must operate the audiographics system themselves, with no technical assistants, training for this form of distance teaching has a greater technical component than audioconferencing. On the other hand, most of the instructional techniques to be learned are similar to what has to be learned in audioconferencing (e.g., maximizing participation and ensuring feedback).

Television

One of the most popular sources of information about teaching by television is *Teaching Telecourses: Opportunities and Options*, a faculty handbook published by the Annenberg/CPB Project in cooperation with the PBS Adult Learning Service (Levine, 1988). While this handbook was developed to prepare faculty to use the PBS/ALS television courses in particular, it serves as a useful primer for any television-based instruction.

The handbook covers some basic questions about television teaching and how to teach, including a discussion of the reasons for using television; how television courses compare to conventional courses; how they are received by students; and some tips about how to teach with television (e.g., preparing, interacting with students; the administrative support needed). However, this handbook is not meant to be a detailed how-to guide but rather an orientation document that aims to motivate faculty to explore the use of teaching by television. Another faculty guide for television teaching is Cyrs and Smith (1990).

Some common elements that must be learned in teaching by television are the following:

- the strengths and limitations of television
- the particular equipment used and how it works
- description of the different people involved and their roles
- general planning steps and procedures
- how to prepare visuals for use with an overhead camera
- how to use the blackboard on camera
- techniques to facilitate student participation/interaction
- considerations associated with the use of video, film, or slides
- on-camera behavior including eye contact, voice, clothing, and movement
- how to respond to technical problems
- copyright considerations
- glossary of television terminology

Some emphasis is necessary to get instructors to pay attention to the monitors during broadcasts as well as watching tapes afterward in order to understand how the instruction comes across to the remote students. Although many guides admonish instructors to "use your own regular teaching style," it is clear that effective television teaching requires changes and adaptations from most traditional classroom instruction styles.

Computers

Because instructors usually initiate and manage conferences, as well as help students use the system, they usually have a good understanding of how the system works. This does not mean that an instructor has to learn computer programming. In fact, once a bulletin board or LISTSERV is set up, it is quite simple to manage, certainly more simple than an audiographics system or most video systems.

Techniques that instructors should learn for facilitating the computer-conferencing component of a course include the following:

- Have each student post a biography at the beginning of class.
- Create a conference that explains conferencing procedures, and encourage students to add their own tips and comments during the course.
- Have students present on-line "book reports" or project results, and encourage other students to add comments.
- Keep assignments, problems, or comments to a single screen, if possible.
- Read and reply to messages regularly (at least daily).
- Establish a positive and helpful tone in replies to messages.
- Be careful not to deal with private issues in public messages.
- Send private messages to students who are not active to encourage them to participate.
- Schedule on-line activities at regular intervals to maintain involvement and prevent procrastination.
- Encourage students to collaborate electronically on projects or assignments.
- Use bulletins to keep students up-to-date on class progress and special events.

Mason (1991) argues that an effective computer conference moderator has three categories of responsibility: organizational, social, and intellectual. The organization role involves managing the conference and providing leadership. The social role entails establishing and maintaining good relationships and a positive learning environment. The intellectual role involves getting all students to participate and weaving their contributions together.

The most fundamental point for instructors to grasp about computer conferencing is that like other forms of teleconferencing, it is primarily suited to inter-learner interactions, such as discussions and collaborative activities, rather than didactic presentation of content.

The Site Coordinator

If a distance education program requires students to meet at distant sites, a local coordinator for that site and those students is needed. The need is acute in programs using real-time interactive technologies, which is what we will have in mind during most of the following discussion. Even programs that are designed for individual study, conducted primarily by correspondence, by recorded audio or video, or by computer modem will benefit from having local coordinators, especially if they hold group meetings at study centers, as is very common in open university systems.

How CMC Affects Teaching

The fact that all interactions in this medium [CMC] are written has forced clarity of expression in developing each weekly lecture surrogate. This in turn has led to a conciseness of ideas that has had positive effects on my classroom performance. I am a better teacher because the topics I have developed for my modem students are expressed with the same conciseness in my classroom. Additionally, I have been able to bring a more active learning orientation to the classroom, making available the automated tutorials and demonstration software experiences as scheduled activities in the labs, and enriching students' learning with memorable hands-on experiences in the labs. Finally, I have gained a new appreciation for the sense of community that can be achieved in either setting, and I see the active learning component and the sharing of ideas as crucial to verbal, face-to-face, and electronic teaching and learning.

Source: Boston (1992, p. 55–56)

The local coordinator should have five characteristics, each of which has a key word that begins with the letter *C*. Here are the "Five *C*s of Site Coordination."

1. Communication

The first requirement of a site coordinator is to be an excellent communicator first with the instructor, then with the students, and after that with the larger community in which the teaching is occurring.

We put communicating with the instructor as the top priority in this list, because if communication should break down between the coordinator and the students or the larger community (which of course should not happen), provided the coordinator has sufficient trust to communicate the problem to the instructor, advice and assistance can be given and action taken to rectify the situation.

Next, the site coordinator must be a good communicator with the students. Since the coordinator speaks on behalf of the instructor and acts as the instructor's eyes and ears to identify problems and opportunities concerning the students in a particular locality, to be effective he or she must have the students' respect and confidence. As instructors, we need to be sure that if a student wishes to raise a problem, that person will know how to contact the coordinator and will have a sufficiently good personal relationship to do so. Provided we have an equally effective channel of communication with the coordinator, we can be sure we will hear of individual student needs as they arise.

The site coordinator must also have good communication with the local community. It is the coordinator who usually contacts the channels of information dissemination in the locality, such as the newspapers, radio, and bulletin boards, to spread information about a forthcoming course, and it is the coordinator who is approached by potential students with inquiries as they think about taking the course. When the course is being planned, the coordinator employs local resource people to undertake such production activities as copying printed materials, or may arrange to make a videotape as part of a class project. Coordinators will negotiate the availability of rooms and teleconference equipment with administrators. They also communicate with administrators on such matters as receiving payment of fees when it is the local college or corporation that enrolls the students rather than the students paying tuition fees personally, as is often the case with foreign sites. Just as we depend on the coordinators to be in close touch with students and to alert the instructor of their problems, so the coordinators should notify the instructor of any difficulty with local administrators. Often, after consulting the instructor, the coordinator can intervene to rectify the situation.

2. Competence

Coordinators should be competent in attending to technical details, to administration, and to instruction. Having technical competence means being able to either install technology themselves or to negotiate and oversee the installation. With most technologies there will be no technicians during the time of instruction, and the coordinators will therefore set up the technology, test it, and during the session, operate it. They must have sufficient technical knowledge to recognize potential faults that may occur during the life of the course, or during a particular session of the course, and be able to take appropriate remedial action. An unexpected and uncorrected technical failure could result in an abandoned session, loss of students' confidence, and the collapse of an institution's presence in a site, a city, or a nation. This could all result from a very minor problem, perhaps just a loose telephone line, that should have been easily dealt with by a coordinator with experience. Thus technical competence means knowing the hardware being used, helping install it, monitoring and testing it, trouble-shooting it, and knowing the actions to take, including calling specialist assistance, to deal with problems arising with it.

A coordinator's competence also covers administrative procedures. Among the most important of these are efficiently receiving materials and distributing them to students and keeping records and reporting them to the instructor, and perhaps to the institution that hosts the local site.

Third, a coordinator should have some instructional competence. The coordinator should be able to discuss the course with the instructor during its design stage and will be indispensable during the interactive stage of teaching it. In our teaching with students in different countries as well as different cities, we depend heavily on the coordinators to ensure that instructions for the group discussions are properly understood and carried out. The importance of the coordinator is very obvious when there are differences of language, but even without this, it is vital that the coordinator knows what the instructor is trying to do and is able to arrange local circumstances to see the goal is achieved. In our teaching, after having given directions to a local site, we do not ask the students if they understand the directions. This is a question addressed to the coordinator; the coordinator is asked to say if the students understand what is required of them. The coordinator understands and has communication with the students, so that if they are in need of help, the coordinator can provide explanations, can act as intermediary, or can give the help directly. Of course, if clear directions have not been given, while students may be diffident about saying so, the coordinators will not be.

Finally, it is helpful if the coordinator is competent in the content being taught in the course. It is better to appoint persons who have previously taken the course as students, so they not only are familiar with the instructional procedures and have a long-standing working relationship with the instructor, but know the subject matter better than the newly enrolled students at their sites. This helps them to interpret the instructor's explanations or questions when the need arises and also to help their students as they struggle to articulate their ideas.

3. Continuity

Having made their best effort to recruit good local coordinators, distance teaching organizations and individual instructors should care for them well (which includes paying them well), because it is essential that they continue in the role and build up experience in the work. There are several reasons why this continuity is important. One is the time and experience that is needed to develop the effective working relationship with the instructor and community and the competence that have been described above. It is much more efficient when the instructor can send materials to a coordinator who has practiced what to do with them in previous iterations of the course, can make plans for a weekly program or discuss a problem student with a colleague who shares memories of similar events in previous courses. While each cohort of students consists of different individuals, their problems are usually similar to those of previous cohorts, and an experienced coordinator is likely to recognize problems and be able to explain them to the instructor with reference to previous experience, or on the basis of previous experience to solve them locally without recourse to the instructor.

4. Control and Confidence

The good coordinator has control of events at the local site, and the students have a comfortable awareness of this. Control is achieved as a result of the other characteristics described above. The technology is set up in advance of students' arrival at the site; the administrative work is done quietly and efficiently; the instructor communicates with the coordinator in ways that reinforces students' sense that they are in the care of a team that works together effectively. The environment at the site should be relaxed and friendly, but there should also be a sense that events are well planned, that everything is under control, and that any problems can and will be resolved. During the sessions, coordinators and instructor handle any unexpected issues or problems with competent professionalism. This sense of control is more important in a distant learning environment than it might be in conventional settings, since it is especially important to instill confidence in the students.

Many students are afraid of being separated from the instructor and others are skeptical about the viability of an environment in which there is no instructor present. To meet these emotional barriers to learning, it is important that the coordinator projects a sense of control, of efficiency, of responsibility, and authority. The instructor should reinforce this style and do what is possible to encourage students to have confidence in the coordinator. The students should be aware, by what is said by coordinators and by the instructor, that not only can any local problems be solved but the instructor has confidence in the ability of the coordinator to solve them; that there is immediate and continous communication between them; that the coordinator will be given any help that is needed to meet the needs of the local students.

5. Caring

Last, but not least in importance, the coordinator has to be a person who cares about the comfort and welfare of the students as well as their success and achievement and is able and willing to communicate this concern. No matter how skillful, the educator at a distance will not be able to establish as good an affective relationship with students as in a face-to-face environment; in fact, because of being at a distance, the instructor is likely to be burdened by the students' fears and anxieties about the teacher's authority that have been inherited from days at school. While the instructor should do everything possible to establish an open, communicative, friendly, and caring environment necessary for learning, it will nevertheless be up to the local coordinator to make up for what the instructor will be unable to do. The coordinator does this in numerous ways: by greeting participants; by ensuring that everyone has freedom to participate in discussions; by private conversation with anyone who is bruised during an oral exchange; by voicing appreciation, approval, or congratulation at an individual's successes.

Tutoring

In some forms of distance education, notably correspondence courses and open university courses, there is little or no use of teleconferencing, little group work, and little or no real-time interaction between the student and an instructor. Instead, the student is assigned a personal tutor, who is usually not the person who designed the course and presents the content of the course. The tutor inter-

Coordinating Distant Sites

Coordinating activities at the distant site is perhaps the most challenging task that distance teachers must accomplish. Distance teachers need to work with support personnel and coordinators at the sites in order to arrange for an effective learning experience. This coordination can be excessively time consuming if several sites are involved. Arranging for a classroom at a remote site and having it ready in time for the first class was my most challenging experience. Imagine the frustration I experienced when I flew to a remote site to conduct my first class and found that the telephone lines were not in place! Unless the distance teacher makes a personal effort to coordinate arrangements at a remote site and works as a team member, the distance learning experience may be a very unsatisfying one for students.

Source: Gunawardena (1992, p. 66)

acts with the student on a one-to-one basis by mail as the student works with the content in a study guide and other recorded materials.

Table 7-2 lists some of the functions that correspondence tutors may perform. While tutors normally interact with students via writing, they may also use telephone, computer networks or even face-to-face meetings. In general, tutoring in distance education courses bears many resemblances to conventional tutoring (see for example, Cohen, Kulik, and Kulik, 1982; Frey and Reigeluth, 1986). In the training world, the role of the tutor can be performed by supervisors or managers.

The primary rationale for having tutors is to provide students with individualized instruction in their courses. In many cases the tutor is the only person a distance education student ever has contact with. Having tutors in a distance education system greatly improves student completion rates and achievement, although such outcomes depend on the nature of the course, the tutor, and the student. Not all students take advantage of tutoring services when they are offered, although most students who do so report that it improves their satisfaction with the course (Ahlm, 1972; Rekkedal, 1983). While there has been ample theoretical discussion about the significance of tutors (e.g., Baath, 1981; Holmberg, 1977), it appears that in practice many tutors are not very sophisticated in their capabilities (e.g., Murgatroyd, 1980), presumably because being drawn from the ranks of conventional teachers they find this different way of teaching to be unnatural.

A number of research studies have examined the relationships between student perceptions and specific teaching strategies or program design characteristics. St. Pierre and Olsen (1991) surveyed the attitudes of students taking

Table 7-2   **Functions of Tutors in Distance Education**

Discussing course content
Providing feedback on progress
Grading of assignments/tests
Helping student plan work
Motivating student
Answering administrative questions
Supervising projects
Teaching face-to-face seminars
Keeping student records
Intervening on behalf of student with the administration
Evaluating course effectiveness

independent study courses from Penn State University. They found that the following factors contributed to student satisfaction:

- the opportunity to apply knowledge
- prompt return of assignments
- conversations with the instructor
- relevant course content
- a good study guide

In addition to grading student assignments and monitoring student progress, tutors fulfill other purposes. They serve as a bridge between students and the institution for the purpose of interpreting policies and solving problems (Coughlan, 1980). They can play an important role in adapting the curriculum to meet individual or local needs—which can be especially critical in international programs that span many countries and cultures (Perraton, 1974). In some programs the tutor has no specific course-related duties and the primary job is to provide counseling and guidance. Given the difficulties that distance learners often encounter, the role of counseling is much more important in distance education programs than traditional courses.

Successful tutoring is a difficult task. Gibbs and Durbridge (1976) identify the following characteristics of good tutors at the British Open University:

- excellent subject matter knowledge
- good general teaching skills
- good communication and social skills
- well organized, flexible, patient
- able to motivate/encourage students
- commitment to students and program

Tutors must also be knowledgeable and proficient with the media used in the program (i.e., writing, audio, video, computer). Most institutions that use tutors extensively have some kind of orientation workshop and printed manuals that outline responsibilities and provide guidelines for effective tutoring. Good institutions monitor the work of their tutors closely and provide continuing in-service professional training.

Tests and Assignments

One of the main features that distinguishes educational programs from informal learning activities is some form of student evaluation scheme involving tests or assignments. In most educational organizations, this provides a means for awarding course grades as well as giving students feedback on their progress. In a distance education setting, taking care to design ways of providing feedback and ensuring that instructors give regular feedback of good quality is of great importance because students are usually isolated and have limited opportunities for comparing their progress with others in the course.

Assignments

Most formal distance learning courses involve a series of assignments, nearly always an essay or other written exercise, to be completed on a regular basis (e.g., every week or two) during the course. This structure serves not only to provide the student with feedback on progress but also to pace the student through the course. In general, setting assignments with cutoff dates motivates the student to keep up with the work, and helps to prevent them from dropping out. However, assignments are only effective if the student receives meaningful feedback from the instructor or tutor. If students only receive a grade or acknowledgment that the assignment was received, the utility and motivational value of assignments is significantly diminished. Instructional designers have to be careful not to overload students with too many assignments, so that the workload of distance education courses does not become unreasonably greater than traditional classes (Malan and Feller, 1992).

Student Expectations

Here is what students say they expect in terms of grading and feedback on assignments (Cole, Coats, and Lentell, 1986):

- fair and objective grading
- to have their work treated with respect
- an explanation and justification of the grade awarded
- a clear indication of how they can improve both in terms of specific responses to questions and in general

- encouragement and reassurance about their ability and progress
- constructive criticism and advice
- an opportunity to respond if desired
- a timely response (i.e., before the next assignment is due)

Satisfying these criteria takes considerable time and effort on the part of the instructor or tutor. However, it must be realized that this is where most of the interaction occurs in a distance education program (as opposed to what occurs in a teleconference course) and therefore this work is central to the whole process of teaching. In the traditional classroom model, little time is allotted for personal interaction with students and therefore teachers are not encouraged to do so; in a distance education approach, this interaction is essential and must be a major part of the teaching process.

Test Security

Testing in a distance education setting presents some special challenges with respect to security. If students were to take an exam or quiz at home or at a learning center with no supervision, it would not be possible to ensure the integrity of the test. Consequently, in most distance education programs, students must complete their final exams in a proctored setting at a learning center or school. Proctors are usually teachers or administrators who are selected by the student and approved by the distance learning institution. Another procedure is to use computer-based testing in which each student receives a different subset of questions randomly selected by the computer. In many adult learning courses, students complete a project report based on a research study instead of a final exam. While these alternative forms of testing and evaluation do not eliminate the possibility of a student cheating, they reduce it to a level of insignificance.

Faculty Perspectives and Training

Dillon and Walsh (1992) reviewed faculty perspectives and evaluations about distance teaching. Here are some of their findings:

- Faculty indicate that distance teaching requires a personalized and empathic rapport with students.
- Communication skills (voice quality, eye contact, body language, clarity) are critical for distance teachers.
- Faculty who teach at a distance are generally positive toward distance education, and their attitudes tend to become more positive with experience.
- Faculty motivation for teaching at a distance comes from intrinsic (e.g., challenge) rather than extrinsic (e.g., financial rewards) motivation.

- Faculty believe that distance teaching experience improves their traditional teaching as well.

Blanch (1994) analyzed the barriers to faculty adoption of distance education approaches at California State Polytechnic University.

The greatest obstacles were:

- a lack of awareness on the part of the university community of the general benefits of distance education;
- lack of incentives for faculty to be involved in distance education;
- the unreasonableness of expecting faculty to commit themselves to a very different teaching approach without any trial period; and
- the faculty's sense that distance education was not integrated within the university's programs and plans. This last obstacle emphasizes the importance of an institution-wide policy regarding distance education.

Based on their experiences at Western Illinois University, Barker and Dickson (1993) offer the following recommendations to administrators who wish to support good distance teaching:

- Hire support personnel to provide assistance with instructional design and the installation, operation, or maintenance of equipment.
- Establish a faculty development laboratory to provide a place to try out and practice with technology.
- Provide administrative support for distance education efforts.
- Be sensitive to faculty's needs for incentives and recognition for distance teaching efforts.
- Provide faculty training, not only in the use of the technology involved but also in presentation and participation skills.

Studies such as these indicate that many changes must take place both institutionally and individually to ensure successful distance teaching; in particular, there is need for more training of persons wishing to teach at a distance. Currently, the procedures used to train teachers for distance education vary from informal orientations to workshops and training manuals that vary greatly in quality. In general, teacher training programs tend to be better planned and more structured in distance education institutions, since that is their sole purpose, and next, in the larger distance teaching units.

Summary

- One of the major prerequisites for effective distance teaching is mastery of the particular delivery technology or technologies involved. Usually the instructor using audio, audiographic, computer, and even some forms of videoconferencing is alone when actually conducting a conference.

Instructors must be able to manipulate the technology confidently and skillfully as a prerequisite to using it creatively in their instruction. In all cases a knowledge of the program planning and development process for the medium is needed.

- In all forms of teleconference teaching, the ability to humanize or personalize the class is important. Techniques to achieve this goal include (1) using names when addressing students, (2) having students begin with their names when speaking, (3) starting class with an informal roll call and greetings, (4) meeting all students in person at least once, (5) showing a positive and caring attitude, and (6) being available for private consultations outside of class.

- Learning how to use a delivery system to make a class of distant groups highly interactive is one of the biggest challenges for any teacher new to distance teaching. Initially, there is a tendency to use the medium simply to present content. To do this involves adopting the presentation styles which work for the particular medium being used. However, it soon becomes obvious to most teachers that the delivery systems used in distance learning are better suited to two-way and multipoint interactions rather than one-way presentations. At this point teachers become very interested in trying out different techniques for facilitating students' participation.

- Surveys of faculty show a demand for training in distance teaching methods. On the basis of the preceding discussion, it can be concluded that a good training program for distance teaching should have at least four ingredients: (1) practice in designing, producing, and presenting content information; (2) ample hands-on practice with the delivery technologies involved; (3) practice with techniques for humanizing a course; and (4) practice with techniques for facilitating student participation.

CHAPTER 8

The Distance Education Student

For anyone designing or teaching a distance education course, it is important to understand the characteristics of distance learners, what affects their success, how they perceive distance learning, and what they expect from a distance learning program. This chapter discusses student-related issues in distance learning, including the nature of adult learners, providing access, factors affecting student success, student attitudes, and student support. While each of these issues is discussed separately, they are all closely interrelated.

The Nature of Adult Learning

While it is true that some forms of distance education are provided to school children in the form of courses that supplement or enrich the regular curriculum, relatively few school or university students depend primarily for instruction on distance education arrangements. On the contrary, around the country and around the world, most distance education students are adults between the ages of 25 and 50. Consequently, the more one understands the nature of adult learning, the better one can understand the nature of distance learning (Kaye and Rumble, 1981). Indeed, theories of adult learning such as those of Cross (1981) or Knowles (1978) provide a very helpful basis for the design and teaching of distance education courses, particularly with respect to motivational aspects (Hough, 1984). Knowles' theory of andragogy is based on what is known about adult learning and can be reduced to the following propositions, all of which should be taken into consideration as we think about adult distant learners, and how to teach them:

- While children trust the teacher to define course content, adults need to define it for themselves, or at least to be persuaded that it is relevant to their needs.

153

- While children accept a dependent relationship with a teacher, adults have a sense of self-direction and personal responsibility.
- Children have little personal experience to draw on, but adults have a lot, which they appreciate being used as a learning resource, and resent being ignored in favor of other peoples' experiences.
- Children will accept the teacher's decisions about what to learn, when, where, and how. Adults like to make such decisions for themselves or at least be consulted.
- Children must acquire a lot of information as the basis of life in the future. For adults the future is now; they have a basis of information and see learning as necessary for using it in solving problems in the present.
- Children may need external motivation to make them learn; adults volunteer to learn because of their intrinsic motivation.

Why Do Adults Enroll in a Distance Learning Course?

For an adult, there are real costs in enrolling in a course of learning, cost that must be measured not only in dollars but perhaps even more important in time and in work that will be added to the existing effort required by the adult's employment and family responsibilities. Virtually all adults enroll voluntarily; very few, if any, are simply continuing in school because they do not know what else to do, which is the case with many younger students. For most, there are very specific and clear reasons for taking a learning program. They are generally highly motivated, task-oriented students.

Unlike younger learners, most adults have experience in employment, and many are seeking to learn more about fields of work in which they already know a great deal. Also unlike younger learners, they know a lot about life, about the world, about themselves, and about interpersonal relations, including how to deal with other persons in a class, and perhaps with a teacher. To the adult student, generally, teachers get authority from what they know and the way they deal with their students, not from any external symbols or titles.

Some adults enroll in courses to compensate for a neglected high school education; others are seeking college credit courses; many take noncredit courses in a plethora of subjects for no other purpose than to improve their general knowledge or to develop satisfying pastimes. Some seek practical knowledge when they first become parents, homeowners, or members of a school board. When you recall the organizations mentioned in this book, the vast range of motivations of adults becomes apparant. They include air force personnel learning the mechanics of a truck by home study, the college dropout trying to catch up with college credit through independent study, the professional engineer keeping abreast of new information through courses offered on NTU, the business manager working on a company-sponsored program about a new product delivered to the personal computer, and the group of homemakers discussing gardening through a co-op extension teleconference. It is impossible to do justice to the range of topics that adults learn; what is certain is that they are almost innumerable and cover every subject under the sun. It is also certain that adult distance students are always very serious about what they are doing, very committed, highly motivated.

Anxiety About Learning

Most adult learners also experience a considerable degree of anxiety about learning. This is not really an anxiety about the teacher, though sometimes it is manifested in emotions about the teacher, but is an anxiety about the ability to meet expectations, both external, and more important, self-expectations. There is a considerable fear of failure. The more accustomed one is to learning, the more confident one is in one's skills, the less important one rates the eventuality of failure, the more experience with previous success, and the less likely one is to be anxious. However, those adults who are inexperienced as learners (not unusual in distance education courses) may have a particularly high degree of anxiety at the beginning of the course. Their fear becomes concentrated when they have to turn in their first written assignment or present their views in a teleconference. Until this anxiety has been relieved by successfully taking the risk involved in handing in the assignment or making the comment, they are not able to enjoy the course, and their learning in fact can be impaired by the anxiety.

One of the first and most important responsibilities of the instructor or tutor is to try to defuse such anxiety in both classes and individual students. This does not mean that the teacher or educational institution should reduce the workload of the course or the standards required of the student. What it means is giving reassurance that mistakes and failures are a natural part of learning; that risk-taking is approved; that there is no such thing as a "dumb question"; that the instructor admires and approves effort and commitment; that the instructor cares about the student being successful and will work toward that goal.

The statements in the following box illustrate some common responses of adult learners, and all say something about the behavior of teachers of adults at a distance:

- Enjoyment, excitement, pleasure—all seven students expressed these emotions. Adults who learn enjoy learning; adults who enjoy learning learn. If they do not enjoy it, they are likely to give up during or after the course, and either do something else with their time or find an alternative way of learning the subject. Enjoyment is a sign of high motivation, and of course it leads the student to be more motivated. The wise instructor tries to keep the work enjoyable, exciting, and pleasurable.
- Most appreciated the convenience of learning at a distance and fitting it into busy schedules. Loretta said "I could not otherwise be going to school"; Richard W. refers to "time-efficient way to pursue a graduate

What Students Say About Distance Education

Here are some comments from students at the conclusion of a course in the Educational Technology Leadership program at George Washington University. This graduate program is delivered via television and computer bulletin board under the auspices of Mind Extension University. These comments were "posted" on the bulletin board as part of the final course assignment and illustrate some of the feelings that adult students have about learning at a distance:

Well, here is my two cents on the good, the bad, and the ugly. I enjoyed the class very much. Distance learning is making a master's degree possible for me. I could not otherwise be going to school. I enjoyed the guests and felt that they add a dimension to the class that we could not get in a traditional classroom. I have never taken a traditional class with a guest speaker almost weekly. I find the application videos interesting to watch and useful for sharing with my colleagues to spark interest. Partnering for assignments was interesting, and it did have us communicate more with our classmates, but I found it a little stressful having someone else depending on me for part of their assignment.
LORETTA A.

I really enjoyed this course—my first in the distance learning format. The highlight for me were the videotapes which clearly showed techniques for using multimedia with children. Although most of the tapes seemed specifically designed to show the actual multimedia product themselves, I found the teaching styles that were demonstrated along with them to be even more interesting. There was a continual emphasis on the role of the teacher as the facilitator of learning rather than someone who simply gives facts and answers. I also really enjoyed the format of the lessons. On the other side of the coin, there was always a lot of anxiety about the final project. I felt a bit in the dark for most of the course about what the expectations were. Although they became clear in the last few weeks, my blood pressure reading could have been helped a bit by having that information earlier.
RICHARD F.

The two courses I've taken have been excellent. I am very excited about the prospects of distance education and graduate study. . . . I think as the program matures it will just get better. It is a very time-efficient way to pursue a graduate degree and you all are doing a great job. Your class preparation is obvious and instructor subject knowledge is outstanding. The guests are informative and the tape demos are good. I would like to see a little more topic-specific information put out during the classes. Humor goes a long way in eliminating topic dryness. The BBS assignments were good and the instructor comments were prompt and to the point, amazing given the number of students in the class. Keep up the good work! I'm looking forward to next semester.
RICHARD W.

I was very pleased with the class, as usual. There is no way I could have possibly taken graduate work in educational technology without this distance learning. The one criticism I have of most of the ed. tech. classes is that they are dry and lack humor. Bill and Greg have outdone themselves with their efforts to include this important aspect. I found the flexibility of the project requirements wonderful. I hate doing

projects that I cannot use in "real life." I like the interaction on the BBS. I feel pairing us in different groups of two for different assignments is great. I hate to sound like such a brown nose, but I even thought the video clips were good.
SUSAN L.

In general, I found this class interesting, full of information, and a real challenge for me. At first, considering that this was my first distance learning class, I felt lost. Using the BBS was a great way to converse with the class once I learned how to navigate through the system. Using the BBS for assignments and discussions proved to be one of the most valuable parts of the class—talk about hands-on interactive learning!! It opened up a new form of interactive multimedia while allowing me to express my ideas and share opinions with the classmates and instructors. I've learned a lot!! I am eagerly looking forward to the Fall class.
CAROLINE B.

I thought it was a great course. I enjoyed it right from the start. I never heard of multi-media before taking this course. Everything I know about multimedia I learned in this course. I think that the use of television and the BBS is terrific. I can come home after a hard day's work and watch the class in the comfort and convienience of my own home. I don't have to waste my valuable time traveling to some distant location to be at a class. If my employer wants me to work late or if I have a social obligation, then I do not lose out, because I have the class recorded on videotape. If there is something I do not understand in the lecture, then I can reverse my tape and play it over again, and no instructor is going to jump on me for not listening well enough the first time. The BBS gives me a chance to make contact with other students from other parts of the country and to work with them on assignments and learn from them.
NORMAN G.

When I first contemplated the course, with my travel schedule limiting my participa-tion in school programs requiring classrooom attendance, I was excited about the prospect of distance learning. The feature of catching up after the fact via videotapes also encouraged my decision. Mechanically, the BBS and the ease of communication by phone, fax, etc., from all over the world has allowed me the feeling of staying con-nected with the class. Although I have not used the BBS much in an E-mail mode, I have enjoyed reading the messages, and have learned from many of them, and rate this facility highly. As a general statement, the televised classes were excellent, with the examples and interview framework interesting and informative, and accomplished well the purpose of introducing us to IMM and its current state. The project assign-ment has greatly improved my computer skills, has been hard work but fun, and has stimulated a strong desire to continue my education in educational technology. Over-all, for me, the course accomplished its purpose, and I give the highest ratings to the tolerance of the instructors (and Catherine) with regard to due dates, and my lack of computer skills in conveying assignments, etc. This created an atmosphere of caring and acceptance that served well as motivation to hang in there. I would recommend this distance learning method to anyone who has similar time constraints and I intend to continue taking courses this way. Thank you!
GEORGE R.

degree"; Susan said "There is no way I could have possibly taken graduate work . . . "; Norman said, "I don't have to waste my valuable time. . ."; George refers to his "travel schedule limiting my participation in school programs requiring classroom attendance."

- Not many of these students mentioned fear, partly because they are successful, experienced, graduate students. Some fear and anxiety was reported by Loretta, "I found it stressful"; Richard F. felt "anxiety about the final project"; Caroline "felt lost" at first.

- They like course activities, especially the project.

- They appreciate humor, which helps reduce tension and develops a playful environment, which is very conducive to learning.

- They like variety, expressed here by appreciation of the mixture of media and the number of different guest speakers.

Perhaps the two most important, typical, adult attitudes that these reports show are an appreciation of efficiency and an appreciation of an enjoyable learning environment.

Providing Access

One special feature of distance education, and perhaps what most people think of when they first think about distance education, is the capability for an organization to give access to education to some learners who could otherwise not have it (Jordahl, 1989). This in fact describes the professional people who we met in the previous section; although some of them lived in major cities, there was no access to the subject that they wanted at times and places convenient to them. However, access is even more important to certain kinds of students—those who are disabled, elderly, or living in rural or remote areas. Here are some stories about such students, reported by Jones (1991):

> Mico Perales was a bright high school student who dreamed of becoming an engineer and attending MIT, but he lived in the tiny Texas town of Norheim (population: 369). Finding teachers who could provide the advanced science and math instruction he needed in order to compete for a spot at MIT would normally be impossible. However, his school arranged for him to take televised courses in these subjects provided by the TI-IN satellite network (see Chapters 2 and 3). In his junior and senior years, Perales took five TI-IN classes, ranking as the top student nationally in two of them. He is now an electrical engineering student at MIT with a full scholarship. Perales credits the advanced science and math classes taken via TI-IN with giving him the background he needed to get into MIT.

> Carolyn Sharp had plenty of free time and a love for learning, but she lived in rural Colorado, 150 miles from the nearest city and college. The 71-year-old Sharp doesn't drive and lives too far out in the country to receive radio or television signals. She loved the peace and beauty of her surroundings but longed for some intellectual stimulation. Things changed when she was given a satellite dish by her sister. Now she could pick up a broad range of television programming including courses provided by Mind Extension University (MEU). She enrolled in the "Hu-

manities Through the Arts" course which she found very rewarding and which helped her with an encyclopedia project she had been working on. She has gone on to take additional MEU courses.

Few people experience a more demanding full-time occupation than stay-at-home parents of small children. Yet while raising their children, many parents want to continue their education. Robin Pappas was an Ohio mother of three small children whose family responsibilities made it impossible for her to attend on-campus classes. However, she needed training that would enable her to manage the family business. In 1988, in the privacy of her living room, she was able to go back to school for the first time in many years. She took an accounting course offered by the University of New Mexico via MEU. After completing this course, she was able to do the bookkeeping for the family business. She subsequently enrolled in other courses related to the business needs as well her own personal interests.

Twyla Hall was born with a physical disability that severely restricts her ability to move about. She completed public school in Woodleaf, N.C., but when it came to attending college, she had trouble finding one that would accommodate her limited mobility. Hall enrolled at University of North Carolina at Greensboro, but had to withdraw after her sophomore year because of the physical burdens of trying to get to classes in buildings not designed for the handicapped. She was extremely disap-pointed and upset that she would not be able to complete her degree. Then she learned about MEU and began to take courses by television. Hall was able to com-plete her degree by distance education and now works as an insurance clerk in the family business.

While the convenience and flexibility of distance education is a benefit to all students, these examples remind us that for some students distance educa-tion makes all the difference between a richer and a poorer quality of life. These stories help also to illustrate the broad range of backgrounds and also the moti-vations that distance education students can have. Thousands of similar stories could be told by every distance education organization. We suggest that you might like to investigate the people behind the statistics, as a class project or as formal research. You will find it a very rewarding activity, because in every pop-ulation of distant learners are found some very exceptional people.

Factors Affecting Student Success

One well-studied aspect of distance education is the factors that affect student success and failure (e.g., Cookson, 1990; Dirr, 1991; Gibson, 1990; Moore, 1989b; Peruniak, 1983; Roberts, 1984).

In most distance education courses and programs, since enrollment is vol-untary, a percentage of the students who begin programs do not complete them. In the past it was not unusual for noncompletion (also referred to as "dropout") rates for distance learning courses to be in the range of 30 to 50 per-cent; nowadays the figure should be near the lower end of that range. For many years administrators and instructors have struggled to understand what causes some students to withdraw, in the hope of being able to improve their comple-tion rates.

Improving the Odds for Minorities Using Two-way Television

In the spring of 1990, California State University-Dominguez Hills installed a two-way classroom-to-classroom compressed video television link at an inner-city high school 15 miles from the campus. Both the university and the high school are located in south central Los Angeles and serve predominantly black and Hispanic populations. The primary goal in installing the two-way video link was to address a major problem for the university and the high school, which was the low rate of attendance and the poor preparation of many minority students for college. It was intended to use distance education to give students exposure to college-level courses and try to improve their motivation to attend college. Two-way video was selected as the delivery technology because it was felt that for this group of students, generally of poor motivation, the ability for students to see the instructors as well as to speak with them was critical to the goal of the project.

Using the two-way television link, Dominquez Hills professors taught a number of college-level courses to the high school students, including advanced algebra, calculus, German, and Mexican-American studies. In addition, there were science demonstrations in physics and chemistry and tutoring programs for help with homework and test-taking skills. The broadcasts were designed to augment regular class instruction and provide the students with enriched educational experiences. A single classroom at the school was used as a receiving site. Because of space limitations and security concerns, the equipment was kept locked in a closet and set up for each broadcast. The project involved 62 students, 4 high school teachers, and 4 college faculty.

Students, teachers, and faculty were interviewed at the end of the school year to assess the success of the project. Students rated the courses as comparable to their high school classes and indicated a desire to receive credit for participation. Students complained about technical problems with the equipment (e.g., broad-

One of the many methodological difficulties of this research is that dropout is usually a result of no one cause, but of an accumulation and mixture of causes. A number of researchers have developed formal models for predicting student completion (e.g., Billings, 1989; Kember, 1989). Figure 8-1 illustrates Billings's model for the completion of correspondence courses. The links shown in the diagram represent the relationships among the variables (i.e., they are causal, additive, and correlational). Billings found that students who made the most progress had the intention of completing the course in three months, submitted the first lesson within 40 days, had higher entrance examination scores and high GPAs, had completed other correspondence courses, had a supportive family, had high goals for completing the program, lived closer to the instruc-

casts were delayed or cancelled because no one was available to set up or operate the equipment), that the course content was too abstract and theoretical, and that there was not enough interaction during the classes. Teachers felt that the exposure to college courses had been beneficial to the students. They reported that getting students to interact during the broadcasts was a problem because they were too anxious or shy. They suggested that students needed to be given a better orientation to the use of the system and that teachers be given better training on how to set up and troubleshoot the system. A high degree of coordination among the teachers and college instructors was required to integrate the content of the broadcasts with regular classes.

The college faculty felt that the broadcasts had improved the self-esteem of the students and their confidence regarding taking college courses and had also increased their interest in the subjects taught. However, faculty found it difficult to teach high school students, especially getting them to participate in the discussions. The instructors had no previous experience teaching at a distance generally, or via television in particular, and this almost certainly limited their effectiveness.

Did the system have any impact on college enrollment? Nearly all the students (93 percent) indicated that they wanted to attend college, but only 8 percent applied and 3 percent were accepted. It appears that despite a number of positive outcomes, this project was too little and came too late in the students' high school careers to have any significant effect on their commitment to further formal education. Furthermore, many mistakes were made in the implementation of the courses which limited their impact.

Source: McGowan (1992).

tor, and had good college-level preparation. The single most important variable was the students' intention to complete.

Educational Background

Not surprisingly, one of the best predictors of success in distance education is the educational background of the student. In general, the more formal education a person has, the more likely he or she is to complete a distance education course or program. For example, Coggins (1989) found significant differences between completers and noncompleters in terms of educational level attained and length of time since last credit course. The latter variable is interesting

Figure 8.1   Model for Completion of Correspondence Courses (Billings, 1989)

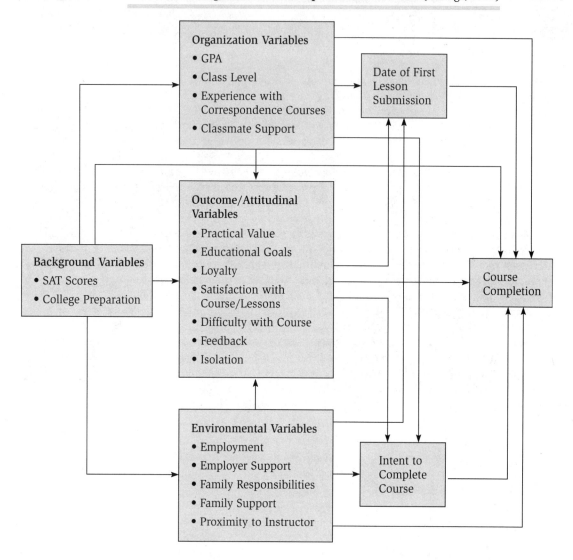

because it suggests that the greater the length of time since completing a formal educational course, the less likely the student will be to complete a new course.

Personality Characteristics

Much less reliable as a predictor of success or failure, but clearly relevant, are the personality characteristics of the student (including what is often referred to as learning style). For example, it has been suggested (e.g, Moore, 1975, Thompson, 1984) that individuals who are more field independent (i.e., less influenced by the surrounding environment, including social environment) are better suited to distance learning than people who are less field independent. Another personality dimension that is often associated with distance education is introversion/extroversion, with introverted individuals being more predisposed to distance learning. Persistance, determination, and "need to achieve" are all qualities that would positively affect a student's success. The nature of the student's motivation for taking a particular course or program (i.e., intrinsic or extrinsic) is also likely to affect success (Atman, 1986).

Extracurricular Concerns

A variety of extracurricular concerns, such as employment (job stability, workload), family responsibilities, health, and social interests/obligations, can positively or adversely affect completion of distance education courses. For example, encouragement from employers, co-workers, friends, and family regarding distance learning can motivate the student to do well; conversely, lack of support from one or more of these groups can result in poor performance and noncompletion. In almost all cases, job or family considerations take priority over distance learning requirements.

Academic Concerns

Many features of the course or program affect the success of students, including:

- the perceived relevance of the content to career or personal interests;
- the difficulty of the course and program (i.e., amount of time/effort required);
- the degree of student or administrative support available;
- the nature of the media used for course delivery and interaction;
- the nature of the pacing or scheduling involved;
- the amount and nature of feedback received from instructors/tutors on assignments and on course progress; and
- the amount and nature of the interaction with instructors, tutors, and other students.

Students are more likely to drop out of a course if they perceive the content as irrelevant or of little value to their career or personal interests, if the course is too difficult and takes too much time or effort, if they become frustrated in trying to complete the course or handling administrative requirements and receive no assistance, if they receive little or no feedback on their coursework or progress, and if they have little or no interaction with the instructor, tutor, or other students and hence become too isolated.

Indicators of Success

Research studies have identified a number of factors which are predictors of probable completion of a distance education course. They include the following:

- **Intent to complete** Students who say they intend to complete a course usually do. On the other hand, students who are unsure about their ability to complete a course are most likely to drop out.
- **Early submission** Students who submit the first assignment early, or punctually, are more likely to complete the course satisfactorily. For example, Armstrong et al. (1985) found 84 percent of the students who submitted the first assignment within the first two weeks successfully completed the course, whereas 75 percent who took longer than two months to submit the assignment did not complete the course.
- **Completion of other courses** Students who successfully complete one distance learning course are likely to complete subsequent courses.

Knowledge of factors such as these can be used by instructors or tutors to identify at-risk students who may need additional support or counseling in order to complete a course. As more and more classes are taught in a distance education form, a full understanding of the circumstances that facilitate student completion is critical to course developers, administrators, and instructors.

Student Reactions

Researchers have examined student reactions from a number of perspectives. Most studies are concerned with assessing the level of learner satisfaction with a particular course or program, or the extent to which students perceive particular instructional media or teaching strategies to be effective. Some studies are concerned with changes in student attitudes to distance learning that come about as a consequence of distance learning activities.

Classroom Versus Distance Learning

A common question that is examined is how students feel about distance learning relative to traditional classroom instruction. In many cases, students say they prefer traditional classroom learning even though they enjoyed their distance learning course and found it worthwhile. For a variety of reasons (e.g., equipment problems, inexperienced teachers/tutors, etc.), there may be problems in a distance education course or program that produces negative attitudes

Cross-cultural Considerations:
Distance Education in Rural Alaska

The University of Alaska provides off-campus classes to the sparsely populated regions of the state. Approximately 12 percent percent of those students are native Alaskans who want to continue their education but do not want to give up their traditional lifestyle to attend university classes in a large city. Audioconferencing and correspondence study are the dominant means used to deliver off-campus courses. To participate in audioconferencing, students often go to a local learning center where the telephone equipment is located. Many of the problems encountered in providing classes to native students have to do with cultural issues. Most of the courses are taught by nonnative instructors who have little understanding of native customs or local conditions that affect learning. Here are some quotes from students and teachers that describe some of the issues involved in this setting:

> It has allowed me to continue my education and stay with my family. I am free to go berry picking in the daytime and still go to college in the evening. I can't just leave and go to university to get a degree. What would my husband and family do?

> It was fifty below and I was a little late for class because of cooking dinner for my family. It was really snowing and I couldn't see anything. It was a whiteout. I used the rope that leads through the village to pull myself to the high school, but halfway up the rope broke. I got to class an hour late and I was freezing. It was hard to concentrate that night.

> It takes a lot of hard work to make these courses good for native students. Lots of natives are not accustomed to the academic life and don't know how to write papers and take tests. When they get to college they get stuck in remedial courses. I am so tired of always having to adjust to the system. The system should try to adjust to us, too.

> When we learn something in the native culture . . . it's different from audioconferencing unless the instructor gives the student a second or third or fourth chance to learn. If you don't do it right the first time in the native culture, you do it again a second time and you do it a third and a fourth time until you master it. Its more like long-term observation.

In addition to the cultural issues there are also language considerations; many natives are not highly proficient with English since they speak Eskimo (Yup'ik) at home. There is also a high percentage of hearing loss in native populations making it difficult for many students to participate fully in audioconferences.

Source: Sponder (1990).

toward distance learning. Very similar problems occur in traditional classrooms, but the absence of the "father figure" or "mother figure" to take care of them is disconcerting for some students. Most students are able to cope with problems, and most students actually enjoy taking responsibility for solving their own problems. However this is obviously harder work than letting a teacher do it, so some of the negative attitude to distance learning comes from reluctance to take responsibility and make an effort. Fortunately this only applies to a minority of students. In well-implemented courses students can be very positive about their distance learning experiences and prefer such courses over traditional classes.

Nelson (1985), for example, surveyed the attitudes of students taking classes via two-way videoconference and reported that 94 percent believed their level of achievement was as high or higher than regular classes, and 97 percent wanted to take further videoconference classes. On the other hand, Barker (1987) evaluated the attitudes of children who had taken classes via the TI-IN satellite video conference system and found that 65 percent believed the video class to be more difficult than regular classes and 70 percent would prefer to take regular classes. It is interesting to note that in this study, numerous problems were mentioned, including difficulty hearing the programs, difficulty contacting the instructor, and inadequate teacher preparation.

One important consideration to keep in mind when analyzing the results of student satisfaction surveys is that there is typically no significant relationship between these attitudes and actual achievement. In other words, students may do well in a course even though they indicate disliking it, or conversely, do poorly in a course that they like. Measures of satisfaction are useful in predicting student course selections and assessing the effectiveness of instructional design or teaching strategies, but they do not indicate learning accomplishment. Perhaps most important, they may be used to predict dropout and be a trigger for counseling intervention.

Resistance to Distance Education

Since most students have little experience learning at a distance, they are unfamiliar with it and may be anxious about taking distance education courses. Indeed, in some situations this unfamiliarity is translated into resistance that must be overcome in order for the courses to have any hope of succeeding. Many students (as well as teachers and training managers) have misconceptions about distance learning that must be changed if they are to profit from it. For example, students may believe that distance education courses are easier than conventional classes and require less work. When they discover that this is not the case and that the opposite is true, they may be unhappy. Students often assume that a distance education course will be of lesser quality than a classroom offering and avoid taking such courses for this reason. And, students frequently do not understand that they must take more responsibility for their learning in a distance education course and not wait for the instructor or tutor

What Students Find Satisfying About Distance Learning

Here are some comments from a student that show some emotional reactions to distance learning:

> The distance learning course was excellent. I would like to emphasize the word "learning" as opposite to the word "teaching." The whole attitude amongst most of us participants was something like this: "Those guys and gals, they respect our professional skills, they honor us. We want to cooperate not only with them but mainly with each other. This is and will be a good exercise/practice for all of us." In the very beginning, the "course masters" gave us the impression that we are here not for receiving highly authorized information but mostly for giving, relaying, distributing the information and skill that we hold. The class is the teacher!

> All of us were not comfortable with the DE course. One of the participants wanted a more authoritarian or school-style education: He disapproved the freedom given adult learners (it is possible that there were more of this kind, but he was the only one who told me so). He would prefer a style where the teacher has more authority. I myself hoped that the teachers or tutors would have gone deeper into my special interest areas.

> The best or most lasting experience is in the cooperation. It was really exhilarating to be a member of an nonhomogenous group (social workers, teachers, engineers, students). I could discuss my ideas and my ways of working with people who were total strangers to my profession and could give me new views to my profession. The teachers taught me to teach and I taught the teachers to co-op with the technology.

> This course lasted half a year. When it was over, I felt sad. Is this all that there is? We have been a good team for a long time and now we must be separated—or must we? We grow together and then we depart; we will have a time to grieve, but the grief will pass by. Now I do not any more miss my fellow students or teachers, I only remember them. But still, I would like to stay in contact with the persons who were a part of my life for six months!

> When I started to write this, I aimed toward "a cool and clean analysis." I gave up to my inner feelings. I still miss those people. Maybe this course will be something that I still miss when I am ten years older than now.

to prompt them. This is the kind of misunderstanding that leads to students falling behind and becoming dissatisfied. For these reasons it is very desirable to include an orientation session/lesson in any distance education course where students can find out about how the delivery system works and what is expected of them.

When properly conducted, however, distance education can be very satisfying, as suggested in the comments above from a student in Finland who expresses some very common feelings about the freedom that being a member of a well-conducted distant learning group can provide.

Student Support

There are a number of things that students expect from a distance education course or program, including:

- information that is up-to-date and authoritative
- courses that are flexible and accommodate different learning styles
- guidance on what and how to study
- opportunities to do something with what they learn (e.g., assignments, projects)
- feedback on their work and progress
- help dealing with administrative or personal problems related to the program

Satisfying these expectations should dictate not only how the course or program is designed and implemented, but also the nature of the teaching/tutoring involved and the student support services provided.

Distance learning institutions, as defined in Chapter 1, tend to have specialist, full-time staff to provide student support services, whereas in program-level delivery, administrators or instructors will be responsible for these tasks along with their other duties.

Guidance/Counseling

Students may need guidance and counseling at a number of different stages in their work as distant learners. At an early stage, they are likely to need advice about whether a particular course promises to suit their particular academic needs at a particular time. They also may need advice about the different degree of responsibility required by the mixture of media in one course as compared with others. Students may want advice about how to study for a particular course given the media used and the format. This kind of guidance should come from an experienced instructor or tutor who is familiar with the media and the teaching strategies used.

Ideally, all students in a program and course receive some sort of orientation that addresses many of these questions in general and minimizes the need for individual counseling. It is particularly important to inform people of the time demands that accompany distance learning and to encourage them to think about the effects their study will have on other members of their family. Even with such orientation counseling, during any course, some students are likely to experience job-, family-, or health-related problems that require special guidance. A counseling service should have a way of identifying these problems and of intervening to offer support if the student does not come forward to request it. Otherwise, these basic concerns will demand the student's complete attention, and there is a good chance the student will drop out of the course or perform poorly.

Students may need guidance and counseling at a number of different stages in their work as distant learners. A counselor advises a student on selecting his next course in an independent study program.

Administrative Assistance

Students often need assistance in dealing with the routine administrative aspects of a course or program: registering, paying fees or getting tuition benefits, obtaining materials, receiving grades, taking exams, etc. In the case of on-campus students, questions or problems can be resolved by visiting the relevant office. However, in the case of an off-campus student, all interaction is likely to be via telephone, fax, or correspondence. Students often have difficulty identifying and reaching the right person to talk to (especially in large institutions) and can become very frustrated. Ideally, students in distance education programs have a single person they can contact for all administrative problems. In addition, all adminstrative requirements and procedures should be described in a student handbook that students receive at the beginning of a course or when they first register in the institution.

Interaction

Most students desire some degree of interaction with their instructor/tutor and fellow students during a course. This may be for the purposes of getting feedback on their ideas and learning progress, or simply for the pleasures of social contact. Whether it is achieved by telephone, mail, fax, or computer messaging, every distance education program needs to provide a means for students to interact when they want to. Instructors/tutors must be accessible to students on a regular basis. A student directory listing contact information should be provided. In a well-designed course, there will be learning activities that provide opportunities for students to work together and interact. Futhermore, students should have a chance to interact with the instructor or tutor when feedback is provided on assignments.

Summary

This chapter has discussed a number of aspects related to the student in a distance learning setting:

- Most students involved in distance education at the present time are adults. Instructors need to understand the adult's motivation(s) for taking a distance learning program, and what this means in terms of the design and delivery of such programs. Adults have many concerns in their lives (job, family, social life), and distance education must accommodate these concerns.

- One of the unique benefits of distance education is that it is able to provide access to education for many students who would not otherwise have the opportunity. This includes rural populations, disabled individuals, mothers with children at home, and the elderly. However, providing effective distance learning experiences to different types of learners requires a good understanding of their particular circumstances and limitations.

- There are many factors that affect the success of students in distance learning programs. These include educational background, personality characteristics, extracurricular concerns, and course-related problems. Factors such as timely submission of assignments, history of previous course completion, and strength of intent to complete the course can be used to predict the success of a student in a distance education course. The design and teaching of the course also affects student success rates.

- Students' reactions are a good source of information about the effectiveness of a particular course and help give ideas for how to design a course for a particular group. Student satisfaction with distance education courses relative to traditional classes can vary according to students' personalities and other characteristics and the design of the course and how well it is taught. Students often have an initial resistance to distance learning that can be addressed by a good orientation segment or session.

- Having a means of providing student support if and when it is needed is critical to the success of distance education programs. There are three categories of student support that are especially critical: guidance/counseling, administrative assistance, and interaction with students and instructors/tutors.

- After overcoming their initial anxiety, most adult learners find distance education that is well designed and well taught to be an exciting, even exhilarating experience because they have the structure and interaction provided by a teaching institution yet have freedom to conduct much of the learning themselves. When this happens in learning groups, it leads to social bonding that for many learners provides great emotional satisfaction.

One fact that should have become clear to you in reading this chapter is how closely related matters to do with the student are to teaching/tutoring considerations as discussed in Chapter 7 and the design of distance education courses and programs as discussed in Chapter 6. As we said in Chapter 1, it is not a bad idea to try to separate the different components of distance education for the purposes of study and discussion, but in reality all the components impact on each other. This is no less true for the topic to which we now turn our attention in Chapter 9, which is the administration and management of distance education and the determination of policies that make it possible for a system to be set up and operated.

Administration, Management and Policy

The management of distance education institutions and the administration of programs is complex. At institutional, state, and federal levels there is need for new policies to support the development of distance education programs, units, institutions, and consortia, and need for procedures to make such policies. In this chapter we discuss issues relating to planning, staffing, resources, budget, scheduling, quality assessment, and how policy is (or is not) made.

The administration of a distance education program, unit, institution, or consortium embraces all the major events and activities that support the teaching/learning process:

- Potential students must be informed about proposed courses.
- Students must be registered and enrolled.
- Fees must be collected and accounts kept.
- Decisions must be made about what courses to produce.
- The process of designing, producing, and delivering course materials must be administered.
- Academic and administrative staff must be hired, supported, and supervised.
- Instructional and counseling services to students must be administered.
- Student grades, diplomas, degrees, and awards must be issued.
- Study centers or other facilities, equipment, and materials must be obtained and maintained.
- The effectiveness and efficiency of the program must be constantly assessed.

While all levels of distance education as introduced in Chapter 1 will involve administration, the extent and complexity of administrative activities will depend on the kind and scope of the type of distance education involved. Thus in many programs the instructor has to handle the administrative duties for a single course, whereas in a distance learning institution an entire department will be needed for each of the administrative activities.

Planning

One of the critical management tasks that administrators must perform is strategic planning. This involves a number of processes:

- formulating a vision and a mission, goals, and objectives for the institution or program
- balancing aspirations with currently available resources and chosing among options so that the priority goals can be achieved with high quality and with the available resources
- assessment of changes in student, business, or societal demands
- tracking emerging technological alternatives
- projecting future resource and financial needs

Good strategic planning begins with a clear understanding of mission or direction. Mission statements often originate from the top leadership of an institution. Since there are many kinds of distance education markets, the organization's leadership should be explicit about who it is attempting to serve, how, and why. Statements of goals and objectives provide guidelines to administrators regarding the ways in which resources (i.e., people, facilities, time, money) should be used. It is the job of the institution's management to determine whether the resources needed to achieve its mission are available or can be obtained, and to select goals and objectives that are realizable within the limits of whatever resources are available. A clear sense of mission and knowledge of what resources are needed together provide the basis for preparing plans to obtain additional resources.

Decision to Offer Distance Education

Another set of issues that must be resolved by the management of an institution (or possibly the administration of a state) relate to the first suggestions that a course or program be offered by distance education. Before offering such a course, the institution must be sure that there is a real demand (or sufficient market) for it. Generally, this would be indicated by market research data showing that there is a sufficiently large number of interested students. However, it has frequently been found that a greater demand exists for educational courses than is revealed by normal market research procedures. Thus when a good distance education opportunity is offered, the number of students who take it up is usually greater than expected.

Second, before deciding to offer a course, the administration must be convinced there is a suitable and cost-effective technology or mixture of technologies available to the institution and to the potential students, and more important, that there is staff capable of designing and teaching the course. Unfortunately, the usual pattern is for the decision to go ahead to be taken after there has been a check of the technology, but not the human resource to use it properly. A suprising number of administrators seem to think that faculty can simply add teaching at a distance to their existing workloads.

Third the institution must determine how to recover the costs of investing in a course or program, including the tuition fees to charge relative to other courses. If a considerable amount of development is involved or new equipment is purchased, how much of these costs should be passed on to the students and how much treated as a normal capital/operating cost?

Finally, there is the issue of faculty workload and compensation. Should teaching a distance education course be treated as equivalent to teaching a traditional class, even though a lot more preparation or student interaction is likely to be required? Olcott (1992) and Whittington (1990) discuss these and other issues as they pertain to universities.

Tracking Technology

Since the cost-effectiveness of distance education is highly dependent on the particular delivery system used, decisions about what technology to purchase may affect the financial viability of an institution and its programs. For example, recent developments in codecs (hardware used to send and receive digital video) have lowered the costs of videoconferencing dramatically, making that form of teleconferencing much more affordable than before. An institution that has not yet invested in classroom videoteleconferencing equipment might delay such a purchase while it waits for a lower cost, and as it studies changes in the direction of workstation delivery. Furthermore, new developments in technology present new instructional capabilities and opportunites as well as cost saving. The emergence of inexpensive bulletin board systems on personal computers made computer conferencing a viable option for distance education, providing a different type of interaction among students and instructors than correspondence or telephone.

Staffing

At the core of any distance education program or institution are the staff who run it. A major administrative task is to recruit, supervise, and train all of the individuals who make up a distance education system. They include the following:

- faculty who teach or tutor courses
- course developers, subject experts, instructional designers, or editors
- media specialists and technicians
- program directors, course managers, and site coordinators
- clerks who process enrollments, grades, or materials
- department heads, deans, vice-presidents, and other administrators

Full-time Versus Part-time

One of the questions associated with staffing is the extent to which employees need to be part-time or permanent. In general, the more part-time staff, the lower the operating costs of the organization.

The principle of division of labor that has been discussed earlier supports the idea of having staff who only work in teaching a small number of students, using teaching materials that other people design, produce, and deliver on a large scale. It is often better to have a lot of part-time staff, so that each person teaches a small number of students and thus maintains a personal student-teacher relationship in spite of the distance, than it is to have full-time personnel with very large student caseloads. Having part-time staff also allows the organization to adapt its curriculum more quickly to changing needs than may be possible if it has a staff locked into the curriculum that may have been relevant 10 or 20 years earlier.

Outside the United States, in open universities it is very common for the organization to have full-time staff to develop distance education courses, and to supplement them with part-time consultants, and then to depend almost entirely on part-time tutors to teach the course. In American independent study units it is usually full-time faculty of the university who design the courses and part-timers, including graduate students, who act as tutors. Other organizations, such as a school district or corporate training department, may use their full-time teachers or trainers and support them with subject experts who are hired for a particular course.

Members of a development team, such as writers, editors, producers, graphics artists, and programmers, are often hired as consultants for a specific project. On the other hand, administrative staff (senior executives, program directors, clerks) tend to be permanent, full-time positions. The ratio of temporary, part-time to permanent, full-time staff is an important factor in the overall effectiveness of an organization since it affects expenses, quality of service, and morale.

Understanding Distance Education

Regardless of their position in the organization, it is imperative that all staff understand and value the nature of distance education and the needs of distance learners. They must appreciate the difficulties that distance education students experience and not only know how to be helpful but want to be help-ful. Distance education is no longer a marginal or second-best option for either students or teachers, and only persons with a professional commitment should be employed. For this reason, hiring staff who have taken distance education courses is a good idea. However, since most people have not had any first-hand experience with distance learning (including teachers and tutors), all staff should receive an orientation that conveys what distance education is like from a student's perspective. Student stories in print or video format may be most valuable for this purpose. After appointment, especially in the early years, staff should be monitored continuously; this is easier in a media-based communications program than in conventional education. They should also be provided with on-going, in-service training.

Training and Qualifications

Until recently, the only qualification a person was likely to have to be a distance education teacher was to have had first-hand experience as a student or teacher in a distance learning program. Indeed, the British Open University and a few other big institutions would be among the few organizations that give staff formal training about how to teach at a distance. Lewis (1992) discusses the development of a competency-based training program for staff at the new Open College in the United Kingdom based upon experiences of the Open University.

Since 1989 the American Center for the Study of Distance Education (ACSDE) at Penn State University has offered a three-course, graduate-level certificate program in distance education which has been completed by students from all over the world. Each course is a three-credit, approximately 150-hour course.

In 1993 the University of Wisconsin began to offer a certificate program in distance education consisting of a number of different courses (see Table 9-1). Athabasca University in Canada now offers a Master's degree in distance education (Coldeway and Spencer, 1993). Several other organizations provide workshops and seminars about some aspect of distance education (see Appendix A).

As degree and certificate programs in distance education proliferate, it will become increasing common for individuals involved in the administration or delivery of distance education to have formal training in the subject. This is likely to result in more effective and efficient distance education efforts at all levels.

Assessment

Good planning also depends significantly on on-going assessment activities. It is important to know how well the institution is doing its job. In the case of distance education, this means finding out whether students and faculty are satisfied with course materials and with the learning accomplished. It is also necessary to examine trends in demography and business to see what changes

Table 9-1   **University of Wisconsin Certificate Program in Distance Education**

Core Modules (all print-based)
Learning at a Distance
Distance Education Technology
Instructional Systems Design
Evaluation in Distance Education

Electives
Learner Support Services (taught in print)
Administration and Management (taught in print)
Designing for Interactive Audio (taught by audioconference)
Interactive Strategies for Video (taught by audioconference)
Next Age Leadership (taught by audioconference)
Site Coordination (taught by audioconference)
Using Multimedia Systems (taught by audioconference)

might be called for in future courses and programs. For example, the increasingly multicultural makeup of the U.S. population makes cultural sensitivity in course content (and perhaps, multilingual versions) more important than it has been in the past. Or the trend for more people to work at home or have home businesses may create a bigger market for distance education in business topics.

Learning Centers

While a large range of materials and services can be delivered to the students at their home or work locations, there are still some that cannot. Most distance education institutions find it necessary to provide students with physical access to resources at a site near their homes or workplaces. In some cases, this is accomplished by establishing regional learning centers where materials and personnel are located.

Setting up and maintaining learning centers require many administrative decisions:

- where learning centers should be located
- when they should be open
- what facilities and equipment are needed
- what staff (administrative and academic) they should have
- how they should relate to the main "campus" (especially degree of autonomy and scope of activities)
- how they should be funded

Staff and students have to learn how to use a learning center. They must be taught to resist the temptation to turn it into a conventional classroom facility. Nearly all the presentation of content is conducted away from the study center, and only those things that cannot be done in any other way are conducted face-to-face. This means such activities as laboratory experiments, role-playing exercises, and above all, learner-learner interaction. It is necessary to remind students and faculty that the learning center is a means of education, just another type of technology, and is not an end in itself.

Libraries

Public libraries frequently play a special role in distance education. The public library is the students' most likely source of "additional" learning resources— that is, books and materials other than those provided by the teaching institution. However, the time and expertise of library staff is limited and may not be very helpful for the specific needs of a distance learner. Distance learning institutions can make libraries more valuable resource centers for their students by forming explicit partnerships and providing the kinds of materials needed. For example, some open universities provide selected libraries with "book boxes" containing multiple copies of the materials needed for specific courses, as well as reference lists of other materials that may be relevant.

This approach may be less appropriate for graduate and other advanced courses where the materials needed are too specialized (e.g., professional journals, technical books) to be found in an ordinary public library, and providing such materials to each library is not feasible. While a variety of solutions are possible (e.g., on-line access, microfiche or CD-ROM, circulating collections, faxing articles), this is a major challenge for designers and administrators of distance education for graduate-level programs.

York (1993) describes a study of the provision of library services at six U.S. university systems engaged in distance education (Cal State-Chico, Colorado State, University of Alaska-Southeast, University of Maine-Augusta, University of Nebraska-Lincoln, and University of Wyoming). The study examined the means of student access to collections, promotion of library services to student and faculty, and relationship to the accreditation requirements.

Kascus (1994) examined the attitudes of deans and directors of American Library Association–accredited library schools in the United States and Canada regarding library support for off-campus and distance education programs. She found the topic is minimally represented in the training of librarians and has a low priority for most deans and directors of library schools.

Latham, Slade, and Budnick (1991) provide a summary of the literature on the relationship between libraries and distance education.

Teleconference Learning Sites

In the context of teleconferencing, the major resource problem for administrators to worry about is to ensure that the learning site is satisfactory for learning and the equipment is working properly. The learning site can range from a small conference room for a group of four to five participants to a large auditorium with hundreds of people. The site coordinator (see Chapter 7) must ensure that every participant has comfortable seating and workspace, that the room acoustics are good, and that everyone has the necessary materials. The site coordinator (or a technician) must also set up and test the teleconferencing equipment and troubleshoot any problems. In addition, the site coordinator may also be responsible for organizing the involvement of local experts at the site in the form of a panel or moderators. It has been well documented that one of the primary reasons for the failure of teleconferences is poor site management (Davis and Elliot, 1992).

Hands-on

A final resource category that has historically posed problems for distance education is equipment needed for hands-on laboratories or job training. One approach to this problem has been to develop "lab kits" that can be shipped to students. Students are provided with microscopes and specimens and told how to conduct experiments at the kitchen sink. Some organizations have developed working models of equipment as well. A good solution to the need for hands-on learning is the development of computer simulations. A computer simulation program can be developed for any piece of equipment, process, or event. Thus there are simulations for high school chemistry or physics experiments, simulations of manufacturing machinery, simulations of petroleum refineries or nuclear plants, and simulations of computer systems and telephone networks. Simulations can be distributed on discs as part of the course materials to be run at home or office, or they can be available on machines in a learning center.

Budgeting

Of all the areas that administrators must deal with, budgeting is probably the most difficult. Budget decisions are basically about priorities and resource allocation. Administrators are always concerned with the question of cost-effectiveness: Are they getting the best value for the money they spend?

In the context of distance education programs, administrators must decide how much to spend on course development, technology, academic staff (teachers, tutors), student support services, learning centers and central facilities, administration, and marketing/promotion.

Budget Allocation

One major question is what relative proportion of funds and resources should be allocated to each of these categories. For example, should more of the budget go toward developing new courses, supporting the existing ones, hiring more academic staff, or improving facilities? In theory, budget allocation should be based on a careful analysis of the critical needs of the distance education program, including current deficiencies and opportunities. For example, if student evaluation data indicates that students want a higher level of interactivity in their courses, more budget could be allocated to a delivery system that allows more interaction, to workshops for teachers on interactive strategies, or to hiring more tutors. On the other hand, if market analysis data indicates that more students would enroll if more (or certain) courses were offered, course development would receive a larger share of the budget. In order to make budget decisions on a rational basis, it is necessary to have reliable evaluation data on all aspects of an organization's distance education efforts. Hence evaluation (discussed in the next section) is fundamental to good budget decision making.

Levels of Decision Making

Budget decisions must be made at many different levels: institutional, departmental, programmatic, and in individual courses. Each level of decision making will have different priorities. For example, senior administrators are likely to be concerned with marketing/promotion (to keep up enrollments and revenue), whereas faculty would probably be preoccupied with maintaining student support services or the number of academic staff (which affects their teaching success). Consequently, budget decisions are often accompanied by power struggles within the organization, as each constituency attempts to obtain as much of the budget as possible. To avoid turning such struggles into acrimonious conflicts, administrators must continually emphasize that all budget decisions are made on the basis of data and all groups wishing to influence the budget must present data to justify their requests or plans.

Administrative Activities

One of the most difficult budget categories to which administrators must allocate funds is administration itself. Most administrators take pride in running a "lean and mean" operation and having the smallest administrative staff possible. However, this may create an administrative function that is understaffed and not able to run things properly. Furthermore, good administration requires extensive planning, and this needs market research and other studies which are more difficult to justify to the faculty or the public than creating new courses, hiring more academic staff, or buying new technology. Thus, many studies that should be done are skipped or done in a very limited way.

On the other hand, institutions sometimes get "top-heavy" in terms of administrative staff (especially assistants and middle managers), and then administration consumes an inordinate amount of the budget while producing little useful work. Senior administrators must continually collect cost-effectiveness data on their administrative operations just like all other aspects of a distance education organization to determine the appropriate portion of the budget that should be spent on administration.

Scheduling

In traditional education all instruction is organized into class sessions and semesters of fixed durations, so a great deal of adminstrative time and effort is devoted to developing and reorganizing schedules (timetables) for students and teachers. Indeed, funding and accreditation of schools is based on student attendance in an exact number of classes. In most forms of distance education, scheduling is far less significant. The key scheduling concerns in the implementation (compared with the design stages) of distance education are course registration, completion dates, and student pacing. Rooms do have to be scheduled of course for teleconference sites.

As we saw in Chapter 6, scheduling of course development (rather than students or facilities) is a very important responsibility of the administration. Because course materials and programs must be prepared far in advance of their use, it is essential that a well-defined schedule be maintained. Usually this takes the form of a work plan that lists all of the tasks that must be completed, the deadlines for each task, and who is responsible for completing the task. It is the responsibility of the administrator in charge of the distance education program to ensure that the development schedule is followed so the materials and programs are ready when the students and instructors need them.

Student Completion

In independent study courses, students are usually responsible for setting their own pace. Most programs establish a maximum period of study (e.g., six months or one year) in which a course must be completed. Within this time period, students can complete their study according to their own timetables. Some programs allow open enrollment while others specify certain registration periods. On the other hand, programs that involve teleconferencing or television broadcasts usually have a fixed class schedule with well-defined beginning and end dates.

For most students, some form of pacing is needed to successfully complete the course (see discussion of student success factors in Chapter 8). Therefore, it is common for instructors or tutors to establish a schedule of due dates for assignments even in an independent study course. It is important that such schedules are reasonably planned and are based on the amount of work involved and turnaround times. Taylor and Reid (1993) discuss the use of PERT techniques to plan appropriate completion schedules for independent study courses.

The Issue of Equivalence

One of the major concerns of administrators responsible for distance education programs is equivalence. They want to be sure that courses offered by distance education meet the same standards of teaching and provide the same learning opportunities as any traditional class in any system or institution. In the absence of physical presence in a classroom, how can the administrator be confident that students are actually receiving the instruction? This concern reflects the historic preoccupation of educational administrators with "seat time" (time spent in the classroom) as a measure of teaching/learning accomplished instead of focusing on the skills and knowledge acquired by the students, (i.e., competency-based instruction). If accomplishment was evaluated by learning outcomes as measured through exams, projects, and assignments, the physical location where the learning occurs would become irrelevant. This is something that would appeal to many learners, but not to some faculty or administrators.

The issue of equivalence also arises in the context of programs that involve multiple providers. For example, many of the satellite teleconference consortia offer courses that originate from a variety of different institutions. How can the administration be assured that all the courses are of equivalent quality? The reality is that this can never be assured, even across courses in the same program from the same institution! However, to the extent that every course offering must pass some sort of curriculum review within its own institution, and the consortium assesses each offering against a quality checklist, a reasonable level of equivalence can be maintained.

Finally, there is the issue of equivalence in terms of disadvantaged or handicapped students. For example, the American Disabilities Act (ADA), which became law in 1993, stipulates that all public institutions must take the needs of the disabled into account in the development and delivery of education. Clearly, this should be a concern of those who design and administer distance education programs (see ITC, 1995).

Quality Assessment

One of the most important administrative functions in an organization is quality assessment (also called quality control). While everyone in an educational institution has a role to play in producing high-quality instruction, administrators are responsible for measuring quality and taking action to improve it. Some of the administrative roles already discussed pertain to this function. A number of other factors can be assessed, including number and quality of applications and enrollments, student achievement, student satisfaction, faculty satisfaction, program or institutional reputation, and quality of course materials. Each of these factors reflects different aspects of quality.

Student application and enrollment trends indicate the overall health of the program or institution, insofar as continually increasing or stable rates of applications and enrollments means that students want to take the courses offered. This suggests that the organization is doing a good job of tracking changes in demographic and socioeconomic variables and adjusting its offerings to changing needs. It also may be an indicator of satisfactory teaching and good word-of-mouth promotion by satisfied students.

Student achievement should be one of the most critical aspects of quality measured; however, it is very difficult to assess. The proportion of students receiving good grades in courses is not always a helpful item since it reflects the grading threshold of instructors, unless, as is usual in other countries, external examiners are employed. In professional areas where students have to take certification exams (e.g., law, medicine, engineering), it is possible to examine the achievement of students relative to other institutions. However, the kind of student achievement data that would be most valuable, namely job performance or work competency evaluations, is almost impossible to obtain due to the complexities of conducting studies in the workplace. Most programs usually settle for anecdotal information about the impact of courses collected from interviews of graduates.

As was pointed out in a previous chapter, student satisfaction data is relatively easy to collect and is important. It is routine for students to evaluate a course at its conclusion, being asked to rate or comment on the content, course organization, the instructor(s)/tutor(s), instructional materials, and the delivery system used. Such data is usually scrutinized by the course manager and sometimes the department head or dean. This provides at least a minimal check on the quality of courses as far as the perceptions of students are concerned. However, student satisfaction data does not measure how effective a course is in terms of students' learning, nor does it assess the validity or relevance of the content taught.

Similarly, faculty satisfaction is an important measure but one that has a number of limitations. Faculty can assess the extent to which existing teaching strategies and materials appear to be effective, whether student support services are adequate, and whether courses appear to meet the needs of students or their employers. Faculty evaluation data tends to be biased and does not present an objective picture of any of these factors. On the other hand, most faculty are very concerned with effective teaching and make recommendations that they believe will improve it. Given the sensitivity of most distance education courses and programs to the effectiveness of the instructor or tutor, it seems highly prudent to pay attention to faculty evaluations (Purdy and Wright, 1992).

To a large extent, enrollments are closely related to the reputation of the program or institution. If graduates are satisfied with their courses, and employers who hire those graduates are also satisfied with their job performance, they will recommend the program to others and this will result in enrollments. Reputation is also enhanced by winning awards and honors from professional associations. Institutions sometimes spend considerable sums of money on marketing and promotional efforts aimed at prospective students or the public in an attempt to establish an image of quality.

Finally, it is possible to assess the quality of course materials or courses in terms of standards established by national associations. For example, NUCEA publishes names of prizewinning independent study courses. The evaluation form that it uses to evaluate potential prizewinners is used internally by many organizations to assess the quality of courses they develop or are considering for adoption. Checklists exist for evaluating all forms of distance education offerings, from satellite teleconferences to home study courses. Note that such evaluations are done on the merits of the course materials or content and are independent of student achievement or satisfaction data. A key element in this kind of evaluation is the extent to which the materials or content match the instructional objectives and reflect appropriate learning strategies for the students and subject matter involved. Recently, there have been attempts to develop national and international quality assessment methods for instructional "products" (Freeman, 1991).

Policy

In Chapter 5 we raised some questions about how policies are made with regard to distance education. Making policy and ensuring it is followed takes a major effort on the part of an institution's management. To the extent that distance education is different from traditional classroom instruction, or involves the collaboration of different groups, or might divert resources of money and people's time from conventional methods, it will raise issues that require policies to be made not only within the institution, but also outside, perhaps at state or even national levels.

For example, the credentialing of teachers and the accreditation of institutions have historically been regional or state matters. However, with distance education, teaching easily crosses state lines, not to mention the borders of countries, which is a reality that is only now emerging (see Chapter 11). This cross-state transmission creates problems for administrators who have to be guided by policies that were written for a single state or geographical region.

The Challenge for Regulators

It is the responsibility of officials in state departments of higher education to monitor higher education offerings and to protect consumers against fraudulent and low-quality providers of distance education programs. This yields two problems: One is presented by the predatory for-profit organization that seeks to exploit a demand for credentials and certification that can be bought in the shortest time and with the least effort. Of course, consumers need help in recognizing such institutions, but their numbers are relatively small, and state regulators are able to control them.

What might be a more difficult problem is whether and how to regulate the growth that can be expected in offerings by reputable institutions that want to use electronic media to transmit their programs across state borders. If a professor at a nationally recognized, fully accredited university offers a course within the state by means of audio-, audiographic, computer, or videoconference and receives a request from a student in an adjacent state to join the conference, should the professor refuse or submit a formal application to the regulators of that state to receive permission to teach? What if there is one student in each of 5 or 10 or 50 states? And what if the professor's colleagues in the department are also offering courses to distant locations. Are there to be multiple sets of applications?

It is hard to see how regulators can hope to control the quality of such offerings or influence the individuals who want to purchase them since the program is received through telephone, modem, and personal computer by the student at home. All the evidence is that with the accelerating development of fiber-optic and ISDN, the extent and frequency of in-home interactive information delivery services will increase to a degree that will confound any attempts at control.

For further discussion of policy issues, see Reilly and Gulliver (1992).

Statewide Planning of Technology

No state has yet worked out a policy that will allow the design of a statewide distance education system, though Florida has come close. Eventually, statewide systems will have to be created, since it is the only way to obtain the economies of scale needed to make proper and efficient use of the technological and human resources that are available.

In the meantime, however, many states have been engaged in analysis and planning concerning the use of technology. It is a very different thing of course to plan to use new technology without inventing new organizational structures to efficiently use it, but that is what has been happening. By now you are aware that distance education requires changes in the use of human resources when designing and delivering programs leading to changes in the schools and universities, changes in the roles of teachers, and changes in the organization of education—in short, much greater changes than can be anticipated by a focus on technology alone.

However, an understanding of the arrangements made by states to govern and coordinate the use of technology gives us a perspective on how they may deal with the larger issues of distance education in the future.

In the 1980s various states began to develop policy concerned with technology, particularly the technology of telecommunications. Many undertook inventories or other systematic studies of their resources, including Texas (1983), Florida (1985), Minnesota (1986), Missouri (1988), and Oklahoma (1981, 1985, and 1988). Most of these studies resulted in recommendations on specific, often regulatory, issues concerning receiving programs from out of state. The Minnesota review addressed out-of-state regulation and also policies regarding funding, faculty development, course development, and protection of property rights. Oklahoma's Regents "Policy and Procedures Pertaining to Off-campus Programs, Electronic Media, and Non-Traditional Methodology" (1988) provided a basis for authorization, purpose, standards, planning coordination, fiscal provisions, reporting, and guidelines for telecourses.

A second approach to policymaking regarding technology at state level has been to set up coordinating "procedures" bodies, intended to provide policies and governance to control resource sharing and to avoid duplication of services. In 1986 the West Virginia Board of Regents recommended ways of improving

Project ALLTEL: A Policy Study for Distance Education

In the mid-1980s, Project ALLTEL (Assessing Long Distance Learning via Telecommunications) was initiated as a joint effort of the Council on Postsecondary Accreditation (COPA) and the State Higher Education Executive Officers (SHEEO). The purpose of the project was to develop a policy framework for the licencing and accreditation of telecommunications-based distance education. In October 1985, the project issued its report which included a template for use by accreditating and state licencing agencies to evaluate distance learning activities. The report stated one of the thorny issues in the regulation of distance education programs:

> The legal issues surrounding the interstate delivery of telecommunications-based higher education are both many and manifestly uncertain. The paucity of legal precedent leaves unanswered such fundamental questions as whether a state can exercise its power to regulate a telecommunications-based provider, how that power can be exercised and what are the basic rights of the learner and of the institution. It is clear that a state has only limited authority to regulate the telecommunications medium, but rather more power to regulate the institutional provider—assuming of course that the institution had created sufficient "physical presence" within the state to trigger its own authorization statute.

From the point of view of distance education providers, the fundamental problem addressed by project ALLTEL is the level of effort and costs associated with obtaining accreditation for their courses in multiple states and regions with differing policies and procedures for accreditation. It was hoped that the ALLTEL template would be adopted by all agencies so that licensing and accreditation would be standardized nationally.

Further discussion of the ALLTEL report can be found in Lenn (1991).

cooperation among providers; similar issues were addressed in a report on the work of the Kentucky Telecommunications Consortium (1988); in 1987 a task force of the Board of Higher Education in Maryland recommended setting up an Advisory Board on Instructional Technologies. In Virginia a task force reported on the need for statewide coordination; since then Virginia has had "Regulations Governing the Approval of Certain Institutions to Confer Degrees, Diplomas, and Certificates" to govern the delivery of programs by out-of-state institutions.

In 31 states, according to Hezel (1987), including Kentucky, South Carolina, and Nebraska, governance and coordination of educational telecommunications is assigned to the public broadcasting board, while in others, such as Florida, Delaware, and New Jersey, it is assigned to an administrative agency such as a department of telecommunications. Still other states, such as Texas, Oklahoma, and Michigan, give governance to state departments of education or higher education.

According to Hezel, the advantage of having educational telecommunications coordinated by public broadcasting organizations is that they have technical facilities and expertise and are aware of technological alternatives. The disadvantage is that public broadcasters tend to be preoccupied with broadcasting as the sole method of transmission, and also to be oriented away from instructional programming toward general audience programming. Where governance and coordination lies with state telecommunications agencies, the advantage is that they tend to cut across institutional boundaries, and coordination can save a lot of money. In very few states do postsecondary institutions participate in planning so that statewide consensus is difficult to achieve. Most higher education institutions plan for their own instructional and marketing needs, and as Hezel says, "Colleges and universities are notoriously independent in adopting technology, and appear to engage in technological competition with other higher education institutions" (p. 4).

State departments of education tend to be strong locations for telecommunications planning. In Kentucky, Virginia, and Florida, the department of education has provided funding for K-12 technology initiatives. Furthermore, many school districts have individual arrangements with colleges and universities to receive advanced placement and enrichment courses via telecommunications systems. Hezel comments, "Those arrangements tend to frustrate planning for a single educational telecommunications system, but they appear to satisfy the immediate needs of the school districts."

In general, says Hezel, statewide educational telecommunications systems are strong in those states where there is firm support from the state government. It follows that the education of politicians in instructional technology (and we would say, distance education more broadly) is a high priority if state funding is to be made available. The possibility of developing a statewide system is much better when the governor and key political leaders are supportive. However, as Hezel says, there needs to be "a realistic understanding about limitations of state resources for telecommunications development."

The Issue of Teacher Certification

The Office of Technology Assessment (OTA, 1989, p. 120) states: "The certification of the teleteacher is the most prominent issue that State Education Agencies (SEAs) are grappling with regarding distance learning. This is particularly true when a complete course of instruction originates in one state and is received in another state." Some clues to the issues involved in teacher certification are provided by England (1991) and shown in Table 9-2.

As seen in England's data, only one state actually required someone who teaches at a distance to be certified to do so. All others assume that if a classroom teacher has a subject or grade-level certification, that person is able to teach distant learners. However, most states do not trust the qualifications of persons who teach in other states, and only one in four will allow an out-of-state distance teacher to teach without obtaining in-state certification. England states that Hawaii said that one reason for this was concern of teachers' unions about teachers from another state replacing them without

Table 9-2   **A Survey of State-level Involvement in Distance Education at the
Elementary and Secondary Levels** (England, 1991)

	Percentage
Proportion of states involved in use of telecommunications	90
Proportion planning or involved in either state networking or regional or national consortia for distance education	93
Proportion having a state level department to coordinate distance education	56
Proportion providing funds for development of distance education	59
Proportion anticipating special legislation to fund distance education	68
Proportion requiring special certification for persons teaching at a distance	2.5 (i.e., one state)
Proportion allowing out-of-state certified teachers to teach without additional certification	27
Proportion with graduate teacher education programs offered by distance education	59
Proportion that would recognize credits earned by distance education for in-service credit	73
Proportion allowing distance education credits for recertification in-state	75
Proportion allowing distance education credits for initial certification in-state	49
Proportion allowing provisional certification for out-of-state teachers arriving in-state	63
Proportion allowing provisional certification for out-of-state teachers teaching from out of state	37
Proportion of respondents believing there will be a move towards a national certification process	44

having the training they thought would be essential to meet the needs of their students (p. 10).

It is also noticeable that while 73 percent of states would recognize credits for teachers earned through distance education programs for in-service training purposes, and 75 percent would accept distance education credits for recertification of persons who physically moved into their state, only 49 percent would accept distance education credits for initial certification. While 63 percent of states welcomed out-of-state teachers who moved in-state by giving provisional certification, a similar welcome was not offered out-of-state teachers who

The Florida Distance Learning Network (FDLN)

In August 1995 the Chancellor of the State University System of Florida established a task force to recommend a policy for setting up a statewide distance education system. The following are extracts from the Report of the Task Force:

> To have a major statewide distance learning system, Florida does not need a substantial increase in resources, but needs to set up mechanisms to use existing resources more effectively. In short, Florida needs to adopt an integrated systems approach to the provision of education and training through distance education.
>
> The Task Force recommends that a public corporation to be called the Florida Distance Learning Network (FDLN) be established to coordinate and link the various existing resources of the state—to plan, design and deliver credit and non-credit distance education on a program by program basis.
>
> The Task Force also recommends that a small number of distance learning projects, designed in 1995 for statewide or regional delivery, begin in October 1995 (or if possible sooner). These will help establish the Florida Distance Learning Network, and also test and demonstrate its effectiveness in coordinating resources to provide high quality, cost effective learning for large numbers of Florida's citizens.
>
> FDLN will be accountable to a Board of Governors, which will be the primary policy making body. The Board will be made up of representatives from the constituent institutional members, with equal representation of the three sectors of public education in Florida, i.e. K-12, community colleges, and state universities, with representation also from public agencies and the private corporate sector.
>
> The Coordinating Center for Distance Learning (CCDL) is the network's management and administrative center. The staff of the CCDL will consist of a Director and six professional staff, one each in charge of a unit responsible for: Planning and Evaluation, Course and Program Design and Development, Media and Program Delivery, Instruction and Learner Support, Training, Documentation and Information.
>
> There will be an Advisory Committee for each of the six units at the Coordinating Center. These Committees represent all agencies of education and training, and provide close links with member institutions of FDLN. They are the principal means of liaison, cooperation, coordination and communication within the Network and between the Network and the Center. Each committee will meet at least monthly.
>
> The Chairs of each of the six Advisory Committees will come from the member institutions of FDLN and will constitute an Executive Committee, the main responsibility of which will be to recommend to the Governing Board course and program projects from among proposals submitted by the member institutions of FDLN assisted by the FDLN Planning and Evaluation Unit.
>
> Florida's universities, community colleges, and public schools have the necessary academic talent and the necessary technology to design and deliver high quality distance education. All that is required to engage the State's existing resources in a cost effective response to the increases in demand for education and training and the changes in the student population, both current and projected, is to systematically organize the human and communications resources that already exist so that they work across institutional and sectorial lines. The establishment of the Florida

(continued)

The Florida Distance Learning Network (cont.)

Distance Learning Network and its Coordinating Center for Distance Learning will provide such a mechanism. It offers the promise of a powerful leveraging of the State's resources, the addition of new programs to complement the existing ones, at a relatively very low cost.

To accomplish this is primarily a role for policy makers, and comes down eventually to a question of political vision and political will. If policy makers will lead on this, the means are at hand to deal with many of the State's educational problems, and in so doing to set an example for the nation.

In March 1995 a bill was presented to the Florida legislature. It contained the following provisions:

It is the intent of the Legislature to establish a cost efficient coordinated system for distance education to:

(a) Increase student access to education,

(b) Maximize the use of telecommunications technologies and their application to provide affordable distance education,

(c) Promote interagency cooperation and promote partnerships,

(d) Secure any federal or private funds and other resources in support of distance education, and

(e) Manage all distance education resources to maximize return on investment with the goal of creating a financially independent, self-supporting, statewide system for distance education.

   (1) There is created a not-for-profit statutory corporation, to be known as "The Florida Distance Learning Network, Inc."

   (2) The Florida Distance Learning Network Inc., shall be governed by a board of directors. The board of directors shall consist of the following members:

   (a) The Governor or designee

   (b) The Commissioner of Education or designee

   (c) The Chancellor of the State University System or designee

   (d) The Executive Director of the State Community College System or designee

   (e) The director of the Florida Public Broadcasting Service

   (f) The Executive Director of the PostSecondary Education Planning Commission

   (g) The Secretary of the Department of Corrections or designee

   (h) The Secretary of the Department of Management Services or designee

   (i) The Secretary of State or designee

   (j) A member of the Senate who shall be appointed by the President of the Senate and serve at the pleasure of the President

   (k) A member of the House of Representatives who shall be appointed by the Speaker of the House of Representatives and serve at the pleasure of the Speaker

(l) Four members from the private sector, appointed by the Governor, one of whom represents the cable industry and one of whom represents the telecommunications industry

    (m) Two school board members, appointed by the Governor, one from a school district with over 50,000 enrollment and one from a school district with under 50,000 enrollment.

Among responsibilities of the Florida Distance Learning Network:

Developing and maintaining a strategic plan for using technology to improve the delivery of and access to education. The initial plan shall be developed by January 31, 1996, and be submitted to the Governor, the President of the Senate and the Speaker of the House of Representatives. The plan shall address the needs of all educational delivery systems and include the following:

> A component of distance learning in which education programs, reports or programs and accountability data are delivered to individuals located in diverse settings, including but not limited to educational facilities, public libraries, state agencies, community facilities, businesses and homes. This component must consider existing public and private networks and comunications systems and their potential in delivering distance learning.

> The Florida Distance Learning Network, Inc., shall annually award grants to school districts, area technical centers, community colleges, state universities, and independent institutions eligible to participate in state student assistance programs established in Part 1V of Chapter 240. The Council shall give priority to cooperative proposals submitted by two or more institutions or delivery systems.

The proposals shall include:

1. Information which describes the educational significance of the program or service in addressing state educational priorities

2. The target population for the program

3. The program content to be transmitted

4. The support services to be provided

5. Provisions to use at least 20 percent of any funds awarded for training both faculty and student learners in the use and application of the products delivered

Source: Addendum to the Master Plan: 1993 through 1997-8. Tallahassee. Florida Board of Regents.

wanted to teach in-state by distance methods. Only one in three states would give such provisional status.

England concludes his commentary on the teacher certification data with some comments on the possibility of national certification:

> With certification requirements set by the state, a more confined locus of control exists and therefore the quality can be monitored more effectively than if requirements were imposed at the national level. National certification is a very complex and highly political issue. Virtually everyone in our society is exposed to some form of formal education for a period of time. This involvement makes education everyone's business, and everyone will have an opinion about students, schools, teachers and ways to improve the system. A move toward national certification may or may not be something to consider. If distance education develops in the future at the same rate that it has developed over the past five years there will need to be rethinking about the requirements to teach in our schools (p.14).

Administrative Barriers to Adoption of Distance Education

What are the barriers that prevent educational institutions and the states from redirecting more of their human and other resources to distance education? One of the reasons for the slow rate of change is found in the administrative procedures that were designed to support an older model of education, and that actually impede the evolution of new systems. These administrative barriers can be found at federal, regional, state, and institutional levels.

At the federal level, barriers include the criteria used to determine what programs are eligible for federal funding and the criteria applied in monitoring and evaluating programs. These are all heavily biased toward traditional forms of provision.

At regional level, the criteria applied in giving institutions their official accreditation to teach are based on the practices of campus-based learning, faculty-centered teaching, and classroom-based instruction. Exceptionally, the Southern Association of Colleges and Schools (SACS) has generated procedures for evaluating distance education when institutions in its jurisdiction undergo the accreditation process.

At state level, there are mechanisms that drive continuing investment in bricks-and-mortar education and prevent the expenditures that would establish virtual universities based on a telecommunications network. The typical funding formulae that states use to decide on allocation of resources, being based on numbers of traditional daytime students, systematically generates on-campus classroom space for 8:00 AM to 5:00 PM teaching, and underprovides not only the communications technology but also the building facilities needed for off-campus learner support and instruction for distance learners.

At the institutional level the barriers include some of the administrative structures and procedures that are supposed to serve students but are often inappropriate for distance learners. They are found in the rules and regulations concerning registration, tuition payment procedures, student support services, library services, examinations, and most especially the provision of instruction at times and places convenient to the learner.

Some of the most serious administrative barriers at institutional level concern the management of faculty. It is unusual for distance teaching to be named in a job description when faculty are being recruited. It is unusual for faculty to be assigned distance teaching as part of their "on-load" teaching responsibilities. Few institutions provide training programs in distance teaching. There are few instances of institutions identifying criteria of good distance teaching and applying them in recognizing and rewarding their faculty. When a professor is considered for promotion or is to be awarded tenure in a university, it is unusual for that person's distance teaching to be as carefully evaluated as conventional classroom lecturing. Rarely does a college dean reward a professor with a salary adjustment in recognition of work in distance teaching.

The administrative structures make it very difficult for faculty to be released to work on the design and production of good-quality distance teaching in conventional institutions. Every teacher is required to present a set number of classes in conventional ways. Procedures do not allow faculty to be organized and administered as design teams, or even to allow them to be released from conventional teaching for substantial periods so they can work with the graphic designers, instructional designers, evaluation specialists, video and audio specialists, and others to develop courses for future presentation to distant learners.

Other administrative barriers include the problems of territoriality and the need to devise ways of rewarding institutions for collaborating instead of competing; intellectual property and the need to reform policies to take into account the different roles of faculty when working in design teams; collective bargaining and the need to encourage experimentation and innovation in faculty hiring arrangements.

Developing a Change Policy at Institutional Level

Most educational and training institutions share three significant problems in introducing distance education:

1. A long-established academic culture that holds a firm view of teaching as an individual's act in a classroom

2. Power to change the system is held by senior faculty and administrators, most of whom are satisfied with the system that gave them power

3. A rich array of technological and human resources is dissipated in a system of faculties, divisions, and departments, each of which guards its own interests

There are only a limited number of options for administrators faced with these issues, and a few key strategies to adopt.

The first key strategy is to identify the innovators in the organization, the small number of people who exist at every level who are interested in change. These people should be helped with money, time, and external assistance to organize themselves, to develop a consensus of ideas and strategies for developing distance education in the organization.

Penn State: A Policy for an Institution-wide System

The issues associated with introducing an organization-wide distance education policy were addressed at The Pennsylvania State University in 1992 by the creation of a task force. The report from the task force concluded:

> In our view, distance education will become a substantial part of the University's future regardless of this report or any actions that are taken as a result of it. We believe that the external forces of an evolving student population, the revolutionary advances in technology, and the changing economic picture for all of higher education will eventually bring an enhanced and expanded use of distance education methodologies into the central strategies of most major universities. . . . However, the Task Force believes that, at this moment, there is a "window of opportunity" that is open to the University that will allow it to capitalize on existing strengths and assume a position of national leadership in distance education. We believe that this could ensure the future viability of our distance education efforts, increase the quality and efficiency of many of our academic programs, bring national recognition and prestige to the University through accomplishments in this area, and serve as a source of both cost-savings and revenue generation.

The recommendations of the task force included:

- the creation of a university-wide unit to facilitate the development of distance education at the university

- the rewriting of tenure and promotion procedures to recognize distance education activities as being equivalent to all other categories of teaching

- the assignment of substantial resources to the distance education unit to support program development and a significant portion of revenue or cost-savings generated by distance education efforts be returned to the unit

- the proposed distance education unit develop demonstration projects throughout the university to establish the potential benefits and applications

The second step is for the innovators to be enabled to undertake a demonstration project. Institutional change will not occur as a result of argument, reasoning, or persuasion alone. The majority of members of the institution will not become persuaded of the viability of distance education until they see the process at work, see a good standard of teaching, see the achievements of the students. They will lose fear of change as they see the professional satisfaction of their peers who engage in the distance teaching activity.

It is critical, absolutely vital, that the demonstration projects be of the highest possible standard, since failure or mediocre results will have exactly the opposite effect from what is desired. For this reason it is imperative that financial, technological, and human resources be ruthlessly focused. The temptation to spread resources over a number of projects must be resisted. For that to hap-

Penn State University has declared leadership in distance education as a strategic goal. Here participants from around the nation attend one of the frequent national conferences held at Penn State.

The task force and its report are illustrative of the kind of policy initiatives that are needed in large organizations (whether universities, school systems, companies, or government agencies) to fully implement distance education.

Source: The Report of the Task Force on Distance Education. The Pennsylvania State University, University Park, PA. November 1992.

pen the organization needs what is probably the most important ingredient if change is to occur—a high-level administrator with a vision of distance education and the courage to implement it.

Given such leadership and a team of innovators, resources can then be organized with the aim of showing how a distance education system works. *All* the technologies of the institution must be brought into play; several million dollars are likely to be required to design, produce, and deliver a single demonstration project of sufficient quality. If someone with true experience of such projects is not available, the temptation to give the job to one of the establishment must be resisted; someone should be brought in from outside, perhaps even from an overseas open university.

Summary

This chapter has discussed a number of major issues related to the administration of distance education and the development of policy regarding distance education at institutional and state levels.

- Planning is one of the critical management tasks that administrators must perform. This includes formulating goals and objectives for the institution; balancing aspirations with currently available resources; assessing changes in student, business, or societal demands; tracking technology alternatives; and projecting future resource and financial needs.

- Some of the staffing issues of concern to administrators in distance education are whether to hire permanant or part-time employees; their knowlege and understanding of distance education; their training and formal qualifications; monitoring and supervising their work.

- There are many policy issues to be addressed at institutional, state, and federal levels, including teacher credentialing and program accreditation; equivalency of course offerings; the process of deciding to offer distance education courses; and conforming with state and federal initiatives in distance education.

- Resource issues include choosing the best delivery system, the proper use of local facilities (especially libraries), hands-on learning activities, and the role of simulations.

- Budget decisions lie at the heart of administration. Some of the most important budget decisions have to do with allocation of funds to different components of the system, dealing with priorities at different levels of the institution, and how much to spend on adminstration itself.

- Scheduling concerns include student completion dates and pacing as well as the development of materials and programs.

- Quality assurance is a primary function of administration. Components that can be evaluated for quality include number of applications or enrollments, student achievement, student satisfaction, faculty satisfaction, program and institutional reputation, and course materials/offerings.

- Distance education cannot simply grow on the back of existing educational structures and policies. Policies must be created, and for that purpose policymaking organs must be set up. Penn State University provides a model at the university level, and the state of Florida provides one at state level. In both, task forces representing the interested parties prepared policies for adoption by university and state administrations.

For further discussion of administrative issues in distance education, see Murgatroyd (1992), Paul (1990), Rumble (1986), or Willis (1993).

CHAPTER 10

The Theoretical Basis for Distance Education

Theory is very, very valuable. A theory is a representation of everything that we know about something. Theory gives us a common framework, a common perspective, and a common vocabulary that help us ask questions in a sensible way and make sense of problems. By summarizing what we already know, theory helps us identify what we don't know, and so it is the starting point for deciding what really needs to be researched. Because most people do not read theory, a lot of the information collected about technology in education is not very important, while questions that are important are neglected. In this chapter we will tell you about one general pedagogical theory of distance education that can be used to guide the creating of useful research questions.

In the summer of 1972, Michael G. Moore made a presentation to the Ninth World Conference of the International Council for Correspondence Education, meeting in Warrenton, Virginia. Moore's paper was called "Learner Autonomy: The Second Dimension of Independent Learning," and, as reported later that year in a Canadian journal, it began as follows:

> We started by postulating that the universe of instruction consisted of two families of teaching behaviors, which we referred to as "contiguous teaching" and "distance teaching." After describing conventional, or "contiguous teaching," Moore defined distance teaching as "the family of instructional methods in which the teaching behaviors are executed apart from the learning behaviors, including those that in contiguous teaching would be performed in the learner's presence, so that communication between the learner and the teacher must be facilitated by print, electronic, mechanical, or other devices. (Moore, 1972, p. 76)

This was the first attempt in America to define distance education. During the presentation, Moore went much further and attempted to lay out a general theory of the pedagogy of distance education. For two years he had worked with Charles Wedemeyer at the University of Wisconsin-Madison on a number of projects using communications technologies. At the same time, he studied educational theory and noticed what had not been noticed before—that there was no theory to account for teaching and learning in which "the teaching behaviors are executed apart from the learning behaviors," nor was this kind of teaching and learning mentioned in the existing theories of education. Moore stated to the conference, reported in a subsequent article:

> As we continue to develop various non-traditional methods of reaching the growing numbers of people who cannot or will not attend conventional institutions but who choose to learn apart from their teachers, we should direct some of our resources to the macro-factors: describing and defining the field; discriminating between the various components of this field; identifying the critical elements of the various forms of teaching and learning; building a theoretical framework which will embrace this whole area of education. (Moore, 1973, p. 661)

History of the Term "Distance Education"

The term "distance education" that Moore chose to define the universe of teaching-learning relationships characterized by separation between learners and teachers was one he first heard in a conversation with the Swedish educator, Börje Holmberg. Holmberg was director of the Hermods Correspondence School in Sweden, and being fluent in German, he had read about the work of a group of German researchers at the University of Tübingen. Instead of talking about "correspondence study," these Germans used the terms "Fernstudium," or "distance education," and "Fernunterricht," or "distance teaching." Prominent among the Tübingen researchers were Karl-Heinz Rebel, M. Delling, K. Graff, Günther Dohmen, and Otto Peters. Since they only published their work in German, it only became generally known to English-speaking scholars in later years, mainly due to the efforts of Desmond Keegan (1986), though Wedemeyer had some communication with Rebel.

The Pioneering Work of Otto Peters

In 1965 Peters published a seminal work, "Der Fernunterriccht. Materialien zur Diskussion einer neuen Unterrichtsform ("Distance Education: Sources for the Analysis of a New Form of Teaching"). In 1967 he wrote "Distance Teaching and Industrial Production: A Comparative Interpretation in Outline," which was published in English in 1983. In this article Peters explained how "it becomes clear that distance study is a form of study complementary to our industrial and technological age" (Peters, 1983, p. 95). His thesis is that distance education allows industrial methods to be applied to the design and delivery of instruction, but that unless industrial methods are used, distance education will not be optimally successful. The principles of industrial production should be applied also to the analysis of distance education.

The industrial techniques include planning, division of labor, mass production, automation, standardization, and quality control. Through the use of industrial techniques we can use expensive communications media and distribute courses to many students, while the economies of scale justify the costs involved. If standardized procedures are followed in the production and administration of such courses, the outcomes are reliable and effective and learning can be ensured.

Although Peters's work was not widely known or circulated in the English-speaking world, the Tübingen group's ideas became known to Wedemeyer through the latter's friendship with Karl-Heinz Rebel, and through Wedemeyer, the ideas found their way into the structures of the British Open University.

Towards a Pedagogical Theory

Peters's theory was an organizational theory, and as explained above, it did not circulate in English until the 1980s. The nearest to a theory in English was Wedemeyer's (1971) attempt to define independent study, and his idea of the correspondence learner as independent not only in space and time but also potentially independent in controlling and directing learning. Moore was attracted by this idea of learner independence and the possibility that distance could actually be beneficial for the independence of the learner. He was working with Wedemeyer, but was more influenced than Wedemeyer by the writings of Carl Rogers, Abraham Maslow, Charlotte Buhler, and other so-called "humanistic" psychologists. At this time also the ideas of andragogy promoted by Malcolm Knowles and the self-directed learning research of Alan Tough were at the height of their popularity.

Moore gathered and analyzed many hundreds of courses of "teaching-learning in which teachers and learners carry out their essential tasks and responsibilities apart from one another" and on this empirical basis, offered his theory at the 1972 ICDE Conference. The theory was intended to be global and descriptive. In other words, it was to be of sufficient generality to accommodate *all* forms of distance education, and to provide a conceptual tool that would help students and others to place any distance education program in relationship to any other. "You are creating an equivalent of the periodic table," advised Professor Robert Boyd; "Follow Linnaeas," said Charles Wedemeyer. Just as that medieval scientist sought to identify the fundamental characteristics that would define living creatures but also assist in classifying them, Moore sought to create a system that would make it possible to classify distance learning courses and programs.

What emerged combines both Peters's perspective of distance education as a highly structured mechanical system and Wedemeyer's perspective of a more learner-centered, interactive relationship with a tutor. It is a global theory because it has a place for both these perspectives, and more important, for every variation of these perspectives. Since 1986 it has been known as the theory of transactional distance.

The Theory of Transactional Distance

The first postulate of the theory of transactional distance is that distance is a pedagogical phenomenon. While it is true that distance education is the universe of all educational activities in which learners are separated by space and/or by time, what is of interest and importance to practitioners and theorists alike is the effect that this distance has on instruction, on the learners, the teachers, the forms of communication and interaction, the curriculum, and the management of the program. When we speak of distance learning, we do not speak of an educational course that is no different from "contiguous" courses except for the physical separation of learners and teacher. This distance is a distance of understandings and perceptions caused by the geographic distance, that have to be overcome by teachers, learners, and educational organizations if effective, deliberate, planned learning is to occur. The procedures to overcome this distance are instructional design and interaction procedures, and to emphasize that this distance is pedagogical, not geographic, we use the term "transactional distance."

Distance Education as a Transaction

The concept of transaction was derived from Dewey and developed by Boyd and Apps (1980). As explained by Boyd and Apps, it "connotes the interplay among the environment, the individuals, and the patterns of behaviors in a situation" (p. 5). The transaction that we call distance education is the interplay between people who are teachers and learners, in environments that have the special characteristic of being separate from one another, and a consequent set of special teaching and learning behaviors. It is the physical distance that leads to a communications gap, a psychological space of potential misunderstandings between the behaviors of instructors and those of the learners, and this is the transactional distance.

This transactional distance is a continuous rather than a discrete variable; in other words, transactional distance is relative rather than absolute. As long as there is a learner and teacher and a means of communication there will be some transactional distance. If there is neither learner nor teacher nor a communication channel, there can be no transactional distance, because there can be no educational transaction! It follows that, as has been pointed out for example by Rumble (1986), there is some transactional distance in any educational event, even those in which learners and teachers meet face-to-face in the same environment. What is normally referred to as distance education is that subset of educational events in which the separation of teacher and learner is so significant that it affects their behaviors in major ways. The separation actually dictates that teachers plan, present content, interact, and perform the other processes of teaching in significantly different ways from the face-to-face environment. In short, the transactional distance is such that special organizational and teaching behaviors are essential. How special will depend on the degree of the transactional distance.

As she thinks about the issues presented in her study guide and audio tape and prepares her responses, the student engages in an on-going dialog with her instructor.

These special teaching behaviors fall into two clusters: dialog and structure. We can describe transactional distance by looking at these teaching behaviors. Similarly, if we are designing courses, we can think about how much to invest in each of these clusters of teaching behaviors, or in other words, how much transactional distance we, or our students, will tolerate.

Dialog

Dialog is a term that helps us focus on the interplay of words, actions, and ideas and any other interactions between teacher and learner when one gives instruction and the other responds. The extent and nature of this dialog is determined by the educational philosophy of the individual or group responsible for the design of the course, by the personalities of teacher and learner, by the subject matter of the course, and by environmental factors. One important environmental factor that affects dialog is the existence and size of a learning group. If everything else is controlled, it is probable there will be more dialog between an instructor and a single learner than with any particular learner in a group of learners. Another environmental variable that influences dialog is language; it is found that persons working in a foreign language are likely to interact less with an instructor than those who share the instructor's tongue.

One of the most important environmental variables is the medium of communication. For example, in an independent study course, each individual learner has a dialog with the instructor as one builds on the ideas of the other in an ongoing correspondence by mail. Because it is in writing, this is a highly structured and slow dialog. More dialog still is likely in a course taught by computer conference, in which there may be fast and frequent responses by teacher and each student to the inputs of each other. Audioconferencing by telephone is usually a highly dialogic process. However, as indicated before, other variables may intervene to lower the dialog. For example, since the audioconference is likely to be group based, there will be less dialog for each individual student. Also, foreign students usually feel more comfortable and engage in more dialog by the text-based, asynchronous computer conference than they do in the faster, synchronous, audioconference.

Some courses, such as those using videotelecourses, have very little or no dialog. It is possible to learn Spanish as an isolated learner using the excellent *Destinos* Annenberg/CPB Project course. When watching these television programs, a student might actually speak out loud, giving a response to something the television teacher says, but since there is no feedback to the instructor, the instructor is not able to respond to the student, and no dialog occurs. Even in such programs it could be said that a form of dialog occurs, with the learner's dialog being with the person who in some distant place and time organized the program. In this way of thinking, the teacher prepared a set of ideas or information for transmission to and interaction with an unknown distant viewer, and the dialog is what Holmberg (see below) would call "an internal didactic conversation."

Internal Didactic Conversation

Working as professor at the Fernuniversität, or Distance University, in Hagen, Germany, Börje Holmberg selected the learner-teacher dialog as the fundamental idea underlying distance education. Distance teaching, suggested Holmberg (1981), should be a conversation, what he called a "guided didactic conversation." Distance education, he said, " . . . as a method of guided didactic conversation implies that the character of good distance education resembles that of a guided conversation aimed at learning and that the presence of the typical traits of a conversation facilitates learning." In other words, Holmberg places the dialog between student and teacher as the critical defining aspect of distance education (see Holmberg, 1986, 1989).

Course Structure

The second set of variables that determine transactional distance are elements in the course's design. The term used to describe this is "structure." A course consists of such elements as learning objectives, content themes, information presentations, case studies, pictorial and other illustrations, exercises, projects, tests. All these may be very carefully composed, very carefully structured. A design team might pilot-test parts of their course on an experimental group, and thus ascertain exactly how long it will take each student to accomplish each objective. They may measure the reading speed of their students and then tailor the number of pages of reading required for each part of the course.

Instructors may be provided detailed marking schemes to ensure all students achieve the criteria of achievement. They may monitor the learning of each student with great frequency, providing remedial activities for those that need them, and so ensure that every student has accomplished each step of the course in a tightly controlled sequence. The students may be admitted into the course as a cohort, and none may be permitted to move into any content area except at the pace of the whole group. In a study guide, each student might follow the same sequence of study and activity; audio- and videotapes are synchronized very tightly to specific pages in the study guide; discussions by teleconference are carefully organized so that each site and each student is included, according to a carefully scripted plan.

By contrast, a different course may permit students to work through a set of videotapes at their own speed, study a set of readings, and submit written assignments when they feel ready. They may be told to call a tutor if, and only when, they wish to receive advice. Such would be a course with much lower structure than the former course, outlined above. These illustrations should indicate the idea that every educational course or other event has a structure and that some are more structured than others.

Like dialog, structure is determined by the educational philosophy of the teaching organization, the teachers themselves, the academic level of the learners, the nature of the content, and in particular, by the communications media that are employed. Courses are structured in different ways to take into account the need to produce, copy, deliver, and control mediated messages.

Since structure expresses the rigidity or flexibility of the course's educational objectives, teaching strategies, and evaluation methods, it describes the extent to which course components can accommodate or be responsive to each learner's individual needs. A recorded television program, for example, not only permits no dialog but is highly structured, with virtually every activity of the instructor and every minute of time provided for and every piece of content predetermined. There is little or no opportunity for any student to deviate according to personal needs. This can be compared with many teleconference courses, which can be structured in ways that allow students to follow several different paths through the content.

Structure and Dialog Measure Transactional Distance

The recorded telecourse program we mentioned above is highly structured, and teacher-learner dialog is nonexistent. This means the transactional distance is high. In the correspondence course there is more dialog and less structure, so it has less transactional distance. In those teleconference programs that have much dialog and little predetermined structure, the extent of transactional distance is relatively low.

The preceding discussion should make it clear that the extent of dialog and the degree of structure varies from course to course, from program to program. In a course or program with little transactional distance, learners receive directions and guidance through ongoing dialog with their instructors and by using instructional materials that allow modifications to suit their individual needs, learning style, and pace. In more distant courses, there is less dialog. If structure is high, learners have guidance; but if there is neither dialog nor structure, they must make their own decisions about study strategies and decide for themselves how to study, what to study, when, where, in what ways, and to what extent.

Learner Autonomy

The greater the transactional distance, the more such responsibility the learner has to exercise. The reader will remember that freedom to carry on self-directed learning was what Wedemeyer proposed as the second important dimension of independent study. Wedemeyer did not actually refer to it as such, but Moore did. Calling his 1972 ICCE presentation "Learner Autonomy: The Second Dimension of Independent Study," Moore declared that models of distance education that only considered the variables of teaching would be flawed. This was at a time when all education, including correspondence teaching, was under the influence of behaviorist learning theory, and the idea of learners being autonomous individuals constructing their own knowledge based on their own experience received little notice outside some adult education circles.

In the behaviorist view, since distant learners were beyond the immediate environment of the teacher, the main problem was how to optimally control them. Instructors were urged to identify their goals in very specific behavioral terms, to prescribe a highly structured regime of presentation, practice, and reward, and to test and measure achievement of all students according to the precise standards built into the objectives. The purpose of interaction was to test the extent to which learners were achieving the instructor's objectives, and to give the successful learners positive reinforcement. The challenge for the educator was to produce a perfect set of objectives, techniques, and testing devices, one that would fit every learner, in large numbers, at a distance so that no one would deviate, no one would fall between the cracks. The parallel of distance education described in this way with the "industrial model" that Peters was working out at that same time is obvious.

Having accepted the importance of structure as a key element of distance education, Moore believed that in a descriptive theory of distance education, a balancing perspective was needed, one that explained the idiosyncracies and independence of learners as a valuable resource rather than a distracting nuisance. In addition to highly structured courses in which passive learners were trained by irresistibly elegant instructional tools, it was necessary to conceptu-

Children begin life with a high degree of learner autonomy.

alize a dimension that would allow for more collaborative relationships of teachers and learners, which would allow for the fact that many learners chose their own learning objectives and conduct, construct and control much of the learning process.

The concept of learner autonomy is that learners have different capacities for making decisions regarding their own learning. These abilities exist. They are fact. The ability of a learner to develop a personal learning plan in some ways different from others, the ability to find resources for study in one's own work or community environment, and the ability to decide for oneself when progress was satisfactory should not be conceived as extraneous and regrettable noise in a smooth-running, instructor-controlled system. Instead, the degree to which these learner behaviors exist are an important dimension for the classi-fication of all teaching programs, in particular all distance education programs. It is a fact that some programs allow for the greater exercise of learners' auton-omy than others. Therefore, programs can be defined and described in terms of what degree of autonomy learners are expected or permitted to exercise.

Applying the Theory

What determines the success of distance teaching is the extent to which the institution and the individual instructor are able to provide the appropriate structure of learning materials, and the appropriate quantity and quality of dialog between teacher and learner taking into account the extent of the learner's autonomy.

The more highly autonomous the learners, the greater is the distance they can be comfortable with—that is, the less the dialog and the less the structure. For others the goal must be to reduce distance by increasing dialog, perhaps through use of computer conferencing or even personal telephone contact, and by developing well-structured printed support materials. At other times it may be appropriate to design highly structured courses or programs but to limit dialog. For practitioners, the theory helps them understand the particular instructional problems they are faced with, without providing a recipe for solving the problem.

Theoretical Refinements

During the decade of the 1980s, considerable writing was done by many experts to clarify and refine the basic concepts and theoretical foundations we have been discussing. Some of the most salient work includes that of Desmond Keegan, Randy Garrison, Doug Shale, and Myra Baynton.

Desmond Keegan

When he founded the Australian journal *Distance Education* in 1980, Keegan published, in the first issue, his own analysis of what he called "four generally accepted definitions of distance education." From his analysis he listed six components of what he proposed would be a comprehensive definition. The four definitions he analyzed were those of Holmberg, Peters, Moore, and (perhaps rather strangely) the July 1971 Law of France, which regulated distance education in that country. Keegan concluded that the following six elements "are to be regarded as essential for any comprehensive definition":

1. separation of teacher and student
2. influence of an educational organization, especially in the planning and preparation of learning materials
3. use of technical media
4. provision of two-way communication
5. possibility of occasional seminars
6. participation in the most industrial form of education

Keegan's summary of the "four generally accepted definitions" became the most widely cited definition of distance education. In 1986 he repeated his technique, this time analyzing Holmberg, Peters, Moore, and Dohmen. He did not change his list of key elements, but he did state them in a longer form. The first element, for example, was "The quasipermanent separation of teacher and learner throughout the length of the learning process; this distinguishes it from conventional face-to-face education." The "possibility of occasional seminars" became "the quasi-permanent absence of the learning group throughout the length of the learning process, so that people are usually taught as individuals and not in groups, with the possibility of occasional meetings for both didactic and socialization purposes" (Keegan, 1986, p. 49).

Garrison, Shale, and Baynton

An interest in telecommunications lead Garrison and Shale (1987) and Garrison and Baynton (1987) to attack Keegan's stipulation that a distinguishing feature of distance education is the "quasi-permanent absence of the learning group." These authors agree that distance education "implies some form of interaction or dialogue between teacher and taught," (Garrison and Shale, 1987, p.11) and that "technical media are required to mediate this communication." However, they argue that Keegan's definition is too limiting and only defines "a private print-based form of study and . . . does not adequately consider new generations of technological delivery" (Garrison and Shale, 1987, p.9).

"Teleconferencing," they say, "is by definition a group method of learning that provides for real-time interaction among all participants in a manner similar to traditional classroom instruction; yet according to Keegan's fifth element, this method cannot be considered a form of distance delivery because people are not taught individually" (p. 9). They propose that the distinguishing feature of distance education is that "it is a means of extending access to education to those who might otherwise be excluded from an educational experience." In our opinion this is too vague, since distance education is frequently chosen by individuals and organizations for reasons besides the unavailability of traditional educational methods. Neither are they correct, bearing in mind we are trying to describe what is, rather than to prescribe what we may prefer, in saying distance education "means something more than simply reading a text or watching a television broadcast."

Sometimes it does and sometimes it doesn't. It is true that most practitioners are especially concerned with the ongoing real-time interaction between teachers and learners. However, as we have discussed earlier, there are different types and levels of interaction, and the concept of dialog also incorporates those interactions that are within a page, a study guide, a text, a television program, or an audiotape as well as those delivered through the more highly "conversational" media of telecommunications. In a television broadcast there is a kind of dialog between the program writers, designers, and presenters and the viewer. It is a minimal dialog, similar to what Holmberg called the internal didactic conversation.

Garrison and Baynton have cast further light on the concept of learner autonomy. As stated above, learner autonomy is a continuous variable. This means that everybody has some element of autonomy in making decisions about learning and carrying them out. Every program has built into it at least some element of personal choice, even those in which the designers try not to give choice. When we classify courses or programs by the variable of learner autonomy we are classifying them by the extent that the learner or the teacher controls the educational processes, especially determining objectives, implementing teaching strategies, and making evaluations.

Obviously, if the learner is exercising a great degree of self-direction in deciding what to learn, or how, or to what extent, then the instructor has less control than when the learner is being directed by the instructor. This is the idea taken up and developed by Garrison and Baynton (1987). Control is not achieved simply by providing independence or freedom from outside influence. It is the dynamic balance between these three components that allows the student to develop and maintain control over the learning process. Garrison and Baynton also discuss the relationship between autonomy and various elements of structure, such as pacing and the negotiation of objectives and dialog, which they describe as frequency and immediacy of communication. For example, it becomes apparent that the greater the pacing, the higher the structure, the lower the autonomy, and the greater the teacher control.

The System Dynamics of Saba

The penultimate theorist we will mention here is Farhad (Fred) Saba. With his colleagues and students, Saba has elaborated the theory of transactional distance by using computer simulation modeling and employed this approach to understanding the use of telecommunications in distance education (Saba, 1988; Saba and Shearer, 1994).

Saba presented a computer simulation research method based on systems dynamics modeling techniques that demonstrates and explains the interactions of different forces in a distance education system. Saba (1988) employed the model to describe the interrelationships of the variables that make up structure and dialog. Here is how he describes the model:

> Integrated systems provide a flexible means for decreasing structure through increased dialogue. They also expedite increased structure so dialogue can be kept to a desirable level. This defines a dynamic relationship between dialogue and the level of required structure. This relationship can be displayed as a negative feedback loop in a system dynamics causal loop diagram.
>
> The negative flow diagram represents an inverse relationship between levels of dialogue and structure. As dialogue increases, structure decreases, and as structure decreases dialogue increases to keep the system stable. In negative feedback loops, the stability of the system depends on interventions from outside the loop. The level depends on the action of teacher and learner. In a plausible scenario, the need for decreasing structure is communicated to the teacher. Consultation

automatically increases dialogue; then adjustments in goals, instructional materials, and evaluation procedures occur and the learner achieves the desired level of autonomy. (Saba, 1988, p. 22)

Saba expanded the systems model in a subsequent project (Saba and Shearer, 1994) when he ran simulations of distance students' exchanges with instructors to measure relationships of transactional distance and autonomy. Using a technique for coding speech called "discourse analysis," the researchers identified the speech content of a number of educational transactions at a distance and classified them into 10 main categories and 20 subcategories. In this way they operationalized dialog, structure, and teacher/learner control and measured the effects that changes in any of these had in the others.

Kember's Open Learning Model

The final theory we will discuss in this chapter is one of the most recent and perhaps the best illustration of how theory should affect practice and vice versa. Kember (1995) presents a model for student progress that focuses specifically on adult learners in distance education courses. Actually, Kember uses the term "open learning" which he considers to be a more general conceptualization that includes distance learning as one form (possibly equivalent). Figure 10-1 shows the basic components of Kember's model. The model focuses on the factors that affect a student's successful completion of a distance education program with particular focus on the extent to which students are able to integrate their academic study with the often conflicting employment, family, and social commitments.

Kember's model suggests that students' entry characteristics (e.g., educational qualifications, family status, employment) direct them toward one of two pathways in a distance education course. Those with favorable situations tend

Figure 10.1 Kember's Open Learning Model (From Kember, 1995. Used by permission.)

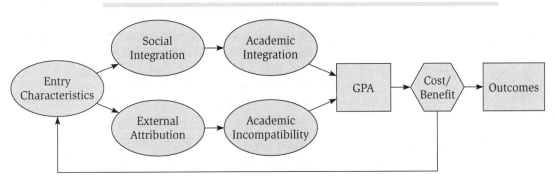

to proceed on a positive track and are able to integrate socially and academically. Other students take a negative track where they have difficulties achieving social and academic integration which affects their course achievement (i.e., GPA). The model also incorporates a cost/benefit decision step in which students consider the costs and benefits of continuing their study. Those who decide to continue will "recycle" through the model for another passage. However, in each pass through the model, the students may change tracks due to their experiences in taking the course.

Kember's model is based on a large body of research and theory about student attrition in both traditional and distance education courses. We reviewed some of this work in Chapter 8 when discussing the dropout problem. However, Kember used empirical data (in the form of interviews and questionnaires) from a number of different sources in the formulation and validation of his model. These sources included students taking courses at the British Open University, the University of Papua New Guinea, the University of Tasmania, Charles Sturt University (Australia), and seven different open learning programs in Hong Kong. In order to collect standardized data for the model, Kember developed and used the Distance Education Student Progress (DESP) questionnaire which consists of 68 items pertaining to the variables in the model (plus demographic information for entry characteristics). Kember also collected student outcome data in the form of grade point average (GPA) and the number of course modules attempted and completed.

To validate his model, Kember used factor analysis on his questionnaire responses to determine the underlying factors. The factor analysis confirmed the four primary variables in the model: social integration, academic integration, external attribution, and academic incompatability. Kember then used path analysis (multiple regression) to identify the causal relationships among the variables in the model. The results of the path analysis confirmed that the basic structure of the model is accurate: 80 percent of the total variance of student completions could be explained by the variables in the model.

Kember outlines the implications of his model. The positive academic integration factor contains the subscales "deep approach" and "instrinsic motivation," while the negative academic incompatibility factor has "surface approach" and "extrinsic motivation" subscales. This suggests that student progress can be enhanced if the design of a course concentrates on developing intrinsic motivation and a deep approach to the subject matter. Academic integration can also be improved by developing collective affiliation and ensuring congruence between student expectations and course procedures. The model also identifies the difficulties students are likely to face in completing open learning courses and can therefore serve as a guide for counseling and guidance activities.

Kember's model is very compatible with the systems approach that is espoused in this book. While Kember does not attempt to relate his model to a systems approach, the major variables of the model do map onto the primary subsystems we discussed initially in Chapter 1.

Conclusion: The Importance of Theoretical Analysis

The primary purpose and value of a theory is that it helps describe and explain a phenomenon. A theory is like a map; in fact, a map is a theory. It shows the general shape of something in a simplified form; it shows the relationships among the constituent parts of the phenomenon; and very important, it shows what areas are *not* known. For a theorist to provide a means of identifying what is not known is extremely important, because in so doing the theory is pointing out areas that need exploration. In other words, a good theory assists in identifying needed research.

The theory of transactional distance has served as a tool that can be used to describe distance education courses and programs and to locate any one in relation to others in the universe of such events. At the same time it provides a framework within which researchers can locate numerous variables of structure, dialog, and learner autonomy, and then ask questions about the relationships among these variables.

It should be emphasised that the theory of transactional distance is a pedagogical theory. Distance education, as conceptualized in the theory is a teaching-learning relationship, so it defines distance education in terms of course variables, learner variables, and instructional variables. As far as the pedagogical conceptualization of distance education is concerned, there is no need for repetition and relabeling of these dimensions. There is, however, need for much more research of an empirical nature to identify the many variables that lie *within* structure, dialog, and autonomy, and to explore them more thoroughly. It is essential that we empirically test specific variables that comprise these broad dimensions, and the relationships among them. There are rich opportunities for graduate students in this unexplored field.

As students look into the possiblities for research, it is important they read as much as possible of the existing distance education literature. The journals mentioned later in this book will provide the basis of this reading. It is also necessary for students to think how they can connect their thinking about research in distance education with their study of the more general body of educational research and theory. For example, there are many aspects of traditional learning theory that are relevant to distance learning (e.g., Schuemer, 1993). Likewise, there is a great deal of research in instructional design and technology-based delivery systems that is directly applicable to distance education efforts. It will help the student to sort out this large volume of literature to have a clear idea of the research question to be addressed, and that means knowing the distance education theory before moving into the more general literature.

The recent work of Saba and Kember are outstanding examples of the power that can be brought to research in distance education by the application of methodologies derived outside the field itself (e.g., system dynamics, simulation modeling, factor and path analysis). By bringing together external methods and a solid foundation of distance education theory, the result is a much more refined explanation of the phenomena of interest, and the ability to explore numerous new relationships among the variables. This is exactly what is needed for good research and also for the further development of the theory of distance education.

For those who have interests other than in the teaching-learning relationship, there are even more opportunities. There is still no historical theory of distance education, theory of organizations, administrative theory, or theory of philosophy. Clearly, as distance education enters the mainstream of educational research these theories will be developed. Now is an exciting time to be a student in the field of distance education!

Summary

- There have been a number of efforts to develop theoretical frameworks to explain distance education. The oldest in English is Moore's theory of transactional distance which suggests that there are two critical underlying variables—structure and dialog—and these are in relationship to learner autonomy. This is a pedagogical theory that explains the nature of programs and courses, and the behaviors of teachers and learners.

- Subsequent theorists have focused on the role of technology, the significance of student versus teacher control, the system dynamics of transactional distance, and causal relationships among factors affecting student success. Future developments in the theory of distance education need to be empirically based rather than philosophical or ideological exercises.

CHAPTER 11

International Perspectives

Almost every country in the world has some form of distance education, and a number of countries have better developed systems than the United States. This chapter describes distance education in a number of different nations. It also discusses the special significance of distance education for developing countries and introduces the idea of internationalism in distance education— that is, teaching from one country to another.

While this book has focused on the U.S. context, distance education is truly a worldwide enterprise. Distance education is, and has always been, one of the most international fields of education. As we saw in Chapter 1, even the term "distance education" is a translation from the German *fernunterricht*, French *tele-enseignement*, and Spanish *educación a distancia*.

Today one of the most important trends in education is to have students in different countries learning together in teleconference groups, and this internationalism is likely to continue and become commonplace in the years ahead.

Internationalism is more firmly established and has a longer history in distance education than other fields of education. For example, the international organization of distance educators is one of the oldest existing international educational organizations. From 1938 until 1982 it was called the International Council for Correspondence Education (ICCE) and is now known as The International Council for Distance Education (ICDE). In 1938 ICCE organized a world conference, and this has been repeated about every four years until recently and now is held about every two years.

As well as having a long tradition of exchanging information and ideas at world conferences, distance educators also have a history of sharing course design techniques and instructional procedures. Such sharing was possible, and likely, because the bulk of instruction was recorded in some way, usually by

print, and in more recent times on audio- and videotape. Because these materials were designed for use by students in distant places, it was natural they would find their way to foreign educators, and thus the spread and adoption of numerous distance education practices and techniques.

Even today students of distance education are encouraged to analyze the printed, audio, and video materials produced by distance educators from overseas as well as at home. Broadcast and teleconference materials, though admittedly more ephemeral than print or recorded materials, are nevertheless more open to analysis and examination than are more traditional forms of instruction. With the development of teleconferencing media, there has been a quickening of the pace and intensity of international learning and borrowing by educators of one country from those of another.

These informal exchanges of knowledge and experiences about distance education have been advanced in recent years by the establishment of such regional associations as the Asian Association of Open Universities, the Latin American Cooperative Network for the Development of Distance Education, and the European Association of Distance Teaching Universities.

A Brief World Tour

In order to convey a taste of distance education in different countries, we present short descriptions of programs in four different nations and continents: China, Norway, Australia, and South Africa. These countries have been selected for several reasons, one of which is that, like the United States, they do not have national open universities.

China

The Peoples' Republic of China is vast in size, about the size of the whole of Europe, with many remote areas and a population of about 1.2 billion people. More than 80 percent of these people live in rural areas. The per capita income is about $400 U.S., and the magnitude of this nation's educational needs is immense. Given these needs, it is not surprising that distance education is extensive. Correspondence study and radio broadcasting have been widely used since the 1940s. When television became available in the 1960s, a number of local "TV universities" were established in major cities. Educational broadcasts were provided in the early morning and late at night for people to watch at their workplace. This worked quite well at a time when television was an attractive novelty to most people and in a political culture in which the workplace played a more central role than in western countries.

In 1979 a nationwide system of Radio and TV Universities (RTVUs) was set up, and that year 400,000 students were enrolled in classrooms all around the country (Wei and Tong, 1994). By 1982 when the first RTVU students in engineering and technology graduated, there were 92,000 of them, which equaled half the number of such students graduating from conventional universities. In

Figure 11.1 Organizational Structure of Distance Education in China (From Wei, 1991)

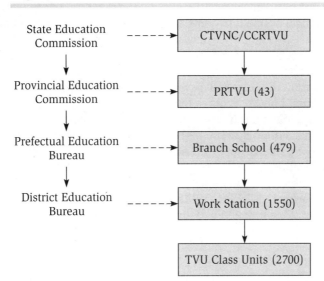

1986 the RTVUs first began to experiment with teaching by communications satellite. In 1988 China launched two of its own communications satellites. Since then satellite television has offered a cost-effective way of taking a giant leap forward in constructing a modern large-scale distance education system. A highly structured organization was necessary to ensure that this satellite delivery system is effective (see Figure 11-1).

In China about one-third of a million students are in higher education correspondence programs offered by 311 of China's 800 colleges and universities. At the national level there are two major institutions engaged in distance education: the China TV Normal College (CTVNC) and the China Central Radio and TV University (CCRTVU). The CTVNC is responsible for teacher training and professional education while CCRTVU provides courses in all subject areas. CTVNC has produced 10,000 hours of television programming, has 1.2 million teachers enrolled in courses and has millions of teachers and administrators involved in continuing education activities. The CCRTVU has published 150 million copies of textbooks and produced 20,000 hours of programming. In 1992 there were over 2 million students enrolled in degree programs and the total number of graduates from RTVUs exceeded 1.5 million, which is equivalent to about 30 percent of that of conventional universities. The total number of degree and nondegree graduates from the national RTVU network over the past 14 years has exceeded 15 million (Wei and Tong, 1994).

The organizational structure of distance education in China has five levels (Figure 11-1). The two major universities are under the direct leadership of the State Education Commission (Ministry of Education) which establishes national policy, direction, and standards. The Provincial Radio and TV Universities (PRTVUs) are under the auspices of the regional governments and are responsible for developing courses and programming to meet local needs. The branch schools come under the control of prefectural or municipal agencies and are responsible for supervising the activities of the workstations (learning centers). The workstations organize classes, register students, collect fees (tuition), distribute course materials, and arrange for tutors. The "class units" provide the direct supervision and support of the students.

This is an organizational system that supports centralized design and delivery of courses and programs, but also allows for considerable decentralization and local application of the subject matter. Considerable research on distance education is conducted by the two central universities as well as the PRTVUs. For example, Jianshu (1990) estimates that no less than 500 articles about distance education are published annually in China! For more information about distance education in China, see Wei and Tong (1994), Chunjie (1993), Gao (1991), Jianshu (1990), and Wei (1991).

Norway

The Scandinavian countries of Sweden, Norway, Denmark, and Finland are a direct contrast to the People's Republic of China. They have small populations (totaling altogether only some 20 million people) and the highest standards of living in the world. They have also been world leaders in distance education for many years.

Although the populations of these countries are small, they are dispersed over a wide distance and isolated due to geography and climate. Futhermore education, like other social services, receives higher priority in the cultures of these countries than in most others, including the United States, so that a high demand exists for instruction and learning in any form. Since the level of basic education is very high, people have good study skills and are therefore able to adapt to distance education quite readily.

Historically, distance education in Norway has been dominated by private institutions. The Norsk Korrespondanseskole (NKS), established in 1914 was the first distance education institution in Norway. Today the NKS has 70,000 enrollments a year in a wide range of courses, from secondary school to university degree levels. The Norsk Korrespondanse Institute (NKI) has an annual enrollment of 45,000 with emphasis on technical, vocational, and administrative courses. While both institutions began during the days when print was the only medium for distance teaching, they now use a variety of media, including audio- and videotapes, television, radio, and CMC. Recently, NKS and NKI have been working with Norwegian Telecom to explore the use of different types of videoconferencing systems for distance learning.

The Norwegian government plays an active role in distance education. In 1948 legislation was passed that regulated correspondence programs and institutions. In 1975 the Parliament decided to provide financial aid to correspondence students in accredited schools, and in 1977 it created the Norwegian State Institution for Distance Education (NFU). The NFU attempts to coordinate the development and distribution of distance education programs in collaboration with the national broadcasting corporation, publishers, and the public schools and university system. In 1991 NFU initiated about 20 projects to encourage the further development of multimedia in distance education courses.

While NKI and NKS are what we described in Chapter 1 as distance education institutions, in recent years Norwegian universities and colleges have started distance education efforts at program level. These include University of Bergen, University of Trondheim, University of Oslo, North Norwegian Conservatory of Music, Opplan College, Stavanger College, Stord College, Tromsoe College, Nordland College, Sagene College, and the Norwegian College of Public Administration and Social Work.

To coordinate this postsecondary provision, the Norwegian Executive Board for Distance Education at University and College Level (SOFF) was established in 1990.

The Norwegian Association for Distance Education (NADE) was established in 1968 as an association of accredited correspondence schools and in 1984 was reorganized to include all institutions in Norway involved in distance education (as well as representatives of the NFU and SOFF). In 1988 the Norwegian Center for Distance Education (SEFU) was created by NFU, NKI, and NKS to conduct research projects. Also in 1988, the Norwegian government established and currently supports the permanent Secretariat of the ICDE, in Oslo.

For further discussion of distance education in Norway, see Paulsen (1992a) and Rekkedal (1983b, 1993).

Australia

Australia is geographically massive, with the land mass equivalent of the United States and with a population equivalent to that of the state of Pennsylvania. Over 70 percent of this population lives in the cities, and because the remainder are so widely distributed over huge areas, distance education has always been an accepted form of teaching and learning for many Australians.

When the University of Queensland was established in 1910, it was required by law to offer correspondence programs. In 1925 it renamed the department of correspondence studies the Department of External Studies. In 1949 this department became an academic unit with its own teaching staff.

At K-12 level, the Melbourne Teacher's College began providing correspondence courses during World War I in response to requests from parents in the outback (isolated rural areas). In 1929 correspondence led to the use of radio broadcasting. In 1951 the School of the Air was initiated, using two-way radio and thus allowing for real-time interaction between teachers and their students on ranches in remote areas.

Today many school systems and most universities provide distance education courses as part of their regular activities—what is often referred to as the "dual mode" structure. (When researching this, it is necessary to keep in mind that the term "external studies" is widely used to include distance education.)

In New South Wales, the Department of Education is empowered by a 1987 law to provide publicly funded distance education to students between the ages of 6 and 15 years, so a full primary curriculum is offered as well as 46 separate subjects at the secondary level. In 1991 the state began to decentralize its distance education program by establishing regional centers (11 for primary and 6 for secondary levels) in order to make learning centers as close as possible to students' homes.

At the level of higher education, most colleges and universities offer distance education courses in parallel with their on-campus classes (so-called "dual mode" institutions). Entry qualifications for accredited distance education courses in Australia are the same as for on-campus courses, so it is common for students to take a mix of on-campus and off-campus courses. This means that Australian distance education students tend to be younger and full-time, rather than older and part-time as is more usual in the United States.

Being a technologically advanced country, Australia incorporates the same wide range of media into distance education as are used in the United States. The most common materials are of course print and audio- and videotapes, with increasing use of computer conferencing, videodiscs, audio- and audiographic conferencing, and satellite-delivered video-/audioconferencing. One of the big differences from U.S. practice is the attempt to rationalize and systematically organize these resources. This has been particularly noticeable since 1990 when it became a matter of government policy.

In 1990 the Australian government set up the National Distance Education Consortium. This rationalized postsecondary distance education and reorganized previously competing institutions into eight major providers, known as Distance Education Centers (DECs): University of Southern Queensland, University of Central Queensland, Deakin University, Monash University, University of South Australia, University of New England, Charles Sturt University, and West Australia Distance Education Consortium (nonamalgamated institutions).

Each of these institutions is responsible for developing and delivering courses that respond to the needs of students in their geographic areas as well as conducting relevant research. For example, the Charles Sturt University (formed by the consolidation of the Riverina-Murry Institute of Higher Education and the Mitchell College of Advanced Education) serves both rural and urban students in New South Wales. It offers more than 100 courses to over 13,000 students, about half of whom are studying at a distance (Meacham, 1990).

One of the distinctive characteristics of Australian distance education is the development of publicly funded courses to meet specific occupational needs. A large percentage of the courses provided are in areas such as agriculture, applied sciences, banking, business, computing, nursing, and management. Futhermore, professional schools offer their courses in distance education format as well. Another characteristic is the significant involvement of the federal and state governments in the planning, implementation, and evaluation of distance education at all levels. Since almost all education in Australia is federally funded, the government exerts considerable influence on the direction and development of distance education programs. On the other hand, each state school system and individual university operates fairly autonomously and implements distance education to meet the needs of its own constituency.

For a critical analysis of contemporary distance education programs in Australia, see Evans and Nation (1989).

The Republic of South Africa

With a population of over 30 million and a very large land area, the Republic of South Africa (RSA) has one of the oldest and largest distance education systems in the world, and by far the most advanced in Africa. The whole educational system of the country is influenced by this long tradition of distance education. There is hardly a school or a university department that does not have faculty with first-hand experience of distance education, as either student or instructor. Even governments at all levels have graduates of the distance education institutions. Where in every other country, distance education is compared with classroom teaching, in RSA there is a quite widespread tendency to compare what goes on in other forms of education with the standard of the major distance teaching institutions. This is mainly because of the dominant part played in distance education and in the whole educational system by the University of South Africa (UNISA).

UNISA was established as a federation of colleges in 1916. As each of the colleges became independent it focused increasingly on "external studies," and eventually, in 1964 became a fully independent, autonomous distance teaching institution as defined in Chapter 1.

In 1993 (historically it should be remembered that majority rule in RSA began in 1994), UNISA had 122,586 registered students, or about one-third of all enrollments in the Republic's universities. Approximately 85 percent of its students enrolled in undergraduate degrees (primarily commerce, science, or education). In 1992 the university awarded 7,615 degrees and diplomas.

The racial composition of the students in 1993 was (in the terms of official UNISA publications) 44.1 percent Black, 43.9 percent White, 8.4 percent Asian, 3.6 percent Coloured. There were equal numbers of male and female students; almost half were over age 30 and a quarter were under age 25.

UNISA has around 3,300 permanent staff, about half of whom are teaching staff. There is a central counseling service and regional learner support centers in the four principal cities. The majority of instruction is by printed correspondence, but for such courses as management, the most modern technologies are used, including all forms of teleconferencing.

Another large distance education institution is the Technikon SA, established in 1980 and focused on tertiary career education (e.g., police adminstration, community services). Technikon SA began with 5,039 students in 1986 and had an enrollment of 63,840 students in 1993 with a faculty of 716.

VISTA University was created in 1981 and dedicated to providing higher education to the urban black population. In 1993 it had an enrollment of 12,869

Telematics in the Outback

In 1993 an evaluation of distance education in the remote areas of Western Australia was conducted by Ron Oliver of Edith Cowan University (Perth) and Tom Reeves of the University of Georgia. Here is an excerpt from trip reports written as part of this evaluation project, in which they describe the use of audiographics in a K-12 project. The Australians use the term "telematics" for audiographics:

> Telematics involves the use of phone lines (one for voice link and the other for computer transmission) to hook up specialist teachers with students in remote schools. The specific telematics application we evaluated in the Pilbara area provides Japanese instruction to students who have no other foreign language instruction available to them. Japanese was chosen because most of the iron ore from Western Australia goes to Japan and because many Australians feel that their economic future is closely linked with that of Japan. Eighth-grade students gather around a speaker phone and a Macintosh PC for two one-hour lessons a week. The teacher uses the color Mac to present material which she explains on the phone. Periodically, she turns control over to the students and they can respond to her queries, either by voice or by drawing Japanese characters on their Mac which then appear on her Mac a thousand kilometers away. Students fax their homework assignments and tests to the teacher who marks them and mails them back to the school. The students who went through a rigorous screening process in terms of both aptitude and motivation handle the technology beautifully themselves. In some schools, they need no adult supervision, even though they are working together in groups of six. The program is quite interactive, and the students are making as much or more progress in Japanese as students studying in face-to-face classes in Perth.
>
> In one group of Aboriginal schools, telematics is being used to provide students with English as a Second Language (ESL) instruction. The ESL teacher, located hundreds of kilometers away, works with small groups of 16-to-19-year-old students who, although they have completed ten years of compulsory schooling, still read and communicate in English at levels that prohibit them from participating in educational, economic and social affairs outside their local communities. According to their community teachers, the Aboriginal students using telematics have made considerable progress in English skills during this school year. However, they report that the most important outcomes are improved self-esteem and confidence, especially among the female students. Most of these students have never used a telephone before, but now they link up via modem and voice phone with their telematics teacher without requiring help from the community teachers. Where telematics is addressing real needs of Aboriginal students (such as improving self-confidence or ESL skills), the program seems to be effective.

However, in another group of Aboriginal schools, telematics is being used to teach introductory computing, but it isn't working as well at those sites. One telling indicator is that in the ESL telematics program, attendance is very high, whereas in the computer education telematics, attendance is below 50 percent, which is supposedly normal for most Aboriginal education programs.

students organized around seven regional contact campuses, plus another 20,120 students at a Pretoria teacher training campus which focuses solely on upgrading of underqualified school teachers.

Technisa is a technical college that provides distance education for vocational and technical training in engineering, business, and general studies. It was founded in 1984 and had an enrollment of 7,607 students in 1992–93.

Like UNISA, Technikon SA, Vista, and Technisa serve a national constituency, primarily through printed correspondence, with other technologies used when the student population has access to the necessary equipment. For most South African students this means the correspondence text is the most common medium of instruction.

The Republic of South Africa passed a Correspondence College Act in 1965 to regulate private correspondence colleges. Today the private market is dominated by five private colleges that together enroll more than 177,000 students a year. It is of great historical interest to note that the Correspondence College Act of 1965 came about as a result of proposals from South Africa's Association of Distance Education Colleges of South Africa (ADEC), an organization that is almost certainly the first in the world to adopt the "distance education" name. (See South African Institute for Distance Education, 1994, p. 15.)

In February 1994, in anticipation of the forthcoming national elections to establish the first popular government in the republic, the African National Congress authorized an examination by an international commission of the state of the South African distance education system and its potential in contributing to the postelection goals of the new government. While on the surface it appears that the distance education system does much to promote equal opportunity and access to education for all South Africans, the commission identified some fundamental problems:

- While access to institutions like UNISA and Technikon SA is quite open, the rate of completion is very poor, typically less than 25 percent. This means that for most students, distance education results in an uncompleted or failed learning experience.

- The overwhelming majority of staff (teachers, adminstrators, course developers) at distance education institutions are from the racial and cultural minority that dominated South Africa in Apartheid days and are not representative of the racial mix of the student body.

- Almost all course materials are developed initially in Afrikaans and embody the cultural biases and attitudes of whites toward other races. Furthermore, these materials are generally uninviting and promote a very passive mode of learning.

- There is a serious imbalance between the number of people and the money spent on course design and teaching from the institution's national centers, and what is spent on the regional and local student support services. Local tutoring and counseling are almost nonexistent in most programs, explaining in part the ineffectiveness of many courses and the low completion rates.

In essence, the present distance education system has an accepted place in society and a structure that could be used as the basis of a national system that could be equal to some of the best in the world, and unequaled in Africa. This system could be the means for equipping millions of South Africans with the skills and knowledge needed to participate fully in the new democracy made possible by the election of the ANC. To do this, however, many changes and reforms to the existing system have to be made.

National Distance Education Systems

Among the largest national distance education systems are the open universities in Asia. India's Indira Gandhi National Open University was established in 1985 with a dual mandate: while functioning as a university like other universities, it was also to coordinate and determine standards for the other distance education institutions in the country. Its student population is around 55,000; it has 123 full-time academics and 590 nonacademic staff, with over 5,000 part-time employees, academic and nonacademic (Koul, 1989).

In Thailand the Sukhothai Thammathirat Open University (STOU) has some 200,000 students in about 400 courses. A bachelor's degree is normally awarded after a four-year program. Other programs focus on professional and vocational training and continuing professional education in such areas as education, management, science, and law (Carr, 1984).

In Pakistan the Allama Iqbal Open University was created in 1974 under an Act of Parliament that stated its purpose "to provide part-time educational facilities through correspondence courses, tutorials, seminars, workshops, laboratories, television and radio broadcasts and other mass communication media" (Fleming, 1982). The major thrust of activity in its early years was teacher training and teacher continuing education. By 1982 some 60,000 of a potential market of 160,000 teachers had taken the primary teachers' orientation course. Among open universities, Allama Iqbal is exceptional in the extent to which it invests resources in nonformal, basic adult education, such as its 18-month village projects that emphasize literacy and the skills needed for rural employment and rural development.

In Germany the FernUniversitat was established in Hagen in 1974 as an institute of higher education of the state of Nordrhein Westfalia. It offers 900 courses, and the student body is around 30,000. The main teaching medium is print, supplemented by audiovisual media. There are 40 study centers where students use study materials and receive tutoring and counseling from "mentors." Full-time academic staff number about 300.

The Open Universiteit of the Netherlands (OU-NL) was founded in 1984. Although an autonomous institution, about half the courses are written by academics of conventional higher education institutions. In addition to written and recorded materials, the OU-NL has arrangements with the Dutch Broadcasting Organization to produce and broadcast television programs. In 1987 there were 33,431 students. Courses lead to a degree that is legally equivalent to degrees of other institutes of higher education. Courses are offered in law, economics, business and administration, technical sciences, natural sciences, social sciences, and cultural sciences.

In Portugal the minister of education announced the creation of the Universidade Aberta in 1988. Educational entry qualifications are as for other universities, and students must be 25 years of age. Teaching focuses on education and teacher training and on economics.

The Universidad Nacional de Educación a Distancia in Spain is one of the oldest and also largest open universities. Approved by Parliament in August 1970, the first students enrolled in 1973. Students must have the same entry certificate as those of conventional universities. Enrollment in 1987–88 was 83,121 with 1,300 graduating each year. The faculties are law, sciences, economics and business administration, philosophy and educational sciences, geography and history, philology, psychology, industrial engineering, and political science and sociology. Media include radio transmissions lasting for two half-hours per day, audiocassettes, video, and telephone tutoring. There are 64 local study centers.

Athabasca University in Alberta, Canada, has around 11,000 students. It offers baccalaureate degrees in liberal studies and administrative studies, using television, audiotapes, print, and telephone. Students are predominantly working adults and a majority are female. The only requirement for admission is that the student be eighteen or older.

Venezuela's Universidad Nacional Abierta (UNA) has 24,000 students. It provides 250 courses in a degree program in various "professional studies"— administration, education, engineering, and mathematics. Before entering the professional studies programs, every student must pass an Introductory Course aimed at orienting them to the practice of learning at a distance and a General Studies Course. UNA has 21 regional centers, where full-time counselors are available for consultation, study groups are organized, and tutorials are provided at General Studies level.

Like UNA, The Universidad Estatal a Distancia (UNED) in Costa Rica at first concentrated on developing a series of professional degrees. It has 260 courses and 12,863 students. Since 1980 it has worked in conjunction with The Ministry of Public Education on developing materials and training tutors for the ministry's distance teaching for secondary schools. As in most autonomous institutions, especially in developing countries, the basic teaching medium is the printed course book. Course texts are written by external authors who are contracted by full-time academic producers. There are limited numbers of television programs and audiotapes. About 80 programs are produced each year and around four hours are broadcast each week. Tutorials take place at the regional centers, of which there are 22 throughout the country. According to Rumble and Harry (1982), dropout is a serious problem, with 74 percent of students who registered in one year no longer being registered two years later.

Consortia

Just as consortia are important in the United States, so has this approach to distance education been preferred by a number of other countries instead of establishing national distance education systems. Here are some examples:

Higher distance education in Belgium dates from a 1986 agreement for Flemish students to study through the Open Universiteit of the Netherlands, by which plan 27 Dutch courses are supplemented by Flemish adaptations and other specifically Flemish courses.

The Deutsches Institut fur Fernstudien (DIFF) was founded in 1967 at the University of Tübingen, in what was then the Federal Republic of Germany, with a charter that stated the aim: "to examine and create possibilities for academic study whereby the continual presence of the student at an institution is unnecessary (distance study)" (Harry and de Vocht, 1988, p. 31). DIFF is a research and development institution, with no students of its own, but it develops materials and teaching-learning models for use by cooperating institutions. DIFF cooperates with radio stations throughout the republic to offer first year undergraduate-level courses to typically over 20,000 students per course.

In France distance education is made available on a regional basis from any of the 22 universities that make up the Federation Interuniversitaire de L'Enseignement a Distance, (FIED). This was created in 1987 to coordinate activities of the distance education centers that are embedded within parent universities, and lecturers who prepare distance education also teach conventional face-to-face classes. The teaching method depends on correspondence, tape-recorded lectures, and radio and television broadcasts. The total number of students served in 1987 was 26,000.

Italy's Consorzio Per L'Universita a Distanza (CUD) was founded in 1984. It is a consortium that designs learning materials and student support services for use by students who register with those Italian universities that are members of the consortium. In 1988 the student population was 1,200. Course materials are prepared by professors of member universities and instructional design is the responsibility of CUD. Courses consist mainly of about 500 pages of print and computer discs. Attendance at study centers is compulsory.

The Irish National Distance Education Centre was established in 1982. It has the status of a Faculty of the National Institute for Higher Education in Dublin and works cooperatively with universities and colleges throughout the country in developing and providing national distance education programs. The Centre offers a baccalaureate degree, and 290 students registered as the first cohort in 1987. The main teaching medium is a printed text, supplemented by recorded audio and video materials.

In Canada "Contact North" is The Northern Ontario Education Access Network. In 1986 the Ontario government granted $16 million, with 40 percent to be in a fund to cover costs of courseware. The network serves 27 communities through coordinating centers in colleges and universities. Any nonprofit group can use the network to deliver distance education courses using print, audio and video media teleconferencing and computer communications. The network has been used for a degree program in nursing, public administration, forestry, and teacher upgrading.

Distance Education in Developing Countries

Throughout Africa, economically the world's poorest continent, the demand for education at all levels is far greater than the resources for providing it. Many African governments have tried to use distance education to make the most of the resources available. As in other parts of the world, distance education in Africa began with private correspondence colleges, established in many countries in the 1940s. Government-supported correspondence programs emerged in the 1960s. For example, the Zambian government created a correspondence unit for secondary study in 1964. At that time, only about 12 percent of children completing primary education were able to find a place in secondary school. Today The National Correspondence College provides instruction at the secondary level to both adults and children and has an enrollment of more than 30,000 students.

In Nigeria the agency responsible for distance education at the primary and secondary educational level is the National Teachers' Institute of Kaduna, which was established in 1978. In common with a number of other developing countries, Nigeria's strategy is to employ distance education for upgrading the skills and qualifications of teachers rather than to deliver programs to children, or even to adults, directly (Brophy and Dudley, 1982).

Where resources are so few and illiteracy rates are high, the idea is to leverage the resources by using distance education to first improve the quality of school teaching, and thus indirectly the quality of education throughout the whole society. The pioneer in this approach in Africa was the University of East Africa in Nairobi in Kenya, today known as the School of Distance Studies at the University of Nairobi. Set up in 1969 with assistance from the University of Wisconsin, what was then called the Correspondence Courses Unit retrained and graduated some 10,000 unqualified teachers between 1969 and 1972. Currently, the school provides in-service training to over 3,000 primary school teachers per year.

According to the Minister of Education, Zimbabwe's expansion of secondary education from 66,000 pupils in 1979 to 700,000 in 1989 was only possible by using school-based distance education programs.

Murphy and Zhiri (1992) provide detailed descriptions of distance education in the sub-Saharan countries of Ethiopia, Kenya, Lesotho, Malawi, Tanzania, Zambia, and Zimbabwe. In many of these countries, distance education is conducted via regional study centers which are operated by the ministries of education. For example, Malawi has approximately 100 such study centers serving 14,000 students at the primary school level and Zimbabwe serves 41,000 students at over 600 study centers (many in existing school buildings). These centers are provided with learning materials (primarily print) and supervised by teachers. The most popular nonprint technology is the radio. Radio receivers use batteries and are not dependent on electricity, which is often nonexistent or unreliable, and the African oral tradition makes listening to a speaker on the radio a popular pastime.

Developing countries in Africa, Asia, and South America have large populations with minimal formal education and are very interested in cost-effective ways to deliver instruction, particularly in the areas of basic literacy and job training. These countries have embraced distance education approaches because they believe it will help them overcome some of the educational disadvantages faced by their population. However, application of the distance education methods as practiced in the developed countries raises a number of economic, technical, political, and cultural issues. Many developing countries lack reliable postal, telephone, or television services (and electrical power) that make even the simplest forms of distance education difficult to conduct. One issue that has emerged in recent years concerns the wisdom of introducing high technology into such environments.

The 1992 ICDE On-line Conference

To introduce some of the different perspectives on this issue we will share some of the comments made by participants in one of the on-line conferences conducted over Internet in conjunction with the 1992 ICDE world conference (see Anderson and Mason, 1993). The discussion begins with the comment of a graduate student and is taken up by respondents from several different countries, as follows:

PARTICIPANT DANA DARBY:

I am a graduate student at the University of Oklahoma in my first distance education course. I try to picture some of the uses of CMC technology in third world countries, but visions of hungry children keep interfering. Aren't we getting the cart before the horse—shouldn't the people of these countries be fed and clothed before we concentrate on issues such as CMC, or will contact with the developed world be an impetus for change?

PARTICIPANT THEO STONE, UNIVERSITY OF MARYLAND:

Dear Dana, the third world is a big place and it doesn't all look like television snippets of the famine in Somalia. The world is increasingly a small place. For any society to thrive, prosper, and compete in the world market, it is imperative that the members of the society have access to training, development, and education. In many environments, distance education is ideal for reaching the people.

PARTICIPANT ROBIN MASON, OPEN UNIVERSITY, U.K.

Thank-you to Dana Darby for putting the viewpoint of the starving children needing to be fed before CMC is relevant. . . . These are views which I have certainly endorsed myself—they seem to reflect the most humanitarian, nontechnology-led approaches to our neighbors. However, I have seen quite a few visitors from developing countries, and they have put forth a very different case for technology in developing countries.

1. *Often they can leapfrog over problems we experience in developed countries because they have no infrastructure (outdated), systems, and equipment. India has in some ways by-passed the evolutionary process of distance education in developed countries by going straight for satellite broadcasting of educational programs into remote villages.*

2. *If developing countries simply sit back and wait for us to iron out all the problems of technologies such as CMC, they do not go through the learning process we do in sorting them out. They are thus doubly disadvantaged—they don't have the benefits of the new technologies and they are even further behind when it comes to the next technology that CMC will inevitably give way to.*

PARTICIPANT JANET POLEY, U.S. DEPT. AGRICULTURE

To play devil's advocate for a moment . . . let me respond on the issue of practicality of CMC in developing countries. My more than 15 years of experience working with developing countries in Africa and Asia . . . causes me to reject some of the conventional wisdom on this issue. Just a couple of facts:

1. *When I first started working with folks from developing countries back in 1976 . . . the most prized item to return home from U.S. study with was a stereo . . . beginning about 1986 that changed dramatically to a portable computer and software!*

2. *In 1981 I helped a group of Tanzanians establish a small computer lab in a rural training center equipped with Apple IIe's. Those machines all still work and have required no servicing, etc. My experience with computers from the earliest days has been that the majority are much more reliable than copying machines, electric typewriters, automobiles, etc.*

3. *Finally, I think the developing world has perhaps the greatest amount to gain from rapidly moving to participate in international networking in the distance education area. BUT, it will require developing country leadership and commitment to do things differently.*

PARTICIPANT FABIO CHACON, VENEZUELA:

This question has been addressed mostly from the hardware-facilities point of view. I do not question the importance of having a modem, a reliable telephone service and so forth. However, as an inhabitant of the so-called developing countries, I think the most central issues have to do with people and educational organizations. So I will try to present a different view on the issue. Here are three factors I see as essential:

1. *To have one or more organizations that support growth and development of CMC. For instance, in Venezuela, this role is taken by the National Council of Science and Technology (CONICIT) which has built a network among the academic institutions.*

2. *To design appropriate pedagogical functions for CMC within the distance education system. Some of these functions may be: to do cooperative research projects, to provide access to knowledge databases, to discuss key topics in some courses, to exchange graphic information or software, to support formative evaluation of materials, to participate in problem-solving, etc.*

3. *To provide familiarization and training to actual and potential uses of CMC, to make them able to start and maintain communications through this medium— with a minimum of effort and a maximum of benefit.*

PARTICIPANT KNUT BRAATANE, NORWAY

I agree with those who say that developing countries need CMC even more than other countries. Of several reasons for this may be mentioned the possibility to compensate for the shortage of educated teachers. And next, teacher education, teacher development, and curriculum exchange may become some of the most promising areas for use of CMC.

Promoting International Distance Education

In June 1994 a conference was held at The Pennsylvania State University on the subject of international distance education. At the concluding plenary session a set of principles was agreed by the participants, and a working group prepared these principles in the form of a communiqué that was subsequently distributed to educational authorities around the world:

It is in the interests of students and society to promote and facilitate distance education across national boundaries. In support of this declaration the conference recommends that education and training agencies:

- promote greater understanding of the cultural, linguistic, pedagogic, administrative, and technological issues associated with studying across national boundaries;

- develop strategies and financial support for further research and the effective dissemination of information about different approaches to distance education in an international context;

- place greater emphasis on minimizing barriers to participation in distance education across national boundaries, including those relating to transfer of course credits, academic calendar and schedule restrictions, and residency requirements;

- ensure that potential students have access to the databases listing distance education courses available to them from outside their country of residence;

- encourage the appointment of sufficient suitably trained and experienced senior staff in posts to develop and facilitate international collaboration;

- seek additional resources and more advantageous financial arrangements, including reallocation of existing resources, for the development of international distance education and for increased student participation in such education;

- initiate a review of the agencies, procedures, and strategies in place for promoting global cooperation in order to ensure their appropriateness for current needs and priorities;

- give careful consideration to the needs of underdeveloped nations and disadvantaged people and encourage their participation in international planning; and encourage further collaboration between educators, learners, international agencies, governments, and business and industry in order to develop effective partnerships for promoting accessible, effective distance education.

Collaboration Between American Institutions and Other Countries

The following are some of the American institutions that have experimented with teaching in other countries by teleconference:

- Pacific Presbyterian Medical Center of San Francisco, with programs in Japan, Belgium, Mexico, Spain, and Taiwan

- Ramapo College of New Jersey, with programs in Montevideo and Monterey

- University of Hawaii Laboratory School students, with programs in Japanese schools

- Harvard University, with programs in China

- Boston University Medical School, with programs in China

- University of California at Los Angeles (UCLA), with programs in Spain and Korea

- AT&T's program to Turkey

- Penn State University (ACSDE), with programs in Finland, Estonia, and Mexico

Most of these programs were experimental. They appear to be essentially of a program level as defined in Chapter 1; they were the fruits of an individual academic's initiative and persistence as much as, or rather than, part of their institution's strategic planning. Among those that appear to have rather more secure funding bases than others are the Pacific Presbyterian project, which received financial support from a major pharmaceutical corporation, while Ramapo College's International Telecommunications Center was supported by a $2.5 million grant from the New Jersey State Department of Higher Education. The UCLA courses were funded largely by a grant from the Korean government.

With the exception of the Pacific Presbyterian Medical Center, where the program was planned by a team of medical experts, what was taught and how it was taught in most of these projects appears to be more the decision of an individual instructor than part of a long-term, institutionally determined plan. It is already apparent that a wide range of content can be taught internationally by teleconference. The subjects taught by the above institutions include continuing medical education for physicians, nurses, and pharmacists; liberal arts and modern languages; mathematics and philosophy; distance education theory and practice. In most programs the primary direction of instruction is from a U.S.-based academic to foreign students, but after this foundation has been built, several programs have gone on to have more two-way, or foreign-originated programs. In programs like Hawaii's, groups in two countries learn their respective languages, while in the Ramapo, UCLA, and Penn State programs, foreign lecturers are brought by teleconference to American classrooms.

The dominant medium in most of these programs is audioconferencing. The Harvard, Boston, Penn State, and UCLA projects also used audiographics systems. These media were supplemented by print in many cases, by slides mailed in advance in some, and by computer conference in the Hawaii and Penn State projects. In most programs the preferred instructional method is a lecture from an expert to one or more groups in distant locations, usually followed by a session of question-and-answer. Students in the UCLA class on fine arts are expected to discuss their artworks; the Harvard and Boston instructors attempt what they refer to as a Socratic method, instructing by means of a series of questions and answers. Being set in a graduate program of study of adult education, Penn State deliberately experiments in nonlecture methods.

Collaboration in Distance Education in North America

In September 1993 around 200 participants, in equal numbers from Mexico, Canada, and the United States, attended the International Symposium on Higher Education and Strategic Partnerships in Vancouver. Most of the people attending were the principal administrators of their organizations, either presidents of universities, corporations, or foundations, or were members of governments or officials in government agencies. They included the Secretary for Education from Mexico who soon after became the President of that country.

At the conclusion of the symposium a statement was issued, containing the following recommendations:

> Innovation and human resource development lie at the heart of our hopes for the future social, economic and cultural development of our countries. The expansion and strengthening of intellectual links, exchanges and collaboration across our region are fundamental to the vitality and health of the democratic life and culture towards which we all aspire. They provide the underpinnings to the stability, civility and respect for human rights and freedoms necessary to democratic civilizations, and they are fundamental to the genuinely sustainable development we need to achieve.

It was recommended that the governments of the three North American countries collaborate in several ways, including the following:

1. The establishment of a North American Distance Education and Research Network (NADERN), a consortium to facilitate access to information and to support education, research and training among participating institutions.

4. The establishment of an electronic information base in each of the three countries, with coordinated sharing of information on academic initiatives and resources for trilateral collaboration, to serve the academic community as well as business, government and foundations.

Other suggestions that were to receive further consideration included:

6. As part of the long-term operations of NADERN, the development of an implementation plan for a North American University (NAU) to operate as a consortium to broker access to recognized graduate distance education courses offered by different institutions, and will (sic) develop a mechanism for awarding graduate degrees for such composite programs.

The idea of establishing a North American University (NAU) is deserving of serious consideration if we abandon the concept of university as bricks and mortar and focus on the university as a North American network of learners and teachers. The idea of university as network is the emerging concept for the next generation of distance education. Meetings of a tri-lateral North American Distance Education Research planning team were held in Texas in April 1994 and in Montreal in November 1994 and in Anaheim in April 1995. The pace of development regarding collaborative distance education policy with Mexico and Canada slowed in 1995 after the economic crisis hit Mexico, but the progress continues and is likely to continue with greater speed once Mexico's currency problems no longer dominate policy making as they did in 1995.

Further Information

The best sources for general information about international distance education are publications of ICDE, that is, the quarterly newsletter and ICDE'S biannual conference proceedings. Other good places to begin to study international developments are Young et al. (1980) for developing countries; Sewart, Keegan, and Holmberg (1983), Moran and Mugridge (1993) and Bates (1990b) for an overview of developments in Europe; Mugridge and Kaufman (1986) describe events in Canada. Demiray (1994) provides a detailed review of the background and research conducted at the Open University of Anadolu University in Turkey. The Asian Development Bank (1986) provides an excellent summary of developments in that part of the world and publications of the South African Institute for Distance Education (SAIDE) will provide up-to-date information about developments in that very important country. The names of other international organizations are given in the appendixes.

CHAPTER 12

The Transformation of Education

As you have seen in this book, distance education represents much more than simply using technology in teaching. It also represents changes in the way we conceptualize education, and the ways we organize the resources of people and capital that are dedicated to the enterprise of education. New technology led to the open university reform movement of the 1970s and 1980s, but we missed out on this in the United States. Now as another generation of technological innovation brings fresh interest in educational reform, there are new opportunities to effect major changes. In this chapter we introduce some of the issues that will have to be resolved as we restructure education, develop new policies, change our institutions, and the roles of teachers and learners in them.

There is a growing awareness in the United States at the end of the 1990s that along with such social structures as the health care system and perhaps the taxation system, education is in need of fundamental reform. While dissatisfaction with the schools and universities is expressed by parents, schoolteachers, students, employers, and politicians, there are no generally accepted ideas about exactly what changes are needed to improve the system. Distance education is frequently mentioned, but most educators and policymakers have only the most simple idea about what distance education means. There is a vague sense that using new communications technologies may help meet some of the problems facing educators, but there is nothing approaching agreement about how this will come about, or about what the effects of such use may be.

In our view, education can and should be transformed at each of the four levels that were introduced in Chapter One. The work of teachers in classrooms can be transformed so that they teach to virtual groups beyond their immediate physical presence. The work of distance teaching units in universities and other institutions is likely to take over a greater proportion of the parent institution's resources and play a greater part in its mission. More institutions specially dedicated to distance teaching, and more consortia of such institutions, are likely to emerge in the years ahead.

Most important, it seems likely that the most advanced form of distance education is likely to be a network of teachers and learners attached to no particular geographic location, a "virtual" institution, an almost infinite bank of teaching programs that can be accessed by every individual learner through communications technologies built on the fusion of digital telecommunications networks that are only now, in the late 1990s, being invented.

As educators and others discuss the transformation of education, here are some of the questions that have to be considered:

- What is the best way for the institution or organization to move from traditional classroom instruction to distance education?
- How does adopting distance education change the nature of the institutions and organizations, particularly the relationships among them?
- What is the likely impact of emerging technology on distance teaching and learning?
- What is the best way to prepare instructors for distance teaching?
- How will distance education affect lifelong learning?
- How will the theory and practice of distance education evolve?

Adoption of Distance Education

There are some precedents for adding on new technology to established teaching structures at program level and there is some experience of attempting to introduce distance education into traditional institutions. There is no precedent to show how to transform an educational institution or system into a distance education system, and no domestic experience of establishing a truly multimedia, integrated, total distance education system. Therefore, the most important research problems in our field concern the processes of transformation and the processes of adoption of new procedures, new ideas, new policies. This transformation cannot be left to speculation by theorists or to *ad hoc* experimentation (which is already happening). To move in this direction we need systematic and carefully designed studies. We need to know:

- Given that we have plenty of evidence of the cost-effectiveness of distance education, what are the factors that lead to rejection of distance education in so many institutions and states?
- In institutions and states where some change has occurred, what are the factors that led to these changes?
- Who are the key individuals making these decisions to change or not to change? What is the relative influence of teachers and faculty, administrators, labor unions, and politicians?

One hypothesis suggested by the literature is that success depends on the extent to which there is a transfer in the motivation for change from external funding to internal commitment by the teachers and others inside an organization. If this is so, how is such internal motivation for change generated and sustained?

The literature also suggests that the effective introduction of distance education is threatened by the too-cautious behavior of educational policymakers and administrators. Institutions and foreign systems that have successfully adopted distance education approaches have in all cases had a senior administrator or political leader prepared to assert the importance of change and to support the minority of individuals within the organization that are prepared to try out the new approach.

In the United States, the role of commercial interests is a matter of particular concern. Vendors have exploited the shortcomings of public education by selling distance education as a profit-making commodity, usually through home study, cable television, or computer network. These commercial providers, by definition, seek to make profits. They charge students as high a price as they can for their courses and spend the least they can in course design, delivery, and learner support. Other vendors press school districts and universities to buy their software and hardware. The vendor's enthusiasm for the product, impacting on busy educational administrators who are usually not well informed about distance education as a total system, results in the purchase of partial technologies. These are technologies that are good in themselves, but they do not lead to significant transformation of the educational system, because they do not fit with other technology, the teacher cadre, and long-term curriculum or instructional planning. They are not part of a well-designed, integrated system.

Changing Nature of Educational Institutions

A long-standing debate in the field of distance education concerns whether it is even possible for existing institutions to adapt themselves to provide distance education, or if there is no alternative to setting up special institutions dedicated to this purpose (e.g., open universities and home study schools). Catchpole (1992) describes the situation as follows:

> Distance education and open learning are being pulled in two directions. Some advocate that they should be moved away from traditional campuses and faculty. They argue for new, improved educational systems in order to better serve distance learners. Others believe that moving distance education to separate institutions (or very independent departments) will compromise the central faculty/student relationship. They believe it will prevent the gradual merging of classroom and distance education. This belief is based upon the idea that, with the tremendous array of communications technologies now available, the innovative classroom teacher can easily provide key features of the classroom experience over a distance and/or with greater openness. (p. 43)

Rumble (1992) discusses this issue from a financial perspective. He explains that dedicated distance learning institutions are the most cost-effective way to provide distance education as long as they offer relatively few courses to large numbers of students. However, as the number of courses offered increases and the student enrollment per course becomes smaller, the economy of scale that favors the institutional model breaks down. For the United States, the lesson to be learned here is that every distance teaching institution should offer to teach a very limited number of courses, but should teach over a very wide geographic area. With a considerable number of such institutions, each teaching a national or at least regional student population, and each one specializing in a limited number of courses, the effect would be a virtual open university in which students benefitted from low costs and high quality that are a consequence of economies of scale.

The case for the smaller, traditional school systems and universities is that they can offer their courses in distance learning format at program level, at a marginal cost once the initial costs of development and delivery technology are accounted for. Furthermore, there is strong financial pressure on many educational institutions (especially private colleges and universities) to "reach out" via distance education and increase their enrollments.

What Rumble suggests is likely to happen is an increasing convergence (and perhaps some actual mergers) between distance education and traditional "classroom-based" institutions. In other words, both types of institution are likely to offer a mix of on-site and off-site courses. In some cases the same course may be taught in both versions (i.e., the on-campus class becomes the local "site"). This situation is becoming increasingly common at many U.S. universities in which an increasing proportion of the courses are offered via some form of distance education. This convergence represents a growing acceptance of the relative benefits of distance education and traditional classroom formats under different circumstances (see Smith and Kelly, 1987). This is a *de facto*, or virtual, division of labor into a design and delivery component (from the distance teaching institution) and a learner support component (from the conventional class with its class teacher).

Impact of Emerging Technology

In Chapter 4 we surveyed the technologies currently used for distance education. However, technologies are changing at a rate probably faster than ever in history, and it seems certain that in the next year or two these are likely to have a major impact on the popularity and cost-effectiveness of distance education (Perelman, 1992). The most significant development in the late 1990s is ISDN (Integrated Services Digital Network). As mentioned in Chapter 4, ISDN is the technical name for the new generation of telephone lines based primarily on fiber-optic cable instead of copper. Fiber-optic cables can carry a tremendous amount of information. Furthermore, the information is transmitted in digital form rather than analog. This latter fact means that information can be compressed, further increasing transmission capacity (and speed). With such increased capacity, it becomes possible to transmit all types of information using telephone lines, including audio, video, images, and data. Thus any home or office with an ISDN connection has the capability to send and receive multimedia information. Computers are already competing with and likely to replace telephones as the primary communications device for learning and teaching as well as other communications needs. Furthermore, since ISDN also takes the place of cable television in terms of providing entertainment, so it enables the computer to supplant the television (or vice versa).

ISDN lines are available to business customers in a growing number of U.S. cities, and before very long, every telephone customer will have an ISDN connection. However, to take advantage of the multimedia transmission capabilities of ISDN, a computer is needed, with a codec (see Chapter 4). It may be some time before such a system is affordable enough for everyone to have one, but when they do, it will be possible for any individual to directly participate in videoconferences or access multimedia materials over networks, making distance education easier and more effective than at present. Perhaps more worrying than the availability of these technologies is the possibility that some sectors of the population do not have them because of cost or lack of awareness of their importance. This could lead to a severe deterioration of the "under class" of already illiterate, since access to the new communications networks will be a prerequisite for functioning in the society of the future.

As new technologies are developed, existing technologies will become more powerful. Satellite receivers are becoming smaller and less expensive, and more satellites and transmission capacity are becoming available (largely due to the use of compressed digital video). As satellite transmission becomes simpler, automated videoconferencing will become even more popular and affordable. Cellular telephone service (using both satellite and ISDN transmission) will become ubiquitous and eventually replace "wired" connections. This will mean that people can engage in technology-based education from any place they choose. Cable television will continue to expand (particularly as a result of cheaper satellites and ISDN), and this opens the possibility of a dramatic increase in the amount of educational (or "edutainment") broadcasting at the local, national, and international levels.

Finally, storage technology for computers will continue to offer more capacity for less money. CD-ROM already offers educators a highly cost-effective means of distributing multimedia materials. If every person owned a computer (preferably handheld) that contained a CD-ROM drive, we would have a very satisfactory technology for learning. In a few years CD-ROM will undoubtedly be replaced by something better (optical cards?) with even more capacity at a lower price, though the growth of on-line access suggests that CD-ROM technology may become outdated before very long.

As communications technologies change, become more interactive and more multimedia in nature, the problem for course developers will change from finding a way to deliver all the materials necessary, to finding enough good-quality material to deliver. The opportunity for learners will be to access programs from an almost infinite number of providers around the world. They will be assisted in this by the use of hypermedia interfaces which make large databases of information easy to use and useful as a learning tool.

Teacher Training

In Chapter 7 we discussed the nature of teaching (and tutoring) in distance education. This chapter showed that teaching at a distance requires additional or different skills than most current classroom teachers possess or new teachers are taught. How do we retrain teachers to be effective in a distance education setting, and how do we change our teacher training programs to properly prepare new teachers for teaching at a distance?

One obvious thing to do is to start converting existing teacher preparation and in-service programs to a distance education format (see Kearsley and Lynch, 1994; Knapczyk, 1991; Stowitschek, Mangus, and Rule, 1986). Then teachers would gain firsthand experience as distance learners. Teacher training curricula must be changed to include distance teaching fundamentals. Eventually, all curricula will need to be modified to incorporate distance learning activities and methods. But who will make these changes? Very few of the faculty at colleges of education (or faculty in general) have any expertise or experience with distance education; in fact, many of these faculty are reluctant to allow transformation in education that might lead to evolution of systems that are very different from those that they understand.

In absence of major initiatives by the federal or state governments, teacher training/retraining for distance education is likely to proceed slowly. This means that many teachers are likely to be thrust into distance teaching situations with little preparation and understanding of how to do it well. Consequently, we can expect a fairly long period of poor-quality distance education, resulting in many frustrated teachers and students. Over time, the proportion of teachers with proper training and experience will increase to the point where distance education becomes reliably effective and worthwhile. This point is likely to be reached more quickly if a state establishes a statewide system that would necessarily include a teacher training program.

Similar remarks can be made about the skills required for the design and development of distance education materials and programs, as discussed in Chapter 6. Instructional designers, writers, media producers, and other specialists involved in the creation of such materials need to be trained about the characteristics of effective distance education programs. This training may come from formal courses, self-instruction, or experience gained in working in distance education projects. In the meantime, a large percentage of distance education materials and programs will be poorly designed.

Lifelong Learning

Most theories and methods of education in North America are grounded in a "schooling" model, a view of education in which students attend schools for most of their youth to be prepared for the adult world of work, family, and social responsibilities. Early in the twentieth century, this model became increasingly inadequate to describe the education of people in a growing number of vocations and professions. A different view of education began with the need of farmers to keep up with changes in agriculture, then of engineers, physicians, lawyers, and others who found it necessary to take "continuing education" courses to keep up with advances in their professions. Over the decades, as the rate of the change of knowledge has quickened, this need for continuing education has broadened to the point where almost all adults need to take courses at some point in their careers to do their job (or retrain for a new one). As work becomes more information-based, and as society becomes more a society of people linked by communications technology, there is a need for all individuals not only to be better educated but to be *continuously* learning. Better education means having not only basic literacy (i.e., reading, writing, arithmetic) but an increasingly advanced technical knowledge to undertake even the most basic occupations. A good example is the change in skills required of someone who works in a factory or office today compared with just a generation ago. In the past such jobs involved mostly physical or psychomotor tasks with relatively little decision making or need to exercise problem-solving skills. Today both the factory and office worker must operate complicated computer systems that require a great deal of thinking power and technical understanding. As a consequence, the demand for basic education and training in all occupations has increased significantly over recent decades and will grow even more dramatically in the future. Traditional classroom instruction cannot cope with the sheer size of such demand for continuing education.

Another interesting development has been the emergence of demand for nonvocational continuing education by "older" students—individuals who decide to take courses or pursue degrees after they have retired from work. Every year, for example, the organization Elderhostel arranges hundreds of programs for senior citizens, mostly of conventional face-to-face type, at colleges and universities. A distance education approach to meeting the needs of this large part of the population is shown in the Seniornet organization. Seniornet is a computer based bulletin board/electronic mail network that provides a national "electronic community" for senior citizens to interact with others in their own homes wherever located in the country (Furlong and Kearsley, 1993). As people retire earlier and live longer, the number of older students will continue to increase substantially. In many cases these students would prefer not to travel far (or at all) for their educational activities. Obviously, this makes distance education of primary interest to them.

What all these changes add up to is a need for lifelong education on the part of most individuals in our society (Peterson, 1979), and for the development of distance education since there is no other way of providing programs

Another interesting development has been the emergence of demand for non-vocational education by 'older' students. This learner uses the traditional library and logs into Seniornet through her laptop computer.

for large numbers at the workplace and home on demand—that is, exactly when and where it is needed. Traditional classroom instruction worked fine for the schooling model because each site (i.e., school) taught essentially the same curriculum. But with lifelong education, the range and volume of learning demanded cannot be accommodated at numerous, redundant sites. People want and need the education to be brought to them, at their workplace, home, or nearby learning center. Furthermore, attending classes for a few days one or twice each year is going to be insufficient for many individuals. They need and want to have education available all year long. Continuing education must become "continuous education." The schooling model must be replaced to make lifelong learning work.

Competition and Cooperation Among Institutions

One of the particularly complex issues that distance education raises is the balance between competition and cooperation among educational institutions. On one hand, the benefits from developing distance education on a large scale and delivering programs over large geographic distances suggests there are tremendous opportunities for institutions to collaborate as members of consortia and to share materials or programs. On the other hand, distance education also makes it easier for institutions to compete against each other for students since there are no geographical constraints on where they operate. Every school, college, university, and training group could easily be in competition with all others in its discipline or subject area on a national or global basis.

A Market-driven Distance Education System?

In the summer of 1990, distance education experts from all levels of education convened at a symposium sponsored by the Los Alamos National Laboratory. Asked to think about future models of educational delivery, one group turned the challenge on its head and proposed that a distance education system should not be driven by designers and providers but by learner demand. A market-driven system is dependent on consumers having information, and therefore the basis of this approach is each potential learner having easy, free access to a real time, interactive database of information about courses produced locally, in-state, nationally, and internationally. The interface of such a system could be located in such public places as libraries and community centers, as well as being accessible from home computers by modem. Some of the resources currently spent on content expertise (teachers of history and mathematics, professors of economics, human resource trainers etc.) are diverted to provide a cadre of readily available expert helpers in accessing and interpreting the database. In response to any learner's inquiry, the system provides information in pyramidal fashion, starting with details of courses that can be accessed locally, perhaps in a distance or face-to-face mode, then if the user desires, giving information about state and nationally or internationally produced courses. The content of courses offered locally is likely to be more specific to the particular locality, while courses offered nationally are likely to be more generic. It is likely that local and national providers would team up to give the benefits of both large-scale production and local learner support. The system gives feedback to course producers to report unmet demand, which in turn brings new courses into the market.

In a significant statement the report from the group stated: "The content of the database would be determined and driven by market forces and the underlying self-interest of participants . . . (On) the issue of quality . . . the assumption is made that the users filter out what is and is not useful to them. However in the long run quality needs to be addressed. The two issues, how do we organize and how do we develop higher quality products, were seen as separate." In spite of this, the group did indicate a direction they thought the course development process might take. In what was called a "regional project level model," a number

Eventually, the increased opportunity that distance education provides for competition between educational providers is likely to result in greater collaboration among potential competitors. Just as the small oil producers early in the century had to combine to raise the capital and develop the movement of materials and people that were needed to make that industry viable, so educational institutions will find they do not have the resources to produce a flow of good programs except when they cooperate with others. They will be forced to form consortia and cooperate in order to be competitive. The pooled resources and economies of scale produced by collaboration will give each member of a consortium a competitive edge over institutions that act alone. Of course, such

of different institutions in a region (which may be as small as counties in a state or as large as a number of states) collaborate to develop and deliver programs and enter them into the database. The potential of this collaborative approach is that it permits individuals and institutions to specialize in such areas as content expertise, course design, contribution of particular media to a multimedia design and the ever-important process of learner support. An institution in, let us say, Switzerland that cooperated with a number of institutions in the United States to produce a course on cooking with chocolate, may arrange with community colleges across the country to provide on-site facilities for monthly meetings of persons in the course who wanted to exchange recipes or organize tastings!

We already have examples of interinstitutional collaboration in the design and delivery of programs by particular media, for example the Telecourse People described in Chapter 2. We have far fewer examples of collaboration *across* media, or between agencies of different kinds, such as universities and corporations. If a market for distance education products and services becomes established, it is likely to favor such collaborative course design and development arrangements since they are likely to produce better courses than single institution or single media efforts.

In most other countries national distance education systems have been set up by decision of central governments, with government funding, and courses are designed centrally and delivered nationally. There is very little competition among providers. The cost of a high-quality distance education course, using a mix of both interactive and recorded media, human- and technology-based delivery, is very high and results in a monopoly market for the producer of that course. An unanswered question is whether market forces are able to bring distance educators and communications specialists, as well as those who decide policy for education and training, into collaborative arrangements to design and deliver the same high-quality programs as are available to our foreign competitors by state planning.

Source: Based on Moore (1990b).

cooperation will not be easy to achieve since most institutions (i.e., faculty and administrators) are not used to extensive collaboration in teaching activities and curriculum development.

The competitive element of distance education will also place increasing emphasis on the quality of programs being offered. Since students can choose from many courses and programs, all of which are equally convenient to take, those which really meet their needs, are enjoyable, and provide good value for the money are going to be the most popular and hence successful. The best courses and programs will establish a reputation and be sought out by students. All aspects (good and bad) of consumer satisfaction and demand that apply to other products and services will operate in the educational world. Marketing will become a major preoccupation of educational institutions in a full-fledged distance learning environment.

This is the optimistic scenario, and one which we are inclined to believe is likely to come about. However, it is also worth bearing in mind that a free market approach has not been successful in providing some other important goods and services, and there is no guarantee that it will succeed in providing good-quality distance education. The use of communications media in the entertainment industry has not had the effect of distributing good-quality entertainment to the mass of the population; competition to provide programs at lower costs than other providers and to satisfy the largest numbers of people at that low cost has led to a downward spiral in aesthetic taste and quality that would be even more disastrous if it were emulated in the field of education. If a market approach to the distribution of distance education is to be contemplated by policymakers in future, it will be vitally important to ensure that there is a very strong regulating authority, with academic representatives in control at all levels.

Third-Generation Distance Education: The Distance Education Network

Bricks and mortar have provided the technology—the classroom—of education for centuries. When distance education was invented in the late nineteenth century, it was the universities of brick and mortar that provided the home and the model of instruction. As we explained in Chapter 2, in this *first-generation* distance education, classroomlike teaching was provided by conventional teachers to learners at a distance by means of correspondence. An essential characteristic of traditional education is that the learning that occurs there is validated and certified by the faculty located in that place, among those bricks and mortar. The certificate of learning—whether it be obtained on campus or at a distance—is named for the geographic location of the faculty.

During the 1970s and 1980s open universities were developed in many countries. These second-generation distance education institutions had no classrooms, and learning occurred in students' own environments. One of Wedemeyer's main contributions to the conceptualization of the open universities (see Chapter 2) was to urge that these institutions have the authority to confer their own degrees. Thus in Great Britain today about one-tenth of all undergraduate degrees are awarded by The Open University; no place name is attached to the certificate, but instead the certificate indicates the process—"open education"—by which the learning was acquired.

Second-generation distance education institutions are only partially place-free. While students have considerable independence with regard to when, where, and to some extent, how they learn, they are as limited in their choice of instructors as are students in a bricks-and-mortar university. Faculty are tied to the distance teaching institution; in fact they must often be physically on a campus to carry out some of their administrative and course design responsibilities. It is true that a second-generation distance teaching institution may contract with external experts to contribute to a course, but they are just that, "external" to the institution. The bulk of teaching has to be done by the tenured, regular, "internal" faculty.

With the emergence of technologies that were not available when second-generation institutions were set up, such restrictions are no longer necessary. With the emergence of ISDN-based electronic highways to our homes and workplaces, we are rapidly approaching technical readiness for the Distance Education Network—a virtual university, school, or training department in which learners anywhere can interact with teachers anywhere. This is not to suggest there will not be a continuing role for institutions of the longer established types. For the foreseeable future it is likely there will continue to be important roles for units working within the framework of brick-and-mortar institutions and for institutions of the open university type.

However, there is a possibility that the United States, having missed the opportunity of participating in the reforms associated with the development of open universities, can reestablish a world leadership in distance education as the latest technologies allow for the setting up of distance education networks.

Such an organization may not be a formally constituted organization at all. It is like an open road where individuals and groups can wander at will. It makes courses prepared by any institution or individual available to students anywhere. A student's faculty is no longer limited to those professors who assemble in any place any more than a teacher's students have to assemble in any one place. Not only can students learn wherever they are located, from instructional resources wherever they are located, but no student of a subject is compelled to take instruction from exactly the same teacher as any other student. Teachers can be accessed from any state, any country, at any time, in any combination of teachers; information resources can be accessed from any state or country and at any time and in any combination. Similarly, advice and guidance can be accessed universally.

Such a network of learners and teachers returns us to the earliest, most basic concept of "university," a point made by Rossman:

> The word university first referred to a guild of students, then to a guild of scholars. From the beginning the universities were international. Students often travelled in search of the course they wanted, wandering from country to country much as some now explore the "electronic highways." The original universities had very little organization, though there was a vigorous intellectual life. Its first charter simply recognized a body of students and teachers that already existed. Similarly today, no international governmental agency is establishing a new global system of higher education. Yet the electronic university seems to be emerging and is closely related to concerns of leading educators. (1992, p. xiii)

While we have not yet been able to organize a viable international university network, there are a number of experiments taking place that can be seen as primitive examples of a distance education network. The example of the

Penn State program teaching students in Finland, Estonia, Mexico, and the United States has already been referred to. From the point of view of the Estonian or Mexican students, they are accessing the best program that they have located anywhere in the world, using computer conferencing and audio- and audiographic conferencing. These are very primitive technologies and also organizational arrangements, but they give some ideas about the direction we will go in as distance teaching networks emerge. Before long it is expected that an organization will be formed that will provide the information and other support that potential students need to access programs from more than just one institution, across state and national borders.

Other illustrations of the emerging global organizations are provided by the University of the World and the Global University Consortium. These are both schemes for international electronic universities that use state-of-the-art computer, satellite, and television technology to disseminate courseware, research data, scientific documents, and other materials over global networks of educational and research institutions.

The University of the World is a concept of Dr. James Grier Miller, a Past President of the University of Louisville. It aims to bring into a worldwide consortium existing educational institutions that will use electronic telecommunication to disseminate educational resources to students and faculties throughout the world. By 1990, using the electronic networks BITNET in North America and EARN in Europe, the University of the World had set up centers in nine countries, besides the United States. As well as Americans on its Board of Trustees were Lord Perry from Great Britain, the first Vice-Chancellor of the British Open University.

The Global Electronic University (GEU) is another proposed worldwide distance education network that would include universities, businesses, governmental and nongovernmental agencies, as well as individual members. GEU hopes to provide a technology package for international access of educational resources via all forms of telecommunications, especially satellite and computer conferencing (Utsumi, Rossman, and Rosen, 1990). GEU demonstrations are already providing experience with multipoint to multipoint, multimedia, interactive international educational teleconferencing. Among future ideas from GEU is " . . . a three space station library system serving the entire globe, each interlinked by laser beam. Each station at a geo-synchronous orbit will be equipped with erasable compact optical disc memory and computers. Hundreds of thousands of these could be stored in space to be accesssed by a juke box type unit. Videos of educational services (courses, seminars, conferences, etc.), as well as all kinds of information can be uplinked to the nearby station and stored in the memory and computers. Individual students with small dish antennae anywhere in the world could receive educational excellence available from any other part of the world" (Utsumi et al. 1990, p. 108). While we are not suggesting that this is a realistic prediction, indeed technology is likely to make such procedures unnecessarily cumbersome, it does show the creative thinking that is going into considerations of how to transform education from what we currently know.

Before such networks can work, however, there is a prior need for inventing a structure to inform students of the learning resources that are available, that recruits and supports instructors in their designing of courses, and organizes, controls, and monitors instruction. There is no organization that links the efforts of one distance education network with others to provide a full curriculum. A particular need that, when met, is likely to boost the evolution of a distance education network is the establishment of valid certification. So far there is no organization that can provide students, wherever located, with an internationally exchangeable, reasonably priced credit toward a degree. In spite of a number of efforts to establish certification of learning by nontraditional methods, there is still no agency in North America that has the power, the recognition, the authority, to provide a certification of independent, individually constructed learning programs, that has credibility in the academic and business environment comparable to the degree awarded by a brick-and-mortar university.

Rossman writes: "The agenda for global higher education begins with questions about who is to coordinate and regulate electronic courses offered on network or satellite; who is to set standards, especially when nations and universities disagree; what technology is to be used and how can it be shared; and who is to arbitrate and decide on such matters as degrees and exchange of course credits. Also, what kind of administration and funding can a worldwide electronic university have if it involves many governments, private colleges, and the teaching programs of business corporations" (1993, p. 13).

Final Thoughts on the Systems Approach

As we think about the emergence of new networks and either the planned construction or market-driven emergence of new organizational structures to support distant learners, we are brought back to one of the fundamental concepts that we wanted to introduce in this book. There cannot be within any unit, institution, or the nation at large, or even in a global network, a viable distance education program in the future that is not in some way integrated into a total system. Making the changes and using the technologies that will bring this about is the biggest challenge of all. It is a task for teachers, school administrators, corporate training directors and government policymakers, and as students who have already taken up such positions, or will soon do so, it is an historically important task that, finally, rests in *your* hands.

Summary

This is an exciting time to be an educator, whether a teacher or administrator. Over the next decade education will undergo a fundamental transformation as teaching and learning at a distance becomes at least as important as the traditional classroom approach that has lasted for more than a century. In this chapter and throughout the book, we have tried to point to some of the important issues that need to be addressed as this transformation occurs, and that will provide challenge and opportunity for the next generation of educators.

These issues include knowing and dealing with the factors that affect the adoption of distance education; understanding and dealing with the changes that institutions will adopt as they adapt greater involvement in distance education; understanding and taking advantage of the impact of emerging technologies; understanding and adapting the institution to the trend toward lifelong learning; understanding and bringing about the changes needed in the training of teachers; understanding and dealing with an appropriate balance between competition and cooperation among institutions; understanding and adapting to the emergence of a worldwide distance learning network.

We hope that reading this book has helped make you more aware than before about what distance education is, what it is not, and how it works. We hope you better understand the many different components of a distance education system and their interdependence. And we hope this book has encouraged you to become involved in distance education, as teachers, administrators, as continuing learners and researchers, to become part of the transformation that is occurring in education and, as a result, in our society generally.

U.S. Organizations

Distance education is becoming of interest to many organizations whose main interest has been traditional higher education, corporate training, etc. It is worth looking out for sessions at conferences and occasional articles in their journals, though you will need to be alert to the various interpretations of the idea and practice of distance education that nonspecialists may hold. Here are a few of the more specialized organizations in the United States:

American Center for the Study of Distance Education (ACSDE)—based at Pennsylvania State University, the ACSDE conducts research and offers graduate courses about distance education, publishes the *American Journal of Distance Education,* organizes conferences, and produces DEOS, the Distance Education Online Symposium, an on-line discussion group/newsletter via Internet.

Address:
Pennsylvania State University
403 S. Allen St., Suite 206
University Park, PA 16801-5202
814-863-3764

American Association for Collegiate Independent Study (AACIS)—a recently established organization of professionals involved in university independent study. Main activities are an annual conference, a newsletter, and on-line listserv, AACIS-L.

Address:
Marie Barber
Department of Independent Study
320 NCCE, University of Nebraska-Lincoln,
Lincoln, NE 68683-0900
Fax: 402-472-1901

American Council for Distance Education and Training (ACDET)—a U.S. affiliate of the International Council for Distance Education (ICDE). Publishes a newsletter, cosponsors the annual conference at University of Wisconsin, and provides U.S. liasion with ICDE.

Address:
16414 San Pedro
Suite 680
San Antonio, TX 78232

Annenberg/CPB Project—based on funding from the Annenberg Foundation, this project began in 1981 and has sponsored research and the development of many alternative educational programs (especially television-based) at the college level.

Address:
901 E St. N.W.
Washington, DC 20004
202-842-9344

Association for Media-Based Continuing Education for Engineers (AMCEE)—consortium established in 1976 which provides hundreds of videotape-based courses on engineering and related topics, derived mostly from university classes. Also offers televised workshops and seminars through NTU.

Address:
613 Cherry St.
Suite 307
Atlanta, GA 30332-0210
1-800-338-9344

International Teleconferencing Association (ITCA)—organization for teleconferencing (audio and video) vendors; holds annual conferences and publishes a newsletter.

Address:
1650 Tysons Blvd.
Suite 200
McLean, VA 22102
703-506-3280

International University Consortium (IUC)—based at the University of Maryland, the IUC is a partnership of colleges, universities, and educational agencies mainly in the United States and Canada that develops and distributes media-assisted courses for adult degree programs.

Address:
University College
College Park, MD 20742-1612
301-985-7845

The Distance Education and Training Council—voluntary association of home study schools, primarily concerned with standards and practices; national accrediting body for for-profit organizations offering correspondence courses (founded in 1926 as the National Home Study Council (NHSC)).

Address:
1601 18th St. N.W.
Washington, DC 20009
202-234-5100

National University Continuing Education Association (NUCEA)—membership consists of 300 colleges/universities; publishes a list of all independent study courses offered by members and presents annual awards for outstanding courses (founded in 1908 as the National University Extension Association). The NUCEA Independent Study Division produces a newsletter.

Address:
1 Dupont Circle
Washington, DC 20036
202-659-3130

U.S. Distance Learning Association (USDLA)—a member organization concerned with teleconferencing; has a journal called *Ed*, published by Applied Business Corporation, which also publishes *Teleconference: The Business Communication Magazine*, and organizes annual TeleCon and IDLCon conferences.

Address:
P.O. Box 5129
San Ramon, CA 94583
510-820-5845

National Distance Learning Center—a computerized on-line database system for listing and accessing programming information on courses offered by correspondence, satellite, videotape, audio, and other technologies. Covers courses from K-12 to Ph.D. Operates as a public service with no charges.

Address:
4800 New Hartford Road
Owensboro, KY 42303
502-686-4556
Fax: 502-686-4558

Western Cooperative for Educational Telecommunications—formed in 1989 by the Western Interstate Commission for Higher Education (WICHE), this consortium coordinates policy and planning for over 100 educational institutions and agencies, spanning 16 western states, and publishes studies and handbooks relevant to the distance education activities of its members.

Address:
P.O Drawer P
Boulder, CO 80301-9752
303-541-0290

Journals, Magazines, and Directories

The following are periodicals that are either devoted solely to the field of distance education or feature articles about related topics of interest to students and practitioners in the field. Note that many of the organizations listed in the previous section publish a newsletter or journal for their membership.

The American Journal of Distance Education
American Center for the Study of Distance Education
Pennsylvania State University
403 S. Allen St., Suite 206
University Park, PA 16801-5202
814-863-3764

Distance Education Newsletter
RRD #2, Box 7290
Winthrop, ME 04364
207-395-4615

Ed (The Journal of the USDLA) and *TeleConference*
Applied Business Telecommunications
Box 5106
San Ramon, CA 94583
510-820-5563

Educational Technology
700 Palisade Ave
Englewood Cliffs, NJ 07632
201-871-4007

THE (Technological Horizons in Education) Journal
150 El Camino Real, Suite 112
Tustin, CA 92680-3615
714-730-4011

TeleConferencing News
Knowledge Industry Publications
701 Westchester Ave
White Plains, NY 10604
914-328-9157

There are a number of journals about distance education published outside the U.S. Some of the major ones are

Distance Education
Distance Education Centre
University College of Southern Queensland
PO Darling Heights
Toowoomba, Qld 4350
Australia

The Journal of Distance Education
CADE Secretariat
151 Slater Street
Ottawa K1P 5NI
Canada

Open Learning (U.K.)
Subscription Dept.
P.O. Box 77
Harlow,
Essex CM19 5BQ
U.K.

Here is a list of directories that describe distance education courses, programs, or providers:

Directory of Courses and Materials for Training in Distance Education
Commonwealth of Learning
#1700-777 Dunsmuir St.
Vancouver, BC
CANADA V7Y 1K4
604-660-4675

The USDLA Funding Sourcebook
United States Distance Learning Association (USDLA)
P.O. Box 5129
San Ramon, CA 94583
510-820-5845

Going the Distance
Annenberg/CPB
901 E St. NW
Washington, DC 20004
202-842-3600

At A Distance
Virginia Ostendorf Inc.
P.O. Box 2896
Littleton, CO 80161-2896
303-797-3131

Distance Learning Projects in the US: K-12 (software)
U.S. Dept Education, OERI
Washington, DC
202-219-1513

The Diversity Directory : Distance_Learn (computer database)
Regents College
7 Columbia Circle
Albany, NY 12203-5159
518-464-8500

The Independent Study Catalog (compiled by the NUCEA)
Peterson's Guides
P.O. Box 2123
Princeton, NJ 08543
800-338-3282

The Business Television Directory
Irwin Communications, Inc.
2000 L St. N.W., Suite 702
Washington, DC 20036
202-223-1016

Directory of Accredited Home Study Schools
Distance Education and Training Council
1601 18th St. NW
Washington, DC 20009
202-234-5100

Campus-Free College Degrees
Thorson Guides
P.O.Box 470886
Tulsa, OK 74147
918-622-2811

Online Networks and Databases

There are a number of online databases and electronic discussion groups, including:

Distance Education Online Symposium (DEOS)
American Center for the Study of Distance Education
Pennsylvania State University
403 S. Allen St., Suite 206
University Park, PA 16801-5202
814-863-3764
DEOSNEWS@PSUVM.PSU.EDU

The Online Chronicle of Distance Education and Communication
NOVA Southeastern University
LISTSERV@ALPHA.ACAST.NOVA.EDU

Ostendorf Online
Virginia Ostendorf Inc.
P.O. Box 2896
Littleton, CO 80161-2896
303-797-3131

The National Distance Learning Center
Owensboro Community College
4800 New Hartford Rd.
Owensboro, KY 42303-9990
502-686-4556
To log-on: 502-686-4555

Distance Education Forum
CompuServe Inc
5000 Arlington Center Blvd
Columbus, OH 43220
800-848-8199

International Center for Distance Learning (ICDL) Database
U.K. Open University
Telnet: ACSVAX.OPEN.AC.UK
[also available in CD-ROM format]

Conferences and Workshops

In addition to the conferences and workshops conducted by the organizations listed in Appendix A, here are some others:

American Center for Study of Distance Education
Holds one or two conferences a year.
For information, check *The American Journal of Distance Education*

Annual Conference on Distance Learning
University of Wisconsin
Dept. Continuing & Vocational Education
225 North Mills St.
Madison, WI 53706
608-262-8611

American Association for Collegiate Independent Study (AACIS)
Annual Conference
(See address in Appendix A)

Certificate Program in Distance Learning
University of Wisconsin
(Same address as above)
608-262-8530

Distance Education for Employee and Customer Training
(3 day workshop)
University of Wisconsin
Dept. Engineering Professional Development
432 North Lake St.
Madison, WI 53706
608-263-3160

Distance Education Research Conference
Texas A&M University (occasional conference)
College Station, Texas 77843-3256
409-845-3016

International Distance Learning Conference (IDLCON)
(Annual conference in Washington, DC)
Telecon (Annual conference in Anaheim, CA)

Basic Seminars (4-day seminar)
Applied Business TeleCommunications
Box 5106
San Ramon, CA 94583
405-743-0320

International Teleconferencing Association (ITCA)
Annual Conference
(See ITCA in Appendix A)

Oregon State University
(Annual conference)
Office of Continuing Higher Education
Oregon State University
503-737-1288

Teaching Through Interactive Television (2-day workshop)
Virginia Ostendorf Inc.
P.O. Box 2896
Littleton, CO 80161-2896
303-797-3131

Teletraining Institute (3-day workshop)
First Friday (monthly audioconference)
Parker Consulting
370 Student Union Bldg.
Oklahoma State University
Stillwater, OK 74078-0801
405-744-7510

University of Maine at Augusta
(Annual conference)
Director of Conferences
University Heights
Augusta ME 04330-9410
207-621-3170

U.S. Distance Education Providers

Here is a sampling of organizations and institutions in the United States providing distance education courses:

Arts and Sciences Teleconferencing Service (ASTS)
Oklahoma State University
401 Life Sciences East
Stillwater, OK 74078-0276
800-452-2787

AT&T Learning Network
P.O. Box 6391
Parsippany, NJ 07054
800-367-7225

Big Sky Telegraph
Western Montana College
710 S. Atlantic
Dillon, MT 59725
406-633-7338
E-mail: Franko@bigsky.dillon.mt.us

Cable in the Classroom
1900 North Beauregard Street
Suite 108
Alexandria, VA 22311
703-845-1400

Calvert School (K-8)
105 Tuscany Rd
Baltimore, MD 21210
410-243-6030

Channel One
Whittle Educational Network
333 Main Street
Knoxville, TN 37902
800-445-2619

Connect-Ed (graduate)
65 Shirley Lane
White Plains, NY 10607
914-428-8766

Educational Satellite Network (K-12)
2100 I-70 Dr., S.W.
Columbia, MO 65203
800-243-3376

EDUNET
P.O.Box 298
Saco, MT 59261
406-527-3531
Computer phone: 406-527-3521

Galaxy Classrooms (K-12)
200 N. Sepulveda Blvd
El Segundo, CA 90245
310-364-7341

The Learning Channel
1525 Wilson Boulevard
Rosslyn, VA 22209
703-276-0881

Massachusetts Corp. for Educational Telecommunications (K-12)
38 Sidney St., Suite 300
Cambridge, MA 02139-4135
617-621-0290

Mind Extension University (undergraduate/graduate)
P.O. Box 6612
Englewood, CO 80155-6612
800-777-MIND

Nova Southeastern University (graduate)
3301 College Ave.
Ft. Lauderdale, FL 33314
800-541-6682

NASA Telelectures
Virginia Air and Space Center
600 Settlers Landing Road
Hampton, VA 23699-4033
804-727-0900

NGS Kids Network
National Geographic Society
Educational Services
Washington, DC 20036
800-368-2728

National Technological University (graduate engineering)
700 Centre Ave.
Ft. Collins, CO 80526
303-484-6050

National University Teleconferencing Network (continuing education)
Old Dominion University
129 Health Sciences Bldg.
Norfolk, VA 23529-0293
804-683-3012

Public Broadcasting System
Adult Learning Service
1320 Braddock Place
Alexandria, VA 22314
1-800-257-2578

Satellite Communications for Learning (SCOLA)
P.O. Box 619
McClelland, IA 51548-0619
712-566-2202

Satellite Telecommunications Educational Programming (STDP)
Telecommunications Division Administrator
STEP
4022 East Broadway
Spokane, WA 99202
509-536-0141

Satellite Educational Resources Consortium (SERC)
P.O. Box 50008
Columbia, SC 29250
803-252-2782

The Telecourse People
South Carolina ETV
Marketing Department
Box 11000
Columbia, SC 29211
803-737-3446

TI-IN Network Inc.
121 Interpark
Suite 300
San Antonio, TX 78216-1803
512-490-3900

University of Phoenix Online (undergraduate/graduate)
101 California St.
Suite 505
San Francisco, CA 94111
415-956-2121

Walden University (doctoral)
801 Anchor Rode Dr.
Naples, FL 33940
813-261-7277

World Classroom
Global Learning Corporation
P.O. Box 201361
Arlington, TX 76006
800-866-4452
E-mail: global@glc.dallas.tx.us

International Research Centers and Organizations

There are a handful of centers around the world that have been set up specifically to conduct research. They include the following:

Centre for Distance Education (CDE)—Part of Athabasca University in Athabasca, Canada. Established in 1986.

Central Institute for Distance Education Research (ZIFF)—Part of the FernUniversität located in Hagen, Germany. Established in 1975.

German Institute for Distance Education (DIFF)—Conducts research on continuing education focusing on learning/teaching models and media. Located at the University of Tübingen, Germany. Founded in 1967.

Instituto Universitario de Educación a Distancia (IUED)—Located at the Universidad Nacional de Educación a Distancia (UNED) in Madrid, Spain.

International Centre for Distance Learning (ICDL)—Located on the campus of the British Open University, the ICDL was orginally established in 1978. The primary function of the ICDL is to serve as a documentation center for distance education. It maintains a computer database listing courses available worldwide that is accessible via Internet.

National Distance Education Center (NDEC)—Located on the campus of the Dublin City University in Dublin, Ireland.

Most major countries in the world have their own distance learning organization that attempts to promote collaboration through annual conferences, publications, and other activities. However, there are some organizations with transnational scope or missions. Here is a brief summary of some of these organizations.

Asociacion Iberoamericana de Educación Superior a Distancia (AIESAD)—Organization of approximately 50 institutions interested in developing distance teaching programs in Spanish and Portuguese. Sponsored by UNED and based in Madrid, Spain.

Asian Association of Open Universities (AAOU)—Organization of Asian open universities. Established in 1987.

Commonwealth of Learning—Established in 1988 to facilitate the sharing of distance education expertise and course materials among the British Commonwealth countries. Headquarters in Vancouver, Canada.

Consorcio-Red de Educacion A Distancia (CREAD)—A consortium intended to facilitate cooperation among distance educators in the Americas, particularly Latin America and the Caribbean. Founded in 1990.

Consortium International Francophone de Formation a Distance (CIFFAD)—A consortium consisting of more than 200 institutions from 25 countries concerned with promoting distance education in French-speaking countries. Established in 1988.

European Association of Distance Teaching Universities (EADTU)—represents over 30 different institutions from 12 European countries. Established in 1987.

European Association of Users of Satellites in Training and Education Programmes (EUROSTEP)—A consortium of more than 100 organizations who produce and share educational programs delivered via the Olympus satellite (more than 500 downlink sites in 32 countries). Established in 1989 when the satellite became operational.

European Distance Education Network (EDEN)—Created to foster collaboration among institutions, networks, and other agencies involved in distance education in Europe, especially central and eastern Europe. First conference was held in Prague, Czechslovakia, in 1991.

European Open Learning Network (SATURN)—An independent association of approximately 80 organizations involved in distance education. Established in 1987 with headquarters in Amsterdam, the Netherlands. European Project of Advanced Continuing Education (EuroPACE)—A nonprofit organization primarily supported by high-tech corporations that delivers technical courses (mostly engineering) via satellite to members (currently 70 organizations) in Europe. Established in 1989. Headquarters in Paris, France.

GLOSAS/Global University—A private organization founded by Takeshi Utsumi to promote the efforts of corporations, universities, and other groups to exchange educational and training courses across international boundaries via computer and telecommunications technologies, including the establishment of a global electronic university (GU). Headquarters in Flushing, New York.

International Association for Continuing Engineering Education (IACEE)—Purpose is to improve the quality of engineering education worldwide with over 500 members representing 71 countries. Headquarters are in Espoo, Finland.

International Council for Distance Education (ICDE)—A worldwide organization dedicated to distance education at all levels. Affiliated with UNESCO as a specialist nongovernmental agency. Originally founded in 1938 as the International Council for Correspondence Education (ICCE) and changed its name in 1982. Coordinates the activities of national/regional distance education associations around the world. Holds a major international conference every two years, with 1997 World Conference at Penn State University, the first in the United States since 1972.

University of the World—A private effort to create a worldwide university using electronic media by linking key members of government agencies and academic institutions. Established in 1983 with headquarters in La Jolla, California.

World Association for the Use of Satellites in Education (WAUSE)—organization dedicated to promoting the worldwide use of satellites for education. Established in 1991 under the auspices of the Community of Mediterranean Universities. Headquarters in Bari, Italy.

GLOSSARY

Analog Information represented and transmitted in the form of a continuous electro-magnetic wave (contrast with digital).

Asynchronous Communication in which interaction between sender and receiver does not take place simultaneously (e.g., e-mail or fax).

Audiographics Transmission of images as well as audio over ordinary telephone lines (includes electronic whiteboards, still video, and computer-based systems).

Bandwidth The range of frequencies that can be carried by a telecommunications carrier (e.g., telephone lines, satellite transmissions) measured in Hertz (Hz).

Bridge A system that allows two or more telephone or videoconferencing lines/sites to be interconnected.

Broadcast The one-way transmission of information (i.e., conventional radio and television).

BBS (Bulletin Board System) A form of computer conferencing system that usually runs on a personal computer.

BTV (Business Television) Private television networks used by organizations for training and other communication purposes.

Byte A unit of computer memory measured in thousands (K), millions (M), or billions (G).

CATV (Cable Television) The delivery of television signals via coax or fiber-optic cable connections, managed by commercial or nonprofit organizations.

C-Band The original frequency in the 4-6 GigaHertz range used for satellite transmission that uses large receiving dishes (3 meter).

CCTV (Closed Circuit Television) A system for transmitting television signals over a private cable network.

CD-ROM (Compact Disc—Read Only Memory) The form of CDs that can store information in digital form and can be read by computers.

CODEC (Coder Decoder) A device used to convert analog signals to digital form (and vice versa), primarily used in video transmissions.

Compressed Video Video images in digital form that allow redundant information to be eliminated, thereby reducing the amount of bandwidth needed for their transmission. The amount of compression (i.e., bandwidth) determines the picture quality.

Digital Information stored in the form of bits (on/off signals) and which can be stored and transmitted via electronic media.

DBS (Direct Broadcast Satellite) A satellite capable of uplinking/downlinking directly to small diameter dishes (1 to 2 feet) at user sites (i.e., offices, homes).

Downlink The transmission of signals from a satellite to an earth station (i.e., receiving dish).

E-mail (Electronic Mail) Messages stored and sent via a computer system.

Fiber-Optics The transmission of audio, video, and computer information in digital form using pulses of light through glass fibers.

Host A large computer (mainframe) that stores and relays information from other computers (usually PCs) in a network.

Hypermedia The storage and retrieval of text, images, audio, and video in computer (digital) form.

Internet The global computer network that interconnects all other networks using a common telecommunications protocol (TCP/IP).

ISDN (Integrated Services Digital Network) A digital telecommunications channel that allows for the integration of voice, video, and data using a single line.

ITFS (Instructional Television Fixed Service) Television channels that use high-frequency channels and microwave transmission to broadcast over a 20-to-30-mile distance (line of sight).

Ku-Band A relatively new transmission frequency in the 12-18 GigaHertz range used for satellite transmission that uses smaller diameter receiving dishes (one meter).

LAN (Local Area Network) Computer networks in a single building or campus connected via coax or fiber-optic cable.

Mainframe A large computer with a lot of storage and processing power.

Modem (Modulation Demodulation) A device that allows computers to send and receive information over conventional (analog) telephone lines.

Multiplexor A device used to combine telephone or video signals from different sources into a single channel.

PC (Personal Computer) An affordable desktop or laptop computer used at home, office, or school.

RAM (Random Access Memory) The memory component of a computer that is used to temporarily store data and programs while processing, measured in bytes.

RS-232 Standard interface for a serial connection to a computer (usually used to connect modems).

Server A computer in a network that serves the role of handling transmissions among other computers in the network.

Slow-Scan A method for transmitting video images over telephone lines (also referred to as freeze frame or still video transmission).

Synchronous Communication in which interaction between sender and receiver takes place simultaneously (e.g., telephone or teleconferencing).

Telecourses Courses in video format that are delivered via television or videotape.

Transponder The component of a satellite that sends and receives the transmissions.

Uplink The transmission of signals from an earth station to the satellite.

VCR (Video Cassette Recorder) Device for playing and recording videotapes in Beta, VHS, or 8mm format.

Videodisc Optical storage medium that allows random access of information when connected to a computer.

VSAT (Very Small Aperture Terminals) Small satellite receiving dishes usually 4 to 6 inches in diameter used for digital transmission.

WWW (World Wide Web) - A hypermedia capability on the Internet.

BIBLIOGRAPHY

Ahlm, M. (1972). Telephone instruction in distance education. *Epistolodidactica, 2*, 49–64.

Anderson, J. S. (1992). A historical overview of telecommunications in the health care industry. In M. G. Moore (Ed.), *Readings in Distance Education*, 3. University Park, PA: ACSDE.

Anderson, T., & Mason, R. (1993). International computer conferencing for professional development: The Bangkok Project. *American Journal of Distance Education, 7*(2), 5–18.

Arias, A. Jr., & Bellman, B. (1990). Computer-mediated classrooms for culturally and linguistically diverse learners. *Computers-in-the-Schools, 7*(1–2), 227–241.

Armstrong, M., Toebe, D., & Watson, M. (1985). Strengthening the instructional role in self-directed learning activities. *Journal of Continuing Education in Nursing, 16*(3), 75-84.

Asian Development Bank (1986). *Distance Education in Asia and the Pacific: Proceedings of the 1986 Regional Seminar*. Manila: The Asian Development Bank.

Astin, A. W. (1975). *Preventing Students From Dropping Out*. San Francisco: Jossey-Bass.

Atman, K. S. (1986). The role of conation (striving) in the distance learning enterprise. *American Journal of Distance Education, 1*(1), 23–29.

Axford, R. W. (1963). Lighty—Fountain of idealism. In C.A. Wedemeyer (Ed.), *Brandenburg Memorial Essays on Correspondence Study*, vol. I. Madison: University of Wisconsin-Extension.

Baath, J. (1981). Introducing the personal tutor/counsellor in the system of distance education. *Epistolodidactica, 1*, 36–48.

Baldwin, T. F., and McVoy, D. S. (1983). *Cable Communication*. Englewood Cliffs, NJ: Prentice Hall.

Banathy, B. (1993). *A Systems View of Education*. Englewood Cliffs, NJ: Educational Technology Publications.

Barker, B. O. (1987). The effects of learning by satellite on rural schools. Paper presented at Learning by Satellite Conference, Tulsa, OK. April 12 (ERIC ED 284693).

Barker, B. O., & Dickson, M. W. (1993). Aspects of successful practice for working with college faculty in distance learning programs. *Ed Journal, 8*(2), J–6.

Barker, B. O., & Goodwin, R. D. (1992). Audiographics: Linking remote classrooms. *Computing Teacher, 19*(7), 11–15.

Barker, B. O., & Platten, M. R. (1989). Student perceptions on the effectiveness of college credit courses taught via satellite. In M. G. Moore & G. C. Clark (Eds.), *Readings in Distance Learning and Instruction*. University Park, PA: ACSDE.

Barry, M., & Runyan, G. (1995). A review of distance learning studies in the U.S. military. Pensacola: University of West Florida. Unpublished paper.

Bates, A. W. (1984). *The Role of Technology in Distance Education*. London: Croom Helm.

Bates, A. W. (Nov. 1988). Technology for distance education: A 10-year perspective. *Open Learning, 3*–12.

Bates, A. W. (1990a). Interactivity as a criterion for media selection in distance education. Paper presented to the Asian Association of Open Universities. ERIC # ED 329245.

Bates, A. W. (1990b). *Media and Technology in European Distance Education*. Milton Keynes, UK: Open University.

Batey, A., & Cowell, R. N. (1986). *Distance Education: An Overview*. Portland, OR: Northwest Regional Educational Lab. (ERIC: ED 278519)

Beare, P. L. (1989). The comparative effectiveness of videotape, audiotape, and telelecture in delivering continuing teacher education. *Amer. J. Dist. Educ., 3*(2), 57–66.

Beijer, E. (1972). A study of students' preferences with regard to different models of two-way communications. *Epistolodidactica, 2*, 83–90.

Berge, Z. (1995). Evaluation of a computer conference used for distance learning. *Amer. J. Dist. Educ.,* in press.

Berge, Z. L., & Collins, M. P. (1993). Computer conferencing and on-line education. *Arachnet Electronic Journal on Virtual Culture, 1*(3). (Archived at LISTSERV@KENTVM as BERGE.V1N3).

Berge, Z., & Collins, M. (1995). *Computer Mediated Communication and the Online Classroom*. Cresskill, NJ: Hampton Press.

Berk, E., & Devlin, J. (1991). *Hypertext/Hypermedia Handbook*. New York: McGraw-Hill.

Billings, D. M. (1989). A conceptual model of correspondence course completion. In M. G. Moore, & G. C. Clark (Eds.), *Readings in Distance Learning and Instruction*, 2. University Park, PA: ACSDE.

Biner, P. M., Dean, R. S., & Mellinger, A. E. (1994). Factors underlying distance learner satisfaction with televised college-level courses. *Amer. J. Dist. Educ., 8*(1), 60–71.

Bittner, W. S. & Mallory, H. F. (1933). *University Teaching by Mail*. New York: Macmillan.

Blackwood, H., & Trent, C. (1968). *A Comparison of the Effectiveness of Face-to-Face and Remote Teaching in Communicating Educational Information to Adults*. Manhattan: Kansas State University, Cooperative Extension Service. (ERIC: ED 028 324)

Blanch, G. (1994). Don't all faculty want their own TV show? Barriers to faculty participation in distance education. *DEOS, 4*(1).

Boone, M. E. (1984). Examining excellence: An analysis of facilitator behaviors in actual audio teleconferences. In L. Parker & C. Olgren (Eds.), *Teleconferencing and Electronic Communications*, III. Madison: University of Wisconsin-Extension, Center for Interactive Programs.

Boone, M. E., & Bassett, R. E. (1983). Training people to audioconference: A review of the current wisdom. In L. Parker & C. Olgren (Eds.), *Teleconferencing and Electronic Communications*, II. Madison: University of Wisconsin-Extension, Center for Interactive Programs.

Boston, R. L. (1992). Remote delivery of instruction via the PC and modem: What have we learned? *Amer. J. Dist. Educ., 6*(3), 45–57.

Boswell, J. J., Mocker, D. W., & Hamlin, W. C. (1968). Telelecture: An experiment in remote teaching. *Adult Leadership, 16*(9), 321–338.

Boyd, R., & Apps, J. (1980). *Redefining the Discipline of Adult Education*. San Francisco: Jossey-Bass.

Briggs, L. J., Gustafson, K. L., & Tillman, M. H. (1991). *Instructional Design: Principles & Applications* (2nd Ed.). Englewood Cliffs, NJ: Educational Technology Publications.

Bronstein, R., Gill, J., & Koneman, E. (1982). *Teleconferencing: A Practical Guide to Teaching by Telephone*. Chicago: American Society of Clinical Pathologists Press.

Brophy, M., & Dudley, B. (1982). Patterns of distance teaching in teacher education. *Journal of Education for Teaching, 8*(2), 156–162.

Bruning, R., Landis, M., Hoffman, E., & Grosskopf, K. (1993). Perspectives on an interactive satellite-based language course. *Amer. J. Dist. Educ., 7*(3), 22–38.

Bruwelheide, J. H. (1994). Distance education: Copyright issues. In B. Willis (Ed.), *Distance Education: Strategies and Tools*. Englewood Cliffs, NJ: Educational Technology Publications.

Burge, E., & Howard, J. L. (1990). Audio-conferencing in graduate education: A case study. *Amer. J. Dist. Educ., 4*(2), 3–13.

Candy, P. C. (1991). *Self-Direction for Lifelong Learning*. San Francisco: Jossey-Bass.

Cannings, T. R., & Finkel, L. (1993). *The Technology Age Classroom*. Wilsonville, OR: Franklin, Beedle & Associates.

Carr, R. (1984). Thailand's Open University. *ICDE Bulletin, 5*, 25–27.

Castleberry, J. (1989). Satellite learning—A vision for the future. *NASSP Bulletin, 73*(519), 35–41.

Catchpole, M. J. (1992). Classroom, open, and distance teaching: A faculty view. *Amer. J. Dist. Educ., 6*(3), 34–44.

Cheng, H. C., Lehman, J., & Armstrong, P. (1991). Comparison of performance and attitude in traditional and computer conferencing classes. *Amer. J. Dist. Educ., 5*(3), 51–59.

Chesterton, P. (1985). Curriculum control in distance education. *Teaching at a Distance, 26*, 32–37.

Christopher, G. R. (1982). The Air Force Institute of Technology—The Air Force reaches out through media: An update. In L. Parker & C. Olgren (Eds.), *Teleconferencing and Electronic Communications*, I. Madison: University of Wisconsin-Extension, Center for Interactive Programs.

Chung, J. (1991). Televised teaching effectiveness: Two case studies. *Educational Technology, 31*(1), 41–47.

Chunjie, X. (1993). An overview and prospect of satellite television in China. In M. Scriven, R. Lundin, & Y. Ryan (Eds.), *Distance Education for the 21st Century*. Proceedings of the 16th ICDE World Conference, Bangkok, Thailand.

Chute, A. G., Balthazar, L. B., & Poston, C. O. (1989). Learning from teletraining. In M. G. Moore & G. C. Clark (Eds.), *Readings in Distance Learning and Instruction*, 2. University Park, PA: ACSDE.

Chute, A. G., Hulik, M., & Palmer, C. (1987). *Teletraining Productivity at AT&T*. Presentation at International Teleconferencing Association Annual Convention, Washington, DC. Cincinnati, OH: AT&T Communications.

Clark, T. (1993). Attitudes of higher education faculty towards distance education: A national survey. *Amer. J. Dist. Educ., 7*(2), 19–33.

CNET Briefing (1994). Briefing on CNET videotele-training. Pensacola, FL: Naval Air Station, Chief of Naval Education and Training. Cited by Barry and Runyan, op.cit.

Coggins, C. (1989). Preferred learning styles and their impact on completion of external degree programs. In M. G. Moore & G. C. Clark, (Eds.), *Readings in Distance Learning and Instruction*, 2. University Park, PA: ACSDE.

Cohen, P. A., Kulik, J. A., & Kulik, C. C. (1982). Educational outcomes of tutoring: A meta-analysis of findings. *American Educational Research Journal, 19*(2), 237–248.

Coldeway, D. O. (1988). Methodological issues in distance education research. *Amer. J. Dist. Educ., 5*(2), 45–54.

Coldeway, D. O. & Spencer, R. (1993). *Curriculum and Instructional Delivery Issues for a Master's Degree in Distance Education*. Proceedings of the Ninth Annual Conference on Distance Teaching and Learning. Madison: University of Wisconsin.

Coldeway, D. O. & Spencer, R. E. (1982). Keller's personalized system of instruction: The search for a basic distance learning paradigm. *Distance Education, 3*(1), 51–71.

Cole, S., Coats, M., & Lentell, H. (1986). Towards good teaching by correspondence. *Open Learning, 1*(1).

Cookson, P. S. (1990). Persistence in distance education. In M. G. Moore (Ed.), *Contemporary Issues in American Distance Education*. Oxford: Pergamon.

Cookson, P. S., Quigley, B. A., & Borland, K. W. (1994). *Audioconferencing in Major Research Universities: A National Survey*. Proceedings, International Distance Education Conference. State College: Penn State University.

Coombs, N. (1990, Feb.). Computing and telecommunications in higher education: A personal view. *Educational Technology*, 46–47.

Coughlan, R. (1980). The mentor role in individualized instruction at Empire State College. *Distance Education, 1*(1), 1-12.

Crick, M. (1980). Course teams: Myth and actuality. *Distance Education, 1*(2), 127–141.

Cross, P. (1981). *Adults as Learners*. San Francisco: Jossey-Bass.

Curtis, J. A., & Biedenbach, J. M. (1979). *Educational Telecommunications Delivery Systems*. American Society for Engineering Education.

Cyrs, T., & Smith, F. (1990). *Teleclass Teaching: A Resource Guide* (2nd Ed.). Las Cruces: New Mexico State University.

Daniel, J. S., & Marquis, C. (1979). Independence and interaction: Getting the mixture right. *Teaching at a Distance, 15*, 29–44.

Davis, D. J. (1990). Text comprehension: Implications for the design of self-instructional materials. In M. G. Moore (Ed.), *Contemporary Issues in American Distance Education*. Oxford: Pergamon.

Davis, S., & Elliot, C. S. (1992). Whose job is teleconference reception? In M. G. Moore (Ed.), *Readings in Distance Education*, 3. University Park, PA: ACSDE.

Deaton, R. & Clark, F. (1987). Teleconferencing and programmed instruction in rural Montana: A case example in foster care education. *Human-Services-in-the-Rural-Environment, 10*(3), 14–17.

Dede, C. (1990). The evolution of distance learning: Technology-mediated interactive learning. *Journal of Research on Computing in Education, 22*(3), 247–264.

DeLoughry, T. (1988, April 6). Interest rises in satellite links to foreign colleges. *Chronicle of Higher Education.*

Demiray, U. (1994). *A Review of the Literature on the Open Education Faculty (1982–1992).* Eskisehir, Turkey: Anadolu University.

Dick, W., & Carey, L. (1985). *The Systematic Design of Instruction.* Glenview, IL: Scott, Foresman & Co.

Diehl, G. (1990, Jan.). Recent research activities of the USAF Extension Course Institute (ECI). *Research in Distance Education, 2*(1), 16–19.

Dillon, C. (1992). The study of distance education in the United States: Programs of study and coursework. *Amer. J. Dist.Educ., 6*(2), 64–69.

Dillon, C. L., & Walsh, S. J. (1992). Faculty: The neglected resource in distance education. *Amer. J. Dist. Educ., 6*(3), 5–21.

DiPaolo, A. (1992). The Stanford Instructional Television Network: A partnership with Industry. *Ed, 6*(7), 4.

Dirr, P. J. (1991). Understanding television-based distance education: Identifying barriers to university attendence. *Research in Distance Education, 3*(1), 2–4.

Doerfert F. Schueme R., & Tomaschewski, C. (1989). *Short Descriptions of Selected Distance Education Institutions.* Hagen, Germany: Institute for Research into Distance Education.

Downing, D. E. (1984). *Survey on the Uses of Distance Learning in the U.S.* Austin, TX: Southwest Educational Lab. (ERIC: ED 246874)

Duchastel, P. (1988). Toward the ideal study guide: An exploration of the functions and components of study guides. *British Journal of Educational Technology, 14*(3), 216–231.

Duffy, T. M. & Waller, R. (1985). *Designing Usable Texts.* New York: Academic Press.

Duning, B. S., Van Kekerix, M. J., & Zaborowski, L. M. (1993). *Reaching Learners Through Telecommunications.* San Francisco: Jossey-Bass.

Dutton, W., & Lievrouw, L. (1982). Teleconferencing as an educational medium. In L. Parker & C. Olgren (Eds.), *Teleconferencing and Electronic Communications.* Madison: University of Wisconsin-Extension, Center for Interactive Programs.

Eckles, S., & Miller W. (1987). *Perceptions of 1987 Master Gardener Participants Toward the Use of Satellite Telecommunications for Educational/Extension Delivery.* (ERIC: ED289042)

Egan, M. W., Welch, M., Page, B., & Sebastian, J. (1992). Learners' perceptions of instructional delivery systems: Conventional and television. *Amer. J. Dist. Educ., 6*(2), 47–56.

Eisley, M. E. (1992). Guidelines for conducting instructional discussions on a computer conference. *DEOSNEWS, 2*(1).

Ellertson, E. K., Wydra, D., & Jolley, H. (1987). *Report on Distance Learning: A National Effectiveness Survey.* Mansfield, PA: Mansfield University and the Pennsylvania Teleteaching Project.

England, R. (1991). *A Survey of State Level Involvement in Distance Education at the Elementary and Secondary Levels.* ACSDE Research Monograph, 3. University Park, PA: ACSDE.

Evans, T., & Nation, D. (1989). *Critical Reflections on Distance Education.* New York: Falmer Press.

Faith, K. (1988). *Toward New Horizons for Women in Distance Education: International Perspectives.* London: Routledge.

Feasley, C. (1983). *Serving Learners at a Distance: A Guide to Program Practice.* Washington DC: ASHE ERIC Higher Education Research Report No.5.

Feasley, C. E. (1984). *Independent Study in 1983: A Research Report of the NUCEA Independent Study Division.* Stillwater: Independent Study Division NUCEA, Oklahoma State University.

Flagg, B. (1990). *Formative Evaluation for Educational Technologies.* Hillsdale, NJ: Erlbaum.

Fleming, A. (1982). The Allama Iqbal Open University. In G. Rumble & K. Harry, *The Distance Teaching Universities.* London: Croom Helm.

Florida Satellite Network Study (1985). Report and Recommendations of the Florida Postsecondary Educational Planning Commission.

Fredrickson, S. (1990). *Audiographics for Distance Education: An Alternative Technology.* Paper presented at the Annual Conference of the Alaska Association for Computers in Education. (ERIC: ED345711)

Freeman, R. (1991). Quality assurance in learning materials production. *Open Learning.*

Frey, L., & Reigeluth, C. M. (1986). Instructional models for tutoring: A review. *Journal of Instructional Development, 1*(1), 2-8.

Furlong, M., & Kearsley, G. (1993). *Computers for Kids Over 60.* San Francisco: Seniornet.

Gagne, R. M., Briggs, L. J., & Wagner, E.D. (1988). *Principles of Instructional Design* (2nd Ed.). New York: Holt, Rinehart & Winston.

Gao, F. (1991). The challenge of distance education in China. *Amer. J. Dist. Educ., 5*(2), 54–58.

Gardner, M. K., Rudolph, S., & Della-Piana, G. (1987). Learning over the lines: Audio-graphic teleconferencing comes of age. *Educational Technology, 27*(4), 39-42.

Garrison, D. R. (1987). Researching dropout in distance education. *Distance Education, 8*(1), 95–101.

Garrison, D. R. (1989). *Understanding Distance Education: A Framework for the Future.* Boston: Routledge & Kegan Paul.

Garrison, D. R. (1990). An analysis and evaluation of audioteleconferencing to facilitate education at a distance. *Amer. J. Dist. Educ., 4*(3), 13–24.

Garrison, R., & Baynton, M. (1987). Beyond independence in distance education: The concept of control. *Amer. J. Dist. Educ., 3*(1), 3–15.

Garrison, R., & Shale, D. (1987). Mapping the boundaries of distance education: Problems in defining the field. *Amer. J. Dist. Educ., 1*(3), 7–13.

Gayeski, D. M. (1993). *Multimedia for Learning.* Englewood Cliffs, NJ: Educational Technology Publications.

Gery, G. (1990). *Electronic Performance Support Systems.* Boston: Weingarten Publishers.

Gibbs, G., & Durbridge, N. (1976). Characteristics of Open University tutors. *Teaching at a Distance, 7,* 7–22.

Gibson, C. C. (1990). Learners and learning: A discussion of selected research. In M. G. Moore (Ed.), *Contemporary Issues in American Distance Education.* Oxford: Pergamon.

Gilbert, J. K., Temple, A., & Underwood, C. (1991). *Satellite Television in Education.* New York: Routledge.

Gilcher, K. W. & Johnstone, S. M. (1989). *A Critical Review of the Use of Audiographic Conferencing Systems by Selected Educational Institutions.* College Park, MD: International University Consortium.

Glatter, R., & Wedell, E. G. (1971). *Study by Correspondence.* London: Longmans.

Gooler, D. (1979). Evaluating distance education programmes. *Canadian Journal of University Continuing Education, 6*(1), 43-55.

Gunawardena, C. N. (1992). Changing faculty roles for audiographics and online teaching. *Amer. J. Dist. Educ., 6*(3), 58–71.

Haaland, B. A., & Newby, W. G. (1984). Student perception of effective teaching behaviors: An examination of conventional and teleconference based instruction. In L. Parker & C. Olgren (Eds.), *Teleconferencing and Electronic Communications* III. Madison: University of Wisconsin-Extension, Center for Interactive Programs.

Hackman, M., & Walker, K. (1990). The impact of systems design and instructional style on student reactions to distance education. *Research in Distance Education, 2*(2), 7–8.

Hansen, E., Chong, S., Kubota, K., & Hubbard, L. (1993). Computer conferencing for collaborative learning in large college classes. *DEOSNEWS, 3*(4).

Harasim, L. (1994). *Global Networks.* Cambridge, MA: MIT Press.

Harasim, L. (1990). *Online Education: Perspectives on a New Environment.* New York: Praeger.

Harris, D. (1987). *Openness & Closure in Distance Education.* London: Falmer Press.

Harrison, P. J., et al. (1990). Development of a distance education assessment instrument. *ETR&D, 39*(4), 65–77.

Harry, K., & de Vocht, C. (1988). *European Association of Distance Teaching Universities.* Milton Keynes, UK: International Centre for Distance Learning.

Hartigan, P., & St. John, R. K. (1989). AIDS training in third-world countries: An evaluation of telecommunications technology. *Educational Technology, 29*(10), 20–23.

Hartley, D. (1992). Anna Eliot Ticknor introduced studies at home. AIS: Newsletter of the Independent Study Division, NUCEA.

Hartley, J. (1978). *Designing Instructional Text.* London: Nichols.

Haaland, B. A., & Newby, W. G. (1984). Student perception of effective teaching behaviors: An examination of conventional and teleconference based instruction. In L. Parker & C. Olgren (Eds.), *Teleconferencing and Electronic Communications*, III. Madison: University of Wisconsin-Extension, Center for Interactive Programs.

Heinich, R. M., Molenda, M., Russell, J. R. (1985). *Instructional Media and the New Technologies.* New York: Macmillan.

Heinzen, T. E., & Alberico, S. M. (1990). Using a creativity paradigm to evaluate teleconferencing. *Amer. J. Dist. Educ., 4*(3), 3–12.

Henderson, E. S., & Nathenson, M. B. (1984). *Independent Learning in Higher Education.* Englewood Cliffs, NJ: Educational Technology Publications.

Her Majesty's Stationery Office (HMSO) (1969). *The Open University: Report of the Planning Committee to the Secretary of State for Education and Science.* London: HMSO.

Hezekiah, J. A. (1986). Teletechniques: A case study in implementation and evaluation. In L. Parker & C. Olgren (Eds.), *Teleconferencing and Electronic Communications*, V. Madison: University of Wisconsin-Extension, Center for Interactive Programs.

Hezel, R. T. (1987). *Statewide Planning for Telecommunications in Education*. Syracuse: Hezel Associates.

Hiltz, S. R., & Turoff, M. (1993). *The Network Nation* (Rev. Ed.). Boston, MA: MIT Press.

Holmberg, B. (1977). Tutoring distance students. *Epistolodidactica, 7*, 4–15.

Holmberg, B. (1981). *Status and Trends of Distance Education*. London: Kogan Page.

Holmberg, B. (1986). *Growth and Structure of Distance Education*. London: Croom Helm.

Holmberg, B. (1989). *Theory and Practice of Distance Education*. New York: Routledge.

Holmberg, R. G., & Bakshi, T. S. (1992). Postmortem on a distance education course: Successes and failures. *Amer. J. Dist. Educ., 6*(1), 27 39.

Holstein, J. A. (1992). Making the written word "speak": Reflections on the teaching of correspondence courses. *Amer. J. Dist. Educ., 6*(3), 22–34.

Hosley, D. L., & Randolph, S. L. (1993). *Distance Learning as a Training and Education Tool*. Kennedy Space Center, FL: Lockheed Space Operations Co. (ERIC: ED355936)

Hough, M. (1984). Motivation of adults: Implications of adult learning theories for distance education. *Distance Education, 5*(1), 7-23.

Howard, D. C. (1987). Designing learner feedback in distance education. *Amer. J. Dist. Educ., 3*(1), 24–40.

Hoyt, D. P., & Frye, D. (1972). *The Effectiveness of Telecommunications as an Educational Delivery System*. Manhattan: Kansas State University. (ERIC, ED 070 318)

Idrus, R. M. (1992). Enhancing teletutorials via collaborative learning: The Malaysian experience. *DEOSNEWS, 2*(14).

Ilyin, V. (1983). The U.S.S.R. Financial and Economic Institute for Distance Education. *Distance Education, 4*(2), 142–148

Irwin, S. (1992). *The Business Television Directory* Washington, DC: Warren Publishing Inc. and Irwin Communications.

ITC (1995). *Federal Disability Law and Distance Learning*. Washington, DC: International Telecommunications Council, American Assoc. Community Colleges.

Jianshu, Z. (1987). Three major events in higher distance education: News from China. *ICDE Bulletin, 13*, 18–20.

Jianshu, Z. (1990). Distance education research in China. *Research in Distance Education, 2*(2), 9.

Johnson, D. A. (1989, August). Training by television. *Training & Development Journal*, 65–68.

Johnston, J., & Brzezinski, E. (1992). Taking the measure of Channel One: The first year. *Ed, 6*(6), 4–9.

Jonassen, D. H. (1982, 1985). *The Technology of Text*. Vols. I & II. Englewood Cliffs, NJ: Educational Technology Publications.

Jonassen, D. H. (1989). *Hypertext/Hypermedia*. Englewood Cliffs, NJ: Educational Technology Publications.

Jonassen, D., & Mandl, H. (1990). *Designing Hypermedia for Learning*. New York: Springer Verlag.

Jones, G. (1991). *Make All America a School*. Englewood, CO: Jones International.

Jordahl, G. (1989). Communications satellites: A rural response to the tyranny of distance. *Educational Technology, 29*(2), 34–38.

Juliussen, K. P. & Juliussen, E. J. (1993). *6th Annual Computer Industry Almanac*. Lake Tahoe: Computer Industry Almanac, Inc.

Kascus, M. (1994). What library schools teach about library support to distant students: A survey. *Amer. J. Dist. Educ., 8*(1), 20–35.

Kaye, A., & Rumble, G. (1981). *Distance Teaching for Higher and Adult Education*. London: Croom Helm.

Ke Ming, G. (1988). The perspective of distance education in China. In D. Sewart & J. Daniel (Eds.), *Developing Distance Education*. Oslo: International Council for Distance Education.

Kearsley, G. (1985). *Training for Tomorrow: Distributed Learning Through Computer and Communications Technology*. Reading, MA: Addison-Wesley.

Kearsley, G., Hunter, B., & Furlong, M. (1992). *We Teach With Technology*. Wilsonville, OR: Franklin, Beedle & Associates.

Kearsley, G., & Lynch, W. (1994). *Preparing Educational Technology Leaders: A Formula That Works*. Technology and Teacher Education Annual. Charlottesville, VA: Association for the Advancement of Computing in Education.

Keegan, D. (1980). On defining distance education. *Distance Education 1*(1), 13-35

Keegan, D. (1986). *The Foundations of Distance Education*. London: Croom Helm.

Keegan, D. (1989). Problems in defining the field of distance education. *Amer. J. Dist. Educ., 3*(2), 4–11.

Keegan, D. (1993). *Theoretical Principles of Distance Education*. London: Routledge.

Keene, S. D., & Cary, J. S. (1990). Effectiveness of distance education approach to U.S. Army Reserve component training. *Amer. J. Dist. Educ., 4*(2), 14–20.

Kember, D. (1989). An illustration, with case studies, of a linear process model of drop-out from distance education. *Distance Education, 10*(2), 196–211.

Kember, D. (1995). *Open Learning Courses for Adults*. Englewood Cliffs, NJ: Educational Technology Publications.

Klinger, T. H., & Connet, M. R. (1992, Oct.). Designing distance learning courses for critical thinking. *THE Journal*, 87–90.

Knapczyk, D. R. (1990). Use of audiographic technology in distance education of practicing teachers. *Educational Technology, 30*(6), 24–27.

Knapczyk, D. (1991). A distance learning approach to inservice training. *THE Journal, 18*(9), 68–70.

Knott, T. D. (1993). Distance education effectiveness. *Ed Journal, 7*(6), 7-16.

Knowles, M. (1978). *The Adult Learner*. Houston, TX: Gulf Publishing.

Koul, B. (1989). Beyond interaction and independence: the IGNOU experience. In A. Tait (Ed.), *Interaction and Independence: Student Support in Distance Education and Open Learning*. Milton Keynes, UK: Open University.

Krebs, A. (1991, Mar.). Funding and policy initiatives in distance learning. *Ed, 5*(3), 9–14.

Kruh, J. (1983). Student evaluation of instructional teleconferencing. In L. Parker & C. Olgren (Eds.), *Teleconferencing and Electronic Communications*, II. Madison: University of Wisconsin-Extension, Center for Interactive Programs.

Kuramoto, A. (1984). Teleconferencing for nurses: Evaluating its effectiveness. In L. Parker & C. Olgren (Eds.), *Teleconferencing and Electronic Communications*, III. Madison: University of Wisconsin-Extension, Center for Interactive Programs.

Laidlaw, B., & Layard, R. (1974). Traditional versus Open University teaching methods: A cost comparison. *Higher Education, 3*, 439–468.

Lane, C. (1992a). A selection model and pre-adoption evaluation instrument for video programs. In M. G. Moore (Ed.), *Readings in Distance Education*, 3. University Park, PA: ACSDE.

Lane, C. (1992b). The IBM approach to training through distance learning: A global education network by the year 2000. *Ed, 6*(1), 10–11.

Latham, S., Slade, A., & Budnick, C. (1991). *Library Services for Off-Campus and Distance Education: An Annotated Bibliography*. Chicago: American Library Assoc.

Lauzon, A. C. (1992). Integrating computer-based instruction with computer conferencing: An evaluation of a model for designing online education. *Amer. J. Dist. Educ., 6*(2), 32–46.

Lauzon, A. C., & Moore, G.A.B. (1989). A fourth generation distance education system: Integrating computer-assisted learning and computer conferencing. *Amer. J. Dist. Educ., 3*(1), 39–48.

Lenn, M. P. (1991). *Distance Learning and Accreditation*. Washington, DC: Council on Postsecondary Accreditation.

Leshin, C. B., Pollock, J., & Reigeluth, C. M. (1992). *Instructional Design Strategies and Tactics*. Englewood Cliffs, NJ: Educational Technology Publications.

Levenson, W. B. (1945). *Teaching Through Radio*. New York: Farrar & Rinehart.

Levine, T. K. (1988). *Teaching Telecourses: Opportunities and Options*. Washington, DC: Annenberg/CPB.

Levine, T. K. (1992). *Going the Distance: A Handbook for Developing Distance Degree Programs*. Washington, DC: Annenberg/CPB.

Lewis, C., & Hedegaard, T. (1993). Online education: Issues and some answers. *THE Journal, 20*(9), 68–71.

Lewis, R. (1992). Approaches to staff development in open learning: The role of a competence framework. *Open Learning*, 7, 7:3 p.20–33.

Lochte, R. H. (1992). *Interactive Television and Instruction*. Englewood Cliffs, NJ: Educational Technology Publications.

Ludlow, N. (1987). Speaking personally with Michael P. Lambert. *Amer. J. Dist. Educ., 1*(2), 67–71.

MacKenzie, O., Christensen, E. L., & Rigby, P. H. (1968). Correspondence Instruction in the United States. New York: McGraw-Hill.

MacKenzie, N., Postgate, R., & Scupham, J. (1975). *Open Learning: Systems and Problems in Post-Secondary Education*. Paris: UNESCO Press.

Major, M. B., & Shane, D. L. (1992). Use of interactive television for outreach nursing education. In M. G. Moore (Ed.), *Readings in Distance Education*, 3. University Park, PA: ACSDE.

Malan, R. F., & Feller, S. (1992). Establishing workload equivalence: U.S. independent study courses and college residence classes. *Amer. J. Dist. Educ.,* 6(2), 56–63.

Mark, M. (1990). The differentiation of institutional structures and effectiveness in distance education programs. In M. G. Moore (Ed.), *Contemporary Issues in American Distance Education.* London: Pergamon.

Martin, E., & Rainey, L. (1993). Student achievement and attitude in a satellite-delivered high school course. *Amer. J. Dist. Educ.,* 7(1), 54–61.

Martin, C. M. (1993). Oklahoma's Star Schools: Equipment use and benefits two years after grant's end. *Amer. J. Dist. Educ.,* 7(3), 51–60.

Mason, R. (1987). Computer conferencing: Its contribution to self-directed learning. Paper presented at the Second Guelph Symposium on Computer Conferencing. Guelph, Canada.

Mason, R. (1991). Moderating educational computer conferencing. *DEOSNEWS, 1*(19).

Mason, R., & Kaye, A. (1989). *Mindweave: Communication, Computers and Distance Education.* Oxford: Pergamon.

Massoumian, B. (1989). Successful teaching via two-way interactive video. *TechTrends,* 34(2), 16–19.

McElveen, L., & Roberts, S. (1992). *Telelearning: A Second Look. 1990–1991, 1991–1992.* (ERIC ED355934)

McGowan, J. (1992). Distance education as a medium for promoting the college preparation of attendance of minority students. *DEOSNEWS, 2*(8).

McGreal, R. (1993). Exemplary programs of secondary distance education in Canada. *DEOSNEWS, 3*(6).

McIsaac, M. S. (1990). Problems affecting evaluation of distance education in developing countries. *Research in Distance Education,* 2(3), 12–16.

McMahill, J. M. (1993). Videotape distance learning courses: Administrative implications for colleges and universities. *Ed Journal,* 7(6), 16–20.

McNeil, D. R. (1980). UMA: Progress of an experiment. In M. N. Chamberlain (Ed.), *Providing Continuing Education by Media and Technology.* San Francisco: Jossey-Bass.

Meacham, D. (1990). Research and development at Charles Sturt University Distance Education Centre. *Research in Distance Education,* 2(1), 2–6.

Miller, G. E. (1992). Long-term trends in distance education. *DEOSNEWS, 2*(23).

Misanchuk, E. R. (1992). *Preparing Instructional Text: Document Design Using Desktop Publishing.* Englewood Cliffs, NJ: Educational Technology Publications.

Moore, D. M., Burton, J. K., & Dodl, N. R. (1991). The role of facilitators in Virginia's Electronic Classroom project. *Amer. J. Dist. Educ.,* 5(3), 29–39.

Moore, M. G. (1972). Learner autonomy: the second dimension of independent learning. *Convergence,* 5(2), 76–88.

Moore, M. G. (1973). Towards a theory of independent learning and teaching. *Journal of Higher Education,* (44), 661–679.

Moore, M. G. (1975). Cognitive style and telemathic (distance) teaching. *ICCE Newsletter* 5(4), 3–10.

Moore, M. G. (1977). A model of independent study. *Epistolodidactica,* (1), 6–40.

Moore, M. G. (1980a). On a Theory of Independent Study. ZIFF Papiere No. 16. Hagen, Germany: FernUniversität.

Moore, M. G. (1980b). Continuing education and the assessment of learner needs. *Teaching at a Distance,* 17, 26–29.

Moore, M. G. (1981). Educational telephone networks. *Teaching at a Distance, 19,* 24–31.

Moore, M. G. (1983). On a theory of independent study. In D. Sewart, D. Keegan, & B. Holmberg (Eds.), *Distance Education: International Perspectives.* London: Croom Helm.

Moore, M. G. (1986). Self-directed learning and distance education. *Journal of Distance Education,* 1(1), 7–24.

Moore, M. G. (1987). Print media. In J. A. Niemi & D. Gooler (Eds.), *Technologies for Learning Outside the Classroom: New Directions for Continuing Education.* San Francisco: Jossey-Bass.

Moore, M. G. (1988). Telecommunications, internationalism and distance education. *Amer. J. Dist. Educ.,* 2(1),1–7.

Moore, M. G. (1989a). Recruiting and retraining adult students in distance education. In P. S. Cookson (Ed.), *Recruiting and Retraining Adult Students.* San Francisco: Jossey-Bass.

Moore, M. G. (1989b). Three types of interaction. *Amer. J. Dist. Educ.,* 3(2), 1–6.

Moore, M. G. (1990a). Recent contributions to the theory of distance education. *Open Learning,* 5(2), 10–15.

Moore, M. G. (1990b). A market-driven distance education system? *Amer. J. Dist. Educ., 4*(2), 1–13.

Moore, M. G. (1991). Developing Cooperation Between Institutions Internationally. Paper given at Association for Educational Communications and Technology Conference, Orlando, Florida.

Moore, M. G. (1993). Is teaching like flying? A total systems view of distance education. *Amer. J. Dist. Educ., 7*(1), 1–10.

Moore, M. G., Candor, K., Collins, M., Cookson, P., & Gayol, Y. (1995). *Offering Penn State's Certificate in Distance Education to Four Countries by Teleconferencing.* Birmingham, UK: Proceedings, World Conference of ICDE Open University and ICDE.

Moore, M., & Thompson, M. (1991). *Effectiveness of Distance Learning: A Summary of the Literature.* University Park, PA: ACSDE.

Moran, L., & Mugridge, I. (1993). *Collaboration in Distance Education: International Case Studies.* London: Routledge.

Mugridge, I., & Kaufman, D. (1986). *Distance Education in Canada.* London: Croom Helm.

Murgatroyd, S. (1980). What actually happens in tutorials. *Teaching at a Distance, 18*, 44–53.

Murgatroyd, S. (1992). Business, education and distance education. In M. G. Moore (Ed.), *Readings in Distance Education*, 3. University Park, PA: ACSDE.

Murphy, P., & Zhiri, A. (1992). *Distance Education in Anglophone Africa.* Washington, DC: World Bank.

Nelson, R. N. (1985). Two-way microwave transmission consolidates, improves education. *NASSP Bulletin, 69*(4), 38–42.

Neil, M. (1981). *The Education of Adults at a Distance.* London: Kogan Page.

Nevada State Dept. of Human Resources, Sparks (1990). Project NETWORC Final Report. (ERIC: ED329073)

Nichodemus, R. (1984). Lessons from a course team. *Teaching At A Distance, 25*, 33–39.

Niemi, J., & Gooler, D. (1987). *Technologies for Learning Outside the Classroom.* New Directions for Continuing Education, no. 34. San Francisco: Jossey-Bass.

Norenberg, C. D., & Lundblad, L. (1987). *Distance Delivery of Vocational Education: Technologies and Planning Matrixes.* St. Paul: Minnesota R&D Center for Vocational Education.

Oberle, E. (1990). The National University Teleconference Network: A living laboratory for distance learning research. In M. G. Moore (Ed.), *Contempo-*

rary Issues in American Distance Education. London: Pergamon.

Office of Technology Assessment (1988). *Power On: New Tools for Teaching and Learning.* Washington, DC: Government Printing Office.

Office of Technology Assessment (1989). *Linking for Learning: A New Course for Education.* Washington, DC: Government Printing Office.

Olcott, D. J. (1992). Policy issues in statewide delivery of university programs by telecommunications. *Amer. J. Dist. Educ., 6*(1), 14–26.

Ostendorf, V. (1989). *Teaching Through Interactive Television.* Littleton, CO: Virginia Ostendorf Inc.

Parker, L. A. (1984). *Teleconferencing Resource Book.* New York: Elsevier.

Parker, L., & Monson, M. (1980). *Teletechniques: An Instructional Model for Interactive Teleconferencing.* Instructional Design Library, 38. Englewood Cliffs, NJ: Educational Technology Publications.

Partin, G. R., & Atkins, E. L. (1984). Teaching via electronic blackboard. In L. Parker & C. Olgren (Eds.), *Teleconferencing and Electronic Communications*, III. Madison: University of Wisconsin-Extension.

Passaro, P. et al. (1991). Using satellite teleconferencing to instruct due process hearing officers. *Journal of Special Education Technology, 11*(2), 108–112.

Paul, R. (1990). *Open Learning and Open Management: Leadership and Integrity in Distance Education.* New York: Nichols Publishing.

Paulsen, M. F. (1992a). Distance education in Norway. *DEOSNEWS, 2*(19).

Paulsen, M. F. (1992b). The NKI electronic college: Five years of computer conferencing in distance education. *DEOSNEWS, 2*(9).

Paulsen, M. F. (1993). The hexagon of cooperative freedom: A distance education theory attuned to computer conferencing. *DEOSNEWS, 3*(2).

Perelman, L. J. (1992). *School's Out: Hyperlearning, New Technology, and the End of Education.* New York: William Morrow.

Perraton, H. (1974). Is there a teacher in the system? *Teaching at a Distance, 1*, 55–60.

Perry, W. (1977). *The Open University.* San Francisco: Jossey-Bass.

Peruniak, G. (1983). Interactive perspectives in distance education: A case study. *Distance Education, 4*(1), 63–79.

Peters, O. (1969). *New Perspectives in Correspondence Study in Europe.* ICCE Proceedings, 94–105.

Peters, O. (1971). Theoretical aspects of correspondence instruction. In O. MacKenzie & E. Christensen (Eds.), *The Changing World of Correspondence Study.* State College: Pennsylvania State University Press.

Peters, O. (1983). Distance teaching and industrial production: A comparative interpretation in outline. In D. Sewart, D. Keegan, & B. Holmberg (Eds.), *Distance Education: International Perspectives.* London: Croom Helm.

Peterson, R. E. (1979). *Lifelong Learning in America.* San Francisco: Jossey-Bass.

Phelps, R. H., Wells, R. A., Ashworth, R. L. & Hahn, H. A. (1991). Effectiveness and costs of distance education using computer-mediated communication. *Amer. J. Dist. Educ., 5*(3), 7–19.

Phillips, G. M., Santoro, G. M., & Kuehn, S. A. (1989). The use of computer mediated communication in training students in group problem-solving and decision-making techniques. In M. G. Moore (Ed.), *Readings in Distance Education,* 2. University Park, PA: ACSDE.

Pisacreta, E. A. (1993). Distance learning and intellectual property protection. *Educational Technology, 33*(4), 42–44.

Pittman, V. V. (1990). Correspondence study in the American university: A historiographic perspective. In M. G. Moore (Ed.), *Contemporary Issues in American Distance Education.* London: Pergamon.

Pittman, V. V. (1986). Station WSUI and the early days of instructional radio. *The Palimpsest,* March-April 1986.

Porter, K. W. (1990, April). Tuning in to TV training. *Training & Development Journal,* 73–77.

Portway, P. S., & Lane, C. (1992). *Teleconferencing & Distance Learning.* San Ramon, CA: Applied Business Communications.

Purdy, L. N., & Wright, S. J. (1992). Teaching in distance education: A faculty perspective. *Amer. J. Dist. Educ., 6*(3), 2–4.

Puzzuoli, D. (1970). *A Study of Teaching University Extension Classes by Tele-lecture.* Morgantown: University of West Virginia. (ERIC: ED 042961)

Radcliff, J. (1990). Television and distance education in Europe: Current roles and future challenges. In A. W. Bates (Ed.), *Media and Technology in European Distance Education.* Milton Keynes: Open University for the European Association of Distance Teaching Universities.

Raybould, B. (1990, Nov./Dec.). Solving human performance problems with computers. *Performance & Instruction,* 4–14.

Reigeluth, C., & Garfinkle, R. (1994). *Systematic Change in Education.* Englewood Cliffs, NJ: Educational Technology Publications.

Reilly, K. P., & Gulliver, K. M. (1992). Interstate authorization of distance higher education via telecommunications: The developing national consensus in policy and practice. *Amer. J. Dist. Educ., 6*(2), 3–16.

Reiser, R. A., & Gagne, R. M. (1983). *Selecting Media for Instruction.* Englewood Cliffs, NJ: Educational Technology Publications.

Rekkedal, T. (1983a). Written assignments in correspondence education: Effects of reducing turn-around time. An experimental study. *Distance Education, 4*(2), 231–252.

Rekkedal, T. (1983b). Enhancing student progress in Norway. *Teaching at a Distance, 23,* 19–24.

Rekkedal, T. (1993). Distance education research in Norway. In M. Scriven, R. Lundin, & Y. Ryan (Eds.), *Distance Education for the 21st Century.* Proceedings of the 16th ICDE World Conference, Bangkok, Thailand.

Richey, R. (1986). *The Theoretical and Conceptual Basis of Instructional Design.* New York: Nichols.

Rifkind, L. J. (1992). Immediacy as a predictor of teacher effectiveness in the instructional television classroom. *Journal of Interactive Television, 1*(1), 31–40.

Ritchie, H., & Newby, T. J. (1989). Classroom lecture/discussion vs. live televised instruction: A comparison of effects on student performance, attitude and interaction. *Amer. J. Dist. Educ., 3*(3), 36–45.

Roberts, D. (1984). Ways and means of reducing early student drop-out rates. *Distance Education, 5*(1), 50–71.

Romiszowski, A. J. (1974). *The Selection and Use of Instructional Media.* New York: Wiley.

Rossman, P. (1992). *The Emerging Worldwide Electronic University.* Westport, CT: Greenwood Press.

Rowntree, D. (1981). *Developing Courses for Students.* London: McGraw-Hill.

Rowntree, D. (1986). *Teaching Through Self-Instruction: A Practical Handbook for Course Developers.* London: Kogan Page.

Rule, S. M., Dewulf, M., & Stowitschek, J. (1988). An economic analysis of inservice teacher training. *Amer. J. Dist. Educ., 2*(2), 12–22.

Rumble, G. (1981). The cost analysis of distance teaching: Costa Rica's Universidad Estatal a Distancia. *Higher Education, 10,* 375–401.

Rumble, G. (1982). The cost analysis of distance learning: Venezuela's Universidad Nacional Abierta. *Distance Education, 3*(1), 116–140.

Rumble, G. (1986). *The Planning and Management of Distance Education.* London: Croom Helm.

Rumble, G. (1989). On defining distance education. *Amer. J. Dist. Educ., 3*(2), 8–21.

Rumble, G. (1992). The competitive vulnerability of distance teaching universities. *Open Learning, 7.*

Rumble, G., & Harry, K. (1982). *The Distance Teaching Universities.* London: Croom Helm.

Russell, F. K. Jr. (1991). Receive-site facilitator practices and student performance in satellite-delivered instruction. In Proceedings of Selected Research Presentations at the Annual Convention of the Association for Educational Communications and Technology. (ERIC: ED335011)

Ryan, R. (1992, Nov.). International connectivity: A survey of attitudes about cultural and national differences encountered in computer-mediated communication. *Online Chronicle of Distance Education & Communication, 6*(1), #1.

Saba, F. (1988). Integrated telecommunications systems and instructional transaction. *Amer. J. Dist. Educ., 2*:3, 17–24.

Saba, F., & Shearer, R. (1994). Verifying theoretical concepts in a dynamic model of distance education. *Amer. J. Dist. Educ., 8*(1), 36–59.

Saettler, P. (1990). *The Evolution of American Educational Technology.* Littleton, CO: Libraries Unlimited.

Saunders, R. (1990). Electronic publishing at the National Distance Education Centre. In A. W. Bates (Ed.), *Media and Technology in European Distance Education.* Milton Keynes: Open University for the European Association of Distance Teaching Universities.

Schaffer, J. M. (1990). Preparing faculty and designing courses for delivery via audio teleconferencing. *Journal of Adult Education, 18*(2), 11–18.

Schieman, E., & Jones, T. (1993). Learning at a distance: Issues for the instructional designer. *Journal of Adult Education, 21*(2), 3–13.

Schnepf, J. A., Du, D. H., Ritenour, F. R, & Fahrmann, A. J. (1995). Building future medical education environments over ATM networks. *Communications of the ACM, 38*(2), 54–69.

Schramm, W. (1977). *Big Media, Little Media.* Beverly Hills, CA: Sage.

Schuemer, R. (1993). *Some Psychological Aspects of Distance Education.* Hagen, Germany: ZIFF.

Schwier, R. A., & Misanchuk, E. R. (1993). *Interactive Multimedia Instruction.* Englewood Cliffs, NJ: Educational Technology Publications.

Sewart, D., Keegan, D., & Holmberg, B. (1983). *Distance Education: International Perspectives.* London: Croom Helm.

Shaeffer, J. M., & Farr, C. W. (1993). Evaluation: A key piece in the distance education puzzle. *THE Journal, 20*(9), 79–82.

Shale, D. G. (1987). Pacing in distance education: Something for everyone? *Amer. J. Dist. Educ., 1*(1), 45–58.

Shapiro, J., & Hughes, S. (1992). Networked information resources in distance graduate education for adults. *THE Journal, 19*(11), 66–69.

Showalter, R. G. (1983). *Speaker Telephone Continuing Education for School Personnel Serving Handicapped Children: Final Project Report.* Indianapolis: Indiana State Dept. of Public Instruction. (ERIC: ED 231150)

Smith, P., & Kelly, M. (1987). *Distance Education and the Mainstream: Convergence in Education.* London: Croom Helm.

Smith, T. W. (1992). Audiographics in continuing engineering education. *International Journal of Continuing Engineering Education, 2*(4).

Snowden, B. L, & Daniel, J. S. (1980). The economics and management of a small post-secondary distance education system. *Distance Education, 1*(1), 68–91.

Souder, W. E. (1993). The effectiveness of traditional versus satellite delivery in three management of technology master's degree programs. *Amer. J. Dist. Educ., 7*(1), 37–53.

South African Institute for Distance Education (1994). Open Learning and Distance Education in South Africa. Draft March 22, 1994. Johannesburg: SAIDE.

Spitzer. D. R., Bauwens, J., & Quast, S. (1989). Extending education using video: Lessons learned. *Educational Technology, 29*(5), 28-30.

Sponder, B. M. (1990). *Distance Education in Rural Alaska.* Monograph Series in Distance Education. Fairbanks: University of Alaska.

St. Pierre, S., & Olsen, L. (1991). Student perspectives on the effectiveness of correspondence instruction. *Amer. J. Dist. Educ., 5*(3), 65–71.

State University System of Florida (1995). Addendum to the Master Plan: 1993 through 1997–8. Tallahassee: Florida Board of Regents.

Stone, H. (1988). Variations in the characteristics and performance between on campus and video-based off-campus engineering graduate students. *Journal of Continuing Higher Education, 36*(1), 18–23.

Stowitschek, J. J., Mangus, B., & Rule, S. (1986). Inservice training via telecommunications: Out of the workshop and into the classroom. *Educational Technology, 26*(8), 28–33.

Summer, J. A., & Spicer, D. (1989). Videotape broadcast as banking: South Dakota's overnight service. *Amer. J. Dist. Educ., 3*(2), 70–75.

Taylor, R. G., & Reid, W. M. (1993). Distance education course sequencing: An application of probabilistic PERT with cycles. *Amer. J. Dist. Educ., 7*(2), 49–58.

Thompson, G. (1984). The cognitive style of field dependence as an explanatory construct in distance education drop-out. *Distance Education, 5*(2), 286–293.

Thorpe, M. (1988). *Evaluating Open and Distance Learning.* London: Longmans.

Tiene, D. (1993). Exploring the effectiveness of the Channel One school telecasts. *Educational Technology, 33*(5), 36–42.

Tight, M. (1985). Do we really need course teams? *Teaching at a Distance, 26*, 48–50.

Tilson, T. (1994). *Instructional radio. International Encyclopedia of Education.* London: Pergamon.

Timmers, S. (1988). Higher Level Distance Education and the Needs of Developing Countries: UNESCO-ICDE Round Table Briefing Paper. Oslo: International Council for Distance Education.

Unwin, D., & R. McAleese (Eds.). (1988). *The Encyclopedia of Educational Media Communications and Technology.* New York: Greenwood Press.

Utsumi, T., Rossman, P., & Rosen, S. (1990). The Global Electronic University. In M. Moore (Ed.), *Issues in Contemporary American Distance Education.* Oxford: Pergamon.

Valore, L., & Diehl, G. E. (1987). *The Effectiveness and Acceptance of Home Study.* Washington, DC: National Home Study Council.

Van Haalen, T., & Miller, G. (1994). Interactivity as a predictor of student success in satellite learning programs. *DEONEWS, 4*(6).

Van Kekerix, J. (1989). The State University of Nebraska: The Life Cycle of an Innovative Organization. Ph.D. dissertation, The University of Nebraska.

Verduin, J. R., & Clark, T. A. (1991). *Distance Education: The Foundations of Effective Practice.* San Francisco: Jossey-Bass.

Von Prummer, C. (1994). Women-friendly perspectives in distance education. *Open Learning, 9*(1), 3–12.

Waggoner, M. D. (1992). *Empowering Networks: Computer Conferencing in Education.* Englewood Cliffs, NJ: Educational Technology Publications.

Wagner, E., & Reddy, N. (1987). Design considerations in selecting teleconferencing for instruction. *Amer. J. Dist. Educ., 1*(3), 49–56.

Wagner, L. (1977). The economics of the Open University revisited. *Higher Education, 6*, 359–381.

Watkins, B. L., & Wright, S. J. (1992). *The Foundations of American Distance Education: A Century of Collegiate Correspondence Study.* Dubuque, IA: Kendall/Hunt.

Wedemeyer, C. (1971). Independent study. In L. C. Deighton (Ed.), *The Encyclopedia of Education, 4.* New York: Macmillan.

Wedemeyer, C. (1981). *Learning at the Back Door: Reflections on Non-Traditional Learning in the Lifespan.* Madison: University of Wisconsin Press.

Wedemeyer, C. (1982). The birth of the Open University—a postscript. *Teaching at a Distance, 21*, 21–27.

Wedemeyer, C. A., & Najem, C. (1969). *AIM: From Concept to Reality. The Articulated Instructional Media Program at Wisconsin.* Syracuse University: Center for the Study of Liberal Education for Adults.

Wei, R. (1991). China's network of radio and television universities. *Amer. J. Dist. Educ., 5*(2), 59–64.

Wei, R., & Tong, Y. (1994). *Radio and TV Universities: The Mainstream of China's Adult and Distance Education.* Nanjing: Yilin Press.

Weingand, D. E. (1984). Teleconferences and the traditional classroom: A study of the delivery of education. In L. Parker & C. Olgren (Eds.), *Teleconferencing and Electronic Communications*, III. Madison: University of Wisconsin-Extension, Center for Interactive Programs.

Wells, R. (1992). Computer-mediated communication for distance education: An international review of design, teaching, and institutional issues. ACSDE Research Monograph #7. University Park, PA: ACSDE.

Westfall, P. (1994). Air Technology Network briefing (video). Dayton, OH: Wright Patterson AFB, AFIT Center for Distance Education. Cited by Barry and Runyan, op.cit.

Whittington, N. (1990). Characteristics of state instructional telecommunications policy for higher education: Some research considerations. In M. G. Moore (Ed.), *Contemporary Issues in American Distance Education.* Oxford: Pergamon.

Whittington, N. (1987). Is instructional television educationally effective? A research review. *Amer. J. Dist. Educ., 1,* 47–57.

Willis, B. (1993). *Distance Education: A Practical Guide.* Englewood Cliffs, NJ: Educational Technology Publications.

Willis, B. (1994). *Distance Education: Strategies and Tools.* Englewood Cliffs, NJ: Educational Technology Publications.

Wolcott, L. (1995). The distance teacher as reflective practitioner. *Educational Technology, 35*(1), 39–43.

Woodley A., & Parlett, M. (1983). Student drop-out. *Teaching at a Distance, 24,* 2–23.

Worley, L. K. (1993). Educational television and professional development: The Kentucky model. *THE Journal, 20*(11), 70–73.

Wright, C. R. (1988, Dec.). The independent/distance study course development team. *Educational Technology,* 12–17.

Wright, S. (1992). Research on selected aspects of learner support in distance education programming. *DEOSNEWS, 2*(4).

York, V. (1993). *A Guide for Planning Library Integration into Distance Education Programs.* Boulder, CO: WICHE.

Young, M., Perraton, H., Jenkins, J., & Dodds, T. (1980). *Distance Teaching for the Third World.* London: Routledge & Kegan Paul.

Zigerell, J. (1991). *The Uses of Television in American Higher Education.* New York: Praeger.

INDEX